LIFE AND THE DIVORCE LAWYER

JOHN LEDBETTER

Cover Design and Formatting by John Amy
www.ebookdesigner.co.uk

Chapter One

The Hawker Hunter jet fighters were flying low around my parents' home in Colchester, that early summer's morning in 1962. I watched with much envy, wishing my brain had been capable, during my school days, of transmitting the correct responses to mathematical and geographical problems.

Not all was lost, however, as the band was achieving more than most in the area during those early Beatle days. A TV appearance and much publicity had followed an offer of a world tour by an Agent who saw us playing a gig in London. Perhaps my drumming would secure a music career. In truth, I sought a more reliable and secure means of earning a living. Moreover I'd fallen for Glenys, and the thought of spending weeks, possibly months, apart was unthinkable.

My mother interrupted my musing, 'A letter for you, postmarked Ipswich.'

That letter heralded the start of a career in the legal profession, a career which was to prove, fulfilling, stimulating, and educational, but also, subsequently, to prove precarious.

The letter offered the post of clerk with a small family legal practice in Ipswich. I had attended an interview with the boss well over a month earlier and had abandoned, given my age (eighteen) any hope of securing the job. I had no 'O' levels, but primarily, no experience. Doubtless my charisma won the day – doubtless, there were no other applicants.

On arrival at the Ipswich office, some two weeks after securing the job, the boss was not in the office, so I was introduced to his son; a very pleasant chap, of similar age to myself, clearly intelligent, clearly a novice. 'My father left a note for you Mr Ledbetter'.

It read, *Will you please see Mrs Caxton at 10.15am and take a proof of evidence.* 'What the hell's a proof of evidence?' I thought. I tried to appear confident but was forced to seek clarification from the boss's son, but he too was uncertain – or was it an initiative test? However, I assumed that it must mean a 'statement'.

Mrs C arrived, a large black lady with smiling face and broken teeth. It is pertinent to mention, at this juncture, that although still in my teens, I was reasonably switched on, but nevertheless, a 'greenhorn'.

Naomi had matrimonial problems and wanted a divorce. I would like to think one of my attributes is that I am not furtive and accordingly attempted to explain my dilemma, which appeared to cause her no concern whatsoever. In fact, I believe that she was simply relieved to find someone she could talk to. Twice during the interview I left the room to ascertain from Michael (the boss's son), whether he considered that the statement would suffice for the purposes of divorce. Like me, he was uncertain.

Married 15 years to the father of her five very young children, when he was not drinking and violently assaulting her, he was otherwise engaged in adulterous relationships; during which he contracted venereal diseases that were 'generously' transmitted to her. An hour and a half later I concluded the interview, having merely scratched the surface of this lady's nightmare. It was then that I experienced, unknowingly, the effects of 'transference of problems'. She was distraught and anxious on arrival, I was in a similar state on her departure.

My boss later appraised the statement and suggested amplification and clarification here and there, complimented me on a good first attempt, and handed me the statement together with a book on divorce procedure. Clearly a man who believed that much benefit would be derived from the practical effects of being ***thrown in at the deep end***.

I had decided, on leaving my previous employer, that it was time to knuckle-down and grasp the opportunity to work hard with a view to providing some stability and security for our future; since Glenys and I were in love and envisaged marriage in the not too distant future.

However, while it would prove possible to 'knuckle down,' my early days with this small family practice would not be distraction free.

The main office, complete with boss, receptionist, book-keeper and secretaries, were situated at the bottom end of Princes Street, and Michael and I shared a small room with two secretaries at the top end of Princes Street. Which effectively meant that supervision was practically non-existent; life was good. Further, Eric (boss) and his son were both car enthusiasts, that regularly resulted in Michael and I grabbing any opportunity, to hit the road in highly tuned, and significantly converted, Volvos, but more particularly a Lotus Elan, and later, an Elva Courier two-seater sports with superb exhaust note. I think it fair to say that while Eric gave Michael and me the benefit of any doubt, we, for our part, did not take advantage of his well-disposed temperament. I respected him, and always delivered where work was concerned.

In securing the job I effectively inherited my predecessor's caseload which mostly comprised of divorce cases, some of which had been pending for years and were categorised as 'long-defended.'

I was determined to make positive progress, so armed with my trusty divorce handbook, and seeking Eric's assistance when required, I began to make minor inroads into the minefield of divorce.

It is strange, but often true, that one person's misfortune can be another's good fortune. This was certainly the case within a very short time of commencing the job, since I was asked by my boss to represent the firm as instructing solicitor to Counsel, i.e. sit with, and assist a Barrister in court. However, the principal reason for requesting my assistance was because the complainant was Eric's daughter, and neither Eric nor Michael felt it ethical, or acceptable, to appear in court as instructing solicitors.

I duly attended the local Magistrates' Court where I was introduced to Counsel, one Francis Petre from London chambers; a very pleasant chap who instilled calmness.

I sat in court next to Eric's daughter, who sought matrimonial orders on the ground of persistent cruelty. I cracked one or two jokes at the expense of her husband, while providing very limited assistance to Counsel. The hearing took much of the day to come to fruition, and included the production of various exhibits by Counsel for the husband, which included items of clothing, in particular a ripped neck tie, that he maintained had been used by his wife in a failed attempt to strangle him. It was this that prompted my muttered jesting.

The magistrate's adjourned, and after an hour, found her case proven, and awarded her custody of the one child. It transpired that Eric's daughter was impressed with the way I conducted myself; that I'd put her much at ease, resulting in my receiving praise from Eric and Michael.

Michael became a close friend, both sharing similar interests, not least cars and music.

Francis Petre of Counsel, as mentioned above, was often my first choice, not least because of his pleasant disposition that was well received by those seeking divorce or family resolution. It was simply a matter of time before he became a Circuit Judge. His persona was such that when, having briefed a barrister in one of my cases in which he was sitting as Judge, he noticed me sitting behind my barrister. Despite the case having proceeded, he leaned forward and waved!

These were busy times while attempting to juggle my career as a young divorce lawyer and **regularly** drumming with the band. However, in the early sixties divorce, unlike today, was still relatively uncommon, thus my caseload was manageable.

Chapter Two

PROGRESSING STEADILY

The law that governed the procedure, then through the Probate, Divorce & Admiralty Division of the High Court, was clearly designed to ensure that the unity and sanctity of marriage was paramount and that divorce should be subject to stringent and uncompromising procedures that once completed, should be placed before a Judge, who would need to be satisfied on the pleadings and evidence laid before him – which would include the oral evidence of the petitioner – that the marriage was at an end and should therefore be dissolved. This rigid procedure applied even if the parties agreed that their marriage was over, or if there was no opposition, and the case proceeded undefended.

The principal grounds for divorce were Adultery, Cruelty and Desertion, but before a party could seek a divorce, the marriage had to have subsisted for a period of three years, unless there had been exceptional hardship suffered by the petitioner, or exceptional depravity on the part of the respondent, in which event an application could be made to the Court for leave to present a petition, notwithstanding the fact that three years had not elapsed since the marriage was solemnised. Such applications were relatively few, not least as the law, and available case law, left little doubt as to the severity and magnitude of the conduct that would have to be proven to justify leave being granted.

Cases involving criminal offences of violence, would invariably merit leave being granted, e.g. a husband convicted of robbery with violence, constituted exceptional depravity, or instances of severe violence upon the applicant, normally the wife, involving the use of a weapon.

Naturally the Court was obliged to have regard to any child of the family, and whether there was 'reasonable probability' that the parties would become reconciled.

In family law the term 'child of the family', is used since the child (or children) may not in every instance be a child of the marriage, i.e. the child may have been born to them both, or to only one of them, prior to the marriage.

My very first client, Naomi Caxton, originally from Jamaica, had been married for more than three years, thus enabling me to proceed on the grounds of cruelty. Since it was not unusual in those days for a divorce petition to be defended, it was essential, particularly in cruelty cases, to plead the case accurately and often in much detail. It was suggested by my boss that initially I should prepare Instructions to Counsel, in London chambers, to settle (draft) the proposed petition, with a view to my drafting petitions once I'd gained some experience.

Accordingly I set to, having first obtained my client a legal aid certificate, which was then available for people on low or no income. Clearly the evidence of cruelty on the part of the husband was overwhelming. He accepted this and indicated as much in his acknowledgement of service, i.e. a document that the recipient completed and signed, confirming receipt of the divorce papers and indicating whether they wished to contest the proceedings, or be heard on any claim for costs. Upon receipt of his acknowledgement of service from the court, I applied to have the case set down for hearing. Notice was subsequently received and I wrote to my client informing her of the date, time, and venue of the hearing; seeking confirmation that she would attend Court. I heard nothing in reply and was therefore compelled to visit her.

Her small and dilapidated rented home comprised of two rooms, and I recall, while speaking with her on the doorstep, a dreadful smell emanating from within the darkness behind her. Of further concern was her apron, which appeared to be covered in blood. I could be forgiven for jumping immediately to the conclusion that she had murdered her husband, but she assured me that he had recently vacated the home. She also assured me that the Council were in the process of moving her to larger accommodation, which was indeed good news given that in the darkness, behind her, I was able to just see a mattress, and upon it, several pairs of eyes, i.e. the five children of the family.

I duly attended Court with Counsel at the Shire Hall, Ipswich, which I believe was then one of the oldest Courts in England, and was still used as the Assize Court. Panelled throughout with wood, it provided little comfort and should have been haunted, not least by those who had been, *taken from here, to the place from whence they came, and from there to a place of execution.*

On hearing my client's oral evidence, the Judge granted her a decree nisi on the grounds of her husband's cruelty, and having been satisfied on the evidence that she was about to be re-housed, certified that the arrangements for the children were the best that could be devised and granted her custody of the five children, which meant that I could apply on her behalf for the decree to be made absolute, which then was three months and one day after pronouncement of decree nisi. Needless to say, my client was pleased, and I (a mere teenager!) was relieved, that all had gone satisfactorily.

If out of the office, Eric, my boss, would see a new matrimonial client in my absence, prepare a statement, and then pass it on to me. One afternoon I arrived back at the office from Court and Eric was in the process of seeing a potential divorce client. He must have heard me and asked me to step into his office, as he did so he smiled as he proceeded to scratch himself around the chest area. On entering his room I was met by an awful smell. The elderly lady client was seeking advice with a view to divorcing her ageing husband, "And another thing", she said, "he's filthy and doesn't wash". She then produced from a carrier bag, various items of her husband's underwear, including an absolutely disgusting pair of 'long-johns'. Eric pleaded with her to remove them from his table, but she wanted him to see just how filthy her 'old man' was. We eventually persuaded her to put the offending items back in her bag, but before doing so she said that she wanted us to keep them as evidence to be produced at the hearing. We assured her that if Counsel considered it necessary, then she would be so advised prior to the hearing. I quipped, as she wrestled with the underwear and carrier bag, that Counsel only handled 'clean' Briefs! She did not hear, Eric laughed and we both scratched uncontrollably.

Another of my early cases – demanded confidence and maturity, which were still in short supply – involved a landlady from a local pub in Ipswich who sought a paternity order against a guy whom she alleged was the father of her baby daughter. He denied paternity, and in those pre DNA days a blood test was the only available means to the party seeking the order. However, in this instance the alleged father would not agree to a blood test, so it was necessary for Eric, who would make the application, to bring this, and our client's evidence, to the attention of the Magistrates.

It was therefore suggested that I obtain further details from our client, since Eric would take the opportunity in Court to cross-examine the defendant as to why he objected to a blood test. I had previously obtained a fairly detailed statement from our client but only scratched the surface of the more intimate details of her relationship. Given that her complaint was to be placed before the Justices the following day, I hastily arranged to see her at her 'pub' during afternoon closing time. She was an extremely mature, no-nonsense lady in her early thirty's, and I, still greenish, and in my teens!

I had already established with her that the alleged father was the only guy with whom she'd had sexual intercourse prior to conception, and that no means of contraception had been used. However, just to complicate the issue, she had mentioned that the guy often withdrew before ejaculation i.e. *coitus interruptus*, and it was in this regard that I needed clarification, so armed with notepad, pen and an air of ill-founded confidence, I duly attended the lady in her 'pub'. "Did he ever ejaculate before withdrawing... he surely must have dribbled... was he ever late in withdrawing?" and so on, and so forth. She, it has to be said, was helpful and displayed not even minimal embarrassment. For my part I concealed any embarrassment, but was relieved to conclude the interview, which actually proved beneficial, since the in depth exploration of bodily fluids actually established a balance of probability that culminated in the alleged father coming clean (excuse the pun) when Eric disclosed the evidence to his solicitor just prior to entering the Court

Chapter Three

By this time some cases were percolating through the procedural avenues, some inherited, some new. I suppose it's fair to say that although inadequately educated but *possibly* of average intelligence, I had the 'gift of the gab,' and accordingly did not have a problem in communicating. Most of my clients appeared to enjoy a good lawyer/client relationship. Furthermore I would like to think that I benefited from a reasonable helping of common sense, which I'm bound to say was, as I discovered with the passage of time, not an attribute found to be universal within the profession.

Some clients, particularly middle-aged, were occasionally perplexed and apprehensive about confiding in this youthful novice, as to their innermost concerns and anxieties, and often having to relate in some cruelty cases, extremely personal and intimate details, particularly if the principal matrimonial offence was of a sexual nature.

It was not unusual when attending a middle aged, or elderly client, for the first time, for them to say, 'I was expecting someone much older.' Some of the younger clients, particularly females in their mid to late twenties, appeared not to have a problem with my age. I think some were flattered or amused by my attempts to appear cool and professional, while often finding it impossible to conceal my blushes. Some females, who'd been assaulted by their husbands, were often only too willing to show me their bruises, one in particular revealing a very shapely leg clad in stockings and suspenders. Due to my obvious vulnerability in this regard, I enlisted the assistance of my secretary who would be summoned to my little room as soon as I envisaged an imminent bruise display. Sadly, I had to curtail future bruise displays and advise clients to consult their GP.

It became increasingly apparent that badly beaten wives were seldom to receive any positive response or action from the police, who would simply dismiss the case as a 'domestic'. Indeed I can recall only one instance during my ten years in Ipswich when my client's husband was arrested and actually prosecuted.

Following a complaint to the local Magistrates Court, based on persistent cruelty, plus three separate applications for injunctions, all of which were completely ignored by the husband, my client was attacked by her husband in public. After a good battering he then attempted to strangle her, but fortunately was seen by a copper who intervened, by which time Hilary (my client) was unconscious.

While I continued to find it inconceivable that most violent husbands could side-step a criminal charge, despite the consistency, and often severity, of such violence; I had to acknowledge the dilemma confronting the police. Not least as many wives inevitably agreed to reconciliation.

On being consulted by a female client, a victim of domestic violence, her case would be immediately prioritised, often involving an application for emergency legal aid. The preparation of an application for an injunction (an order restraining the husband from further acts of violence) involved the preparation of a lengthy and detailed affidavit to be sworn and filed in support of her application. The Court would then be asked to allocate the earliest possible date for hearing. Often I would attend Court and the applicant would not. 'Telephone call for Mr Ledbetter' would often greet me from the Clerk of the Court or, in later years, the P.A. system. 'I've decided to give him one final chance.' To which I often replied, "You said that last time".

I would be a far wealthier lawyer, had I received £10 every time a client subsequently said to me, 'Oh you were so right, I should have divorced the bugger in the first place'.

'What about wives assaulting their husbands?' I hear you ask. Well, during my lengthy career, I never received instructions from a husband to seek a restraining order against his wife. I acknowledge, however, that this scenario has become more common of late.

My knowledge of divorce law and practice was still in its infancy, when a lady, who'd married a Polish guy, consulted me. It was immediately apparent that injunctive action was necessary, given that she bore the scars of battle, i.e. her teeth had literally been knocked into her mouth so that, although still in her gums, the upper and lower front teeth were almost horizontal, and her nose was bloodied and broken. Also, an injury to her hand rendered her incapable of writing. Inconceivably, it took fifteen minutes to ascertain her name. 'What is your name?' Was followed by this poor woman's attempts to pronounce a Polish name, which it transpired, would probably have been unpronounceable in the absence of her injuries.

What followed would be seen as fundamental part of my learning curve.

Every application for an injunction, combined with any ex-parte orders (orders made in the Respondent's, invariably the husband's, absence) required to be personally served upon the Respondent.

I arrived at the Respondent's home, just as he was parking

his bicycle behind a low picket fence, and access gate. I had obtained a photograph and asked him to confirm that he was Mr X (I still hadn't mastered the pronunciation) and handed him the papers. Instead of making a hasty retreat, I explained to this perplexed pole-axed Pole, the purpose of my visit. He spoke some English, and clearly understood what I was saying, given that he grabbed the dividing fence and began to shake. I attempted to pacify him as his cold grey eyes dilated and darkened.

'All's well that ends – well I must be going', I said, as he caught his ankle on his bicycle pedal, while attempting to join me, brandishing his bicycle pump. I maintained eye contact and attempted to reassure him while backing towards my car. It's truly amazing, but when you need brown trousers, you're never wearing them. Suffice it to say that I lived to tell the tale.

Thereafter, save for a few occasions when I was feeling lucky, or had a death wish, I would instruct an Enquiry Agent in the process of personal service. Most were retired coppers and were used to dealing with assailants armed with bicycle pumps.

However, of the few occasions when I ventured forth, one particular case is perhaps worthy of mention.

I was acting for a husband whose wife had committed adultery with a number of men, and four of them, were cited in the divorce petition. It was normal practice to name the person with whom your wife/husband had committed adultery, not least as an order for costs could be sought against them. It was, however, relatively uncommon for four Co-Respondents to be cited. Three of those named in my chap's petition, filed their acknowledgements of service, but the fourth, one Leroy P, failed to return his to the Court. I was therefore unable to proceed to trial.

My client instructed me that he understood that LP was

about to stand trial for GBH, and that due to previous form, he was likely to receive a custodial sentence. I was asked if I would arrange personal service immediately as LP was to stand trial the following day. Needless to say I was apprehensive but was left with little alternative, so armed with the Court documents I arrived at the address of LP that was situated in a rough area of Ipswich. I climbed the steps and knocked on the door there was no reply. After three attempts a door, below in the unseen basement, opened, and a guy called, "yeah, what d'yer want?" I looked down and asked if he was LP. It is still firmly imprinted on my brain, the sight of this guy literally unfolding himself from the doorway. 'Oh shit, was this to be my stairway to heaven?'

As he came up the steps to confront me, he literally dwarfed my six foot and one inch medium build frame. I attempted to maintain a polite and relaxed stance, and tried not to stutter. What transpired simply supported my theory based on experience and findings during school days, and indeed to the present, i.e. that most guys who are eager to pick a fight, are often short and stocky. This guy, despite his imminent trial for GBH, was pleasant and completely reasonable. He took the papers and signed the acknowledgement of service, indicating that he did not wish to be heard on any aspects, and joked that my client was unlikely to ever see any costs given that he expected a lengthy stay in Dartmoor Prison. He returned to the basement and half way down the steps turned, his handsome face grinning broadly and exclaimed. 'The guy was really pissing me off, so I hit him, wouldn't you?' He was still laughing as he bent his enormous frame through the basement doorway. I doubt he heard me concurring, and wishing him luck.

Chapter Four

THE GROUNDS

ADULTERY: The most commonly committed matrimonial offence, and often regretted, but not necessarily immediately!

Throughout the sixties, adultery was increasingly the ground upon which a Petitioner would rely. However, if the Respondent denied the offence, then it would invariably be necessary to instruct an Enquiry Agent (Private Investigator) to investigate the movements of the Respondent with a view to proving, on the balance of probability, that he or she was committing adultery.

Occasionally a couple would be discovered in a swaying motor vehicle, with obligatory steamed windows, or as in one of my cases, a telephone box, with obligatory steamed windows – 'Dial 'A' for Adultery'! (For those not of my era, 1960's TV included a drama, 'Dial 'M' for Murder')

Adultery could also be inferred if the parties spent the night in a hotel. The most common scenario, however, would involve the sighting of a Respondent entering the home of the potential Co-Respondent, or vice versa, usually at night, and then seen leaving the following morning, the Enquiry Agent having possibly seen them enter a lighted bedroom, and then switching the light off. Either way, the task was simplified if the accommodation was small and bed-space limited, thus enhancing the balance of probability.

Once sufficient evidence had been compiled, the Respondent and Co-Respondent would be challenged and invited to make confession statements. If they refused then the matter would proceed on the evidence of the Petitioner and Enquiry Agent, plus any other corroborative witnesses.

One particular Enquiry Agent, actually confronting a couple in the act of sexual intercourse, proceeded thus: "I am instructed by your wife's solicitors in connection with divorce proceedings – would you kindly refrain from doing that!" Naturally I jest. Or do I?

Most Respondent's co-operated, and made confession statements when challenged by an Enquiry Agent.

If following an admission, or other supporting evidence, of adultery, the parties attempted a reconciliation that exceeded a period of three months, the adultery would be seen to have been condoned, and once condoned, could not be revived. If, however, the guilty party re-offended, then the earlier offence could be revived i.e. used as evidence in the divorce proceedings.

Reverting for a moment to the role of Enquiry Agents, I was acting for a lady who was anxious to divorce her husband but had no grounds. She was convinced, however, that her husband was associating with another woman i.e. out most evenings and seldom home at weekends, leaving her with little else to conclude. An Enquiry Agent was instructed, but was unsuccessful in collating sufficient evidence to prosecute a suit for divorce. My lady was at her wits end, since she had attempted many times to confront her husband, but he simply shrugged his shoulders and went out.

In an effort to assist, I decided to try my hand at a spot of investigation, so armed with a recent photograph of the guy, I sat with Glenys in our car one freezing winter's night (no heater) for about an hour outside my client's home in Ipswich. I was about to give up, when he appeared. Whether it was my frozen condition that restricted my immediate response remains to be seen, but this guy was fit and quick. He mounted his bicycle and sped off down the road at such speed as to render those competing in the Tour de France sluggish. We made some progress in that he was still in sight, but as if by magic, disappeared into the darkness. I got out of the car and walked in the direction he was travelling, thinking that he may have escaped down an alleyway, but nothing. Just as well I didn't join the police force!

The twist in this tale is that I was subsequently able to petition for divorce, her husband having requested her to do so, as he'd fallen for another bloke!

I referred earlier to costs being claimed by a Petitioner against the Co-Respondent. In addition a Co-Respondent ran the risk of a claim by the Petitioner for damages for enticement in the event of the Co-Respondent knowing that the Respondent was married. Although I was obliged to advise Petitioner clients that a claim could be made, I considered the law in this regard to be out-of-date. However, despite my misgivings, it would be a few years before the modus operandi was abolished, but I have to confess to finding the law and case law applicable to such action, both interesting and amusing.

During my introduction to the realms of divorce law, it was necessary in the event of the Petitioner having also committed adultery, to seek the Court's discretion in granting a decree of divorce, notwithstanding his or her own adultery. The procedure deemed it essential that a discretion statement, signed by the Petitioner, should be placed in a sealed brown envelope, which would be placed before the Judge at the hearing. The respondent was permitted to know that the petitioner was seeking the discretion of the Court, but was not entitled to know the content of the discretion statement. It was of minimal concern if my client had committed adultery following the break-up, but I was always concerned if adultery had been committed prior to the break-up, particularly if there were children to be considered, and their custody was in issue. I recall a few instances when taking details from female clients, and becoming increasingly concerned as the number of other men reached three, and then four! I would wait, with bated breath, for the Judge's reaction on opening the envelope and reading the discretion statement. Often the reaction would be no more than a raised eyebrow, but depending on the content, the Judge invariably asked a few more questions than usual to satisfy himself that any children were being adequately catered for.

It was emphasised by the Courts that damages for enticement were to be seen as compensatory only. It was not the job of the Court, nor indeed, in some cases, the jury, to punish the adulterer, but to compensate the Petitioner for his/her loss. That said, I recall that the conduct of the adulterer, i.e. his 'treachery or deliberation' or 'wanton attack on family honour', were deemed to be of relevance to any potential claim. Further, the loss of one's spouse, and the resulting injury to feelings, then defined as a, *blow to his honour*, were all aspects for consideration.

Having concluded that the Applicant should be compensated, the Court would assess the amount to be awarded, and woe betide any Co-Respondent who had used his, *wealth, rank or position*, to seduce the Respondent!

It's fair to say that I soon formed a viewpoint (that would remain steadfast during my career) that I preferred to act for females, not least as they mostly (not always) responded sensibly to advice given.

DESERTION: Which during the early sixties, and indeed for many years prior thereto, required both parties to have lived completely separate and apart for a period of at least three years from the date the Respondent deserted the Petitioner, immediately preceding the date the petition was presented.

Also available to some petitioners, was the ground of constructive desertion. This means of divorce applied when the Petitioner had left the Respondent because his/her conduct was so intolerable that it rendered the continuation of the marriage impossible. However, it was still necessary for the parties to have lived apart for at least three years. Accordingly if consulted by a party prior to the expiration of the three years period, I would try to establish whether the conduct complained of was sufficient to merit a petition on the grounds of cruelty. Often, during the desertion period one of the parties would enter into another relationship, thus providing the other party with a means to an end.

Occasionally a Petitioner was unaware of the Respondent's whereabouts, in which event, attempts would first be made to trace the Respondent from his/her last known address, followed mostly by an application to the Court for an order for substituted service of the petition by advertisement in a local newspaper, in the town or area where the Respondent last resided, plus the London Gazette. Alternatively the Court could, in some exceptional circumstances, be invited to dispense with service of the divorce papers upon the Respondent.

Chapter Five

=SEXUAL DEPRAVITY/WEIRD RELATIONSHIPS

Occasionally, if the evidence was overwhelming, an Enquiry Agent would not be required. This was apparent in one of my early (teen) cases.

The young, and indeed attractive, woman sought my advice regarding her husband's adulterous activities. It transpired that her husband, carpenter and part time footballer, having provided her with three children in three years, was mostly playing away.

My lady instructed me that prior to consulting me she had established the identity of the other woman, and had confronted her. A blazing argument ensued culminating in a fight, but once exhausted, they began to converse, and it became patently obvious that the other woman initially, and erroneously, thought that my client's husband was single. Accordingly, they decided to confront him. The following day, shortly after the husband came home from work, the other woman arrived at the matrimonial home. The husband was in the sitting room, and clearly must have heard the woman being invited into the house by his wife; however, there was no means of escape. The women entered the sitting room and the husband momentarily disappeared, but only until his wife spotted, his toes sticking out beneath drawn curtains. I appreciate that you are waiting for something akin to Laurel and Hardy, possibly something china, or perhaps in view of sixties fashion, a stiletto heal buried into one of his feet. In fact, the husband appeared from behind the curtains with penis in hand, and enquired, 'which of you wants this?'

A letter, or letters, from a male or female, containing intimacies, could also be sufficient evidence to prosecute a suit for divorce.

The husband, for whom I acted, had found letters to his wife from an American serviceman who was based at a local USAF base. Graphic and intimate details of sexual acts were contained in most of the letters, but one in particular has remained in my memory bank. It chivalrously read, 'Honey, I could eat the shit out of your ass.' It also detailed an act that made me realise that for some, sexual fulfilment could include somewhat bizarre (whatever turns you on) activities. In this particular instance a 'Golden Shower.'

Not that I can recall acting for a clergyman, I do recall that adultery could result in a Vicar being deposed, which succinctly suggests, 'You may take your vest off in the pantry, but must never take your pants off in the vestry!'

Many, many years later my client was convinced that while her husband was working away in Scotland he was having an affair. I therefore advised that she would require evidence to support a divorce petition. Subsequently, she informed me that she'd found cards and letters in her husband's travel case, from another woman.

I prepared and filed her petition that, once served, was not contested by her husband. However, my client upon swearing her affidavit in support of her petition was insistent that I see the many letters and cards from her husband's lover. She then placed a large bulging envelope on my table.

'No, I don't need any further evidence, your husband is not contesting the petition.' I urged.

She pleaded with me to extract any of the cards or letters. So, with a sigh, I started to randomly pull a card (any card!) or letter from the vast selection. Simultaneously she informed me that *some* were of an intimate nature. Yes indeed, since (I must have a nose for aspects of this nature) the card displayed, neatly glued thereon, the other woman's pubic hair! Cooley I responded, 'a genuine red-head?'

An early case for me in Cornwall involved the unreasonable and somewhat bizarre behaviour of the husband. That said, given that this was Cornwall, and the lawyer, Essex born and bred, perhaps the sexual activities pleaded should not be dismissed as unusual. Either way, my lady took exception to her husband's insistence that she, while naked, be generously covered in Cornish clotted cream. (Excluding, I presume, scone and jam – jam first!)

With the exception of various sexual aids or toys, some tolerated, some not, the parties to divorce proceedings were, in the main, without depravity. That said, one lady instructed me that while she had no proof, circumstances left her with little doubt that her husband was probably committing bestiality with his pet German Shepherd bitch.

Of concern was the apparent increase in possible rape and intolerable sexual conduct of husbands. A few wives instructed me that they'd been assaulted and/or raped, some wrongly assuming that marriage afforded unquestionable consent to such offences, and all for whom I acted chose not to report those offences to the police.

One lady sought legal redress for her husband's persistent violent sexual assaults that followed his admission of regularly viewing (during work hours) pornographic material.

I stress that those who warranted petitions for unreasonable behaviour – and cruelty prior to Divorce Reform – were the subject of instructions and pleadings last prepared by me long ago. Given technology and the access to pornography, I assume cessation of the sanctity of marriage has been a contributory factor.

Chapter Six

JUDGEMENT

I consider myself fortunate in those early days in Ipswich, that the Judge often sitting to hear divorces, and also who I often appeared before when pursuing case applications in Chambers, was Judge Drabble, the father of author, Margaret Drabble. Though always insistent that cases were correctly and competently presented, he was of pleasant disposition, and in my opinion, very well suited to family law, not least, as he always ensured that children received 'paramount consideration', an obvious prerequisite, but one, as I would discover with time, often inanely and ineffectually rolled off the tongues of Judges and lawyers, with scant regard. I should emphasise, however, that fortunately this was the exception, rather than the rule.

In addition to Judge Drabble, I also had the pleasure of gaining advocacy experience before a portly senior Registrar, who was flamboyant in manner and style: often wearing brightly coloured waistcoats and displaying a jovial disposition. I was encountering some unnecessary flack from a senior lawyer who was opposing my application for a maintenance order in my client's favour. He was capitalising on my inexperience but I was not prepared to submit. The Registrar sat quietly with a grin on his round ruddy face until deciding to intervene with, 'Do either of you gentlemen ever go dog racing?' A pregnant pause preceded, 'Not recently Sir,' I replied. 'But as a child I sometimes went to the White City Stadium with my grandfather'. The other lawyer looked completely dumfounded and spluttered, 'Dog racing? – No.' 'Oh, what a pity,' said the Registrar. 'I thought I'd ask, since I have a greyhound for sale!'

As mentioned earlier, when I commenced my job as a lawyer, I inherited various cases from my predecessor, including some *long defended* divorce cases, as they were then known.

One of these cases finally came to fruition in the month following my marriage, and had taken six years to arrive at the court doors. It provided a good grounding in court procedures and pleadings in that they (the pleadings) consisted of the husband's (my client's) petition, his wife's Answer and Cross Petition, the husband's Reply, the wife's Request for Further and Better Particulars, the husband's Further and Better Particulars in response, his Request for Further and Better Particulars, and, the final pleading, his wife's Further and Better Particulars in response.

Reference is made above to the wife's 'cross petition'. In that document she alleged her husband's cruelty and desertion i.e. constructive desertion based on her assertion that her husband's conduct forced her to leave him. Even with my limited experience, I viewed her defence as feeble, and I preferred my chap's version of events that led to the end of their marriage.

The case came before Mr Justice Baker at The Royal Courts of Justice on 19th October 1965. This was to be my first experience of a contested hearing, and having briefed Counsel to represent my chap, I settled down and began to make notes to assist Counsel. As the hours passed, listening for the first time to a husband and wife telling the Judge how dreadful the other had been, I came to the conclusion that there had to be a better way of resolving matrimonial disputes. At some stage, it is reasonable to assume that this couple had been in love. Now, however, they were forced to relate their innermost secrets and while my client attempted to maintain some dignity and reasonableness, the wife's somewhat frivolous assertions against him resulted in his response that his wife had frequently killed any passion within the matrimonial bed by wearing bed socks!

The hearing lasted two days and Mr Justice Baker granted my chap a decree nisi on the grounds of his wife's desertion. In his judgement he said, *I have never heard more trivial circumstances for the break-up of a marriage.*

The case received wide national newspaper coverage with headlines, 'Why A Countryman Lost His City Wife' and 'Bored Wife Got Out Of Bed And Went Home To Mother', and the News of the World, 'Town Girl Was Bored In The Country.' Which succinctly summed it up, given that my chap's roots were in the country and his wife preferred London life. The beginning of the report in the News of the World read thus: 'The marriage of the pretty London bred girl, with Marxist views, to 'a good solid countryman', who was a Tory with his roots in the country where he was born, just did not work out'. Most newspapers carried large photographs of the defeated wife looking extremely happy. Apparently she'd met, and fallen for, a city dweller!

Chapter Seven

Earlier I alluded to 'exceptional hardship' and 'exceptional depravity' as grounds for seeking leave of the Court to divorce within three years of marriage.

One of my early cases involved such relief being sought, and it is fair to say that the circumstances had quite a profound effect upon me not least as only about eight months had passed since my initiation.

My client was a Ward Sister, of pleasant disposition, in her mid-twenties. Approximately a fortnight prior to consulting me, she had married a colleague, a male nurse. She was extremely distressed, anxious, and very angry, given that it transpired that her husband was homosexual, had confessed as much, and administered salt to the wound, by telling her that he was missing his boyfriend. She kept repeating that she should have known, particularly because of her status and experience. I attempted to reassure her, but my experience and knowledge of such disastrous scenarios were nil, as indeed was my experience, and knowledge, of homosexuality.

The following day I received a telephone call from my client's very anxious mother, who asked if I would speak again with her daughter, as she feared that she was suicidal. I immediately drove, with the boss's son, Michael, to her home. I recall en route thinking how bizarre this matter was, not least as this experienced nurse was looking to me, a nineteen year-old *naive* novice who simply, but erroneously, thought from his own chemistry, and that of his mates (I think they mostly did in those days!) that lads lusted after lasses.

We arrived at a very nice cottage in the Suffolk countryside, where we attempted to pacify and reassure this very unfortunate lady. Perhaps a small part of our chat proved beneficial as she subsequently returned to her job, working all hours, in an effort to combat the effects of her traumatic experience. I still vividly recall my somewhat inane comments to this lady during our conversation, not least, "You are a very attractive and intelligent young lady, and you are bound to meet someone else". True, but somewhat pathetically predictable!

I successfully obtained leave of the court to petition for divorce.

Given that I'm now in my seventies, I have to acknowledge that homosexuality has been, and always will be, part of our lives, but I still don't fully understand the causation, save that it may originate from early conception, and be combined with a neurological disparity – or perhaps, given what appears to be a surge since the 1950's – the birth pill, resulting in too much oestrogen in the water! 'What about lesbians?' I here you ask – answers on a postcard please.

However, whatever the cause, one cannot ignore possible scenarios, not least when a young woman or lad experience a preference for a person of the same sex, then indisputably they (may) require help during what can be a desperately unhappy and confusing time – some attempting, and some actually committing, suicide. This, needless to say, is nothing short of a tragic consequence.

Staying for a moment with 'exceptional hardship' and/or 'depravity', case law provided that where one's spouse deserted and committed adultery within the first three years of marriage, this would not singularly, amount to exceptional hardship or depravity. Accordingly I had to advise a young man that the Court was extremely unlikely to grant him leave to present a petition, despite the fact that his wife had left him at the wedding reception, to pursue an adulterous relationship with his best man! However, the marriage having not been consummated, a decree of nullity could be sought.

Chapter Eight

ACTING FOR DIFFERENT PROFESSIONS

Acting for different professions, proved to be another part of my learning curve, and which followed a trip to The Royal Courts of Justice, in connection with another long defended divorce case that proved surprisingly beneficial.

Having briefed my usual barrister I was advised the day before the hearing that he was part heard in another case so a colleague from his Chambers accepted the brief on behalf of my lady client. In this case the wife alleged cruelty and it was quite apparent from my initial conversation with Counsel – a short, ruddy faced, rotund, lively middle-aged chap with character, and gold watch and chain – that he derived much enjoyment from defended divorce cases, in particular the opportunity to cross examine nasty husbands.

Before long the 'bully' husband was showing his true colours while undergoing a brilliant piece of cross-examination by my Counsel. Though I was still of the opinion that there must have been better ways of ending one's marriage, I have to confess that I too derived some satisfaction, as I was convinced, from the outset, that the husband was lying. The Judge clearly shared this view, and granted my client a decree nisi, plus an order that the husband pay his wife's costs. There were no children to consider.

The parties had been in Court for several hours so the husband paid dearly for his day and a half in Court.

After the hearing I grabbed a late lunch with Counsel and as we chatted about the case, I mentioned that I imagined that the husband had been a difficult guy to act for. Counsel then gave his opinion, based on his many years experience, of the most difficult people to act for in divorce cases, and I'm bound to say that his observations proved consistently accurate during my lengthy career.

A client's response to: 'What do you do for a living?' would invariably predict the degree of difficulty:

'I'm a housewife.' Mostly rational.

'I'm a builder.' Mostly ok.

'I'm an engineer.' Good.

'I'm a farmer.' Difficult - and most have guns!

'I'm a shopkeeper.' Often strange.

'I'm a teacher.' Pause, and reply, 'I'd like to be able to assist you, but I'm extremely busy.'

Many times, when bashing my head against a brick wall in attempting to advise a teacher, have I recalled Counsel's poignant observation, 'You'll find it fucking impossible to **advise** teachers!'

Chapter Nine

Highly Strung Wife Gets Decree For Cruelty: Was the
headline to follow my next long defended divorce case, which,
on this occasion, was heard at the Assize Court in Ipswich on
6th April 1967. Like the cases that preceded it, this case was
inherited from my predecessor, but in this instance, it must have
been one of the longest pending cases of all time, certainly the
longest I was ever to conduct. When I took over the case in 1962
it had already been pending for five years, so effectively took ten
years to come to fruition.

When meeting my client at the Court, in the company of her
sister, both were relaxed and laughing, which naturally
appeared somewhat outré given the circumstances, until she
revealed that as I arrived, wearing my three piece 60's style
(wedding) suit, her sister remarked that I looked like Tom
Jones, whereupon we all had a good laugh. Upon reflection I
could see the likeness – NOT!

The case took several hours to be heard, and in his summing
up Commissioner Tolstoy said, ['Mr Ledbetter looks about as
much like Tom Jones as my cat. What's new pussycat?'] 'I am
quite satisfied that the parties were not suited to each other
sexually...' (It had clearly taken them some time to come to this
conclusion, given that they married in 1955) '...but I think the
real crux of the matter was that the husband did drink and the

wife did not, and I think on frequent occasions he had more than was good for him.'

In those days defended divorces were invariably reported and there was no exception in this case in that the following day the East Anglian Daily Times provided a detailed account of the evidence of both parties as adduced during the lengthy hearing.

Another of my early inherited cases proved very much a challenge since it provided an insight into aspects unknown to this young lawyer.

My client, a lady in her early thirties was seeking an annulment of her marriage on the ground that it had not been consummated due to the husband's wilful refusal. Although somewhat puzzling, the husband was intent on defending his wife's petition, maintaining that he had not wilfully refused and that his wife was incapable of having sexual intercourse due, primarily, to a mental condition that prevented her from performing the sexual act. This resulted in medical reports and opinions, which, in the main, appeared to support her case. The case was set down as a lengthy contested suit for hearing in February 1969 at the Royal Courts of Justice before Mr Justice Ormrod, a Judge of much experience, who was both legally and medically qualified.

At this time, Glenys and I, plus baby Gareth, were still living in our semi bungalow in Somersham, Suffolk, a pretty little rural village, particularly when covered in six inches of snow, which was the scene that awaited me on the morning of the hearing. Our home had no garage so my Mini Cooper (A Morris 1275 'S' for like-minded petrol heads) was buried beneath the snow, but sadly much more than six inches due to drifting. I had purchased this brilliant little second-hand motor during 1968 to replace the Morris 1100, as it would achieve, unlike the 1100, a good level of performance and mechanical reliability. Truth is, I was (Glenys was not) quite obsessive about cars and speed – still am!

Having cleared enough snow I began my drive to Ipswich Railway Station on roads of virgin snow. Eventually I reached the Sproughton straight, a piece of road approximately two miles long, and as I was determined not to miss the train, and as there were no other vehicles, I gradually increased my speed to about 60mph whereupon the car turned abruptly to the right. Front-wheel drive enabled me to correct this, so I steadily increased speed until a repeat performance, this time the car turning abruptly to the left necessitating an opposite lock and me looking through the driver's side window. I arrived at the station, shaken, but not stirred, only to discover that all trains were running significantly late due to frozen points. Should I have foreseen this?

I eventually made it to Court and fortunately counsel had anticipated my delay due to the appalling weather and had commenced his pre-trial conference with my client who had stayed in London. Once concluded, counsel had the customary chat with his opposite number. Mr Blofeld, my lady's barrister, concluded that if Counsel for the husband was intent on raising new evidence that had not been pleaded, Lord Justice Ormrod would be far from impressed, and that I should watch for his reaction.

Mr Blofeld attempted, one last time, to dissuade the other barrister from raising the new evidence and warned him of Lord Justice Ormrod's probable reaction. He, Mr Blofeld, outlined the case for the wife and as Counsel for the husband rose to his feet Mr Blofeld nudged me and whispered, 'Wait for it.' Ormrod's response was such that I am convinced that his face turned grey. He left Counsel, for the husband, in no doubt that he should not attempt such tactics if ever appearing before him and also humiliated him by relating both basics in regard to adducing fresh evidence and making the obvious point that the case had been pending for so long as to render the raising of further evidence, of questionable significance, wholly incomprehensible. He concluded by indicating that he then intended to leave the courtroom and that Counsel should speak with Mr Blofeld with a view to achieving a sensible solution to a case where clearly the marriage was at an end.

Agreement was eventually reached whereby the wife achieved her annulment. I confess that I cannot recall whether an order for costs was made against the husband but clearly an aspect that would have been pursued at some point of the negotiations. Either way, the intervention of the Judge meant that the parties, particularly the wife, were saved the distress and anxiety of a lengthy hearing that would have included medical evidence and much delving into matters of an extremely personal nature.

It was just a few months later that Lord Justice Ormrod dealt with the case of Corbett v Corbett in December 1969, involving transgender model April Ashley. Subsequently Lord Justice Ormrod became Lord Justice of Appeal.

Of my various visits to the Royal Courts of Justice I invariably had difficulty in finding a particular courtroom but experienced more of a problem when attempting to find a Master's chamber i.e. a room in which a slightly lesser mortal than a Judge would sit and hear all manner of legal applications e.g. maintenance orders for wife and children, leave to amend pleadings and so on. I sought directions but found myself in a tight corridor, which it transpired, led to the corridor dividing Judges. I knocked on one door, entered and found a Judge while in the process of being robed for court. Both he and his dresser stared at me in astonishment. I apologised and retreated. So much for security, and sadly I cannot report having seen any whips or other sadistic weaponry that one may have expected to see in a Monty Python sketch.

Chapter Ten

CONTROVERSIAL DECISION

In early 1971, following a child custody decision in the Bromley County Court, my client, a mother of three children, became the subject of Appeal proceedings brought by her former husband who was advised to appeal the decision which awarded custody of the children to their mother.

My client had been divorced and had commenced a relationship with the Co- Respondent cited in the divorce proceedings. Both were of very pleasant dispositions, and we enjoyed a very good lawyer/client relationship.

There were many procedural measures to be implemented, not least a detailed and lengthy affidavit for swearing by my client in support of her response to her former husband's application to the Court of Appeal.

I chose to prepare the affidavit, instead of instructing Counsel, since by 1971 I had gained sufficient experience and was therefore able to draft all pleadings, including divorce petitions.

The application was lodged and a date fixed for hearing in the Royal Courts of Justice, but a part heard case had over-run, which resulted in our case commencing after lunch. Despite pleas and submissions from my Counsel to the presiding Lord

Justices to hear the case without delay, the case was adjourned, Counsel having warned both client and myself that his attempts to persuade the three Lord Justices would probably fall on deaf ears due to the Lord Mayor's Banquet taking place that evening!

It is still firmly imprinted on my brain the sight of three Lord Justices effectively ignoring Counsel's submissions, chatting to each other throughout, and adjourning the case to be returned to them the following day.

The father's Appeal commenced before those presiding: Lord Justices Karminski, Davies and Megaw .

Ld Karminski commented on part of my client's affidavit and agreed with certain paragraphs the content of which I had included with some reservation and caution, but was obviously encouraged and reassured by his comments. Not least as this was my introduction to the Court of Appeal, in a case where three children's present and future welfare hung in a somewhat precarious balance.

As a loving mother, my client was in a state of desperation and anxiety during the two-day trial and this prevailing state of mind, perhaps unsurprisingly, boiled over during a short recession. The Appellant father was represented by a female barrister of grim disposition and appeared devoid of basic compassion, culminating in her, very unprofessionally, making very audible comment to her client outside the court room affectively criticising my client, clearly with the intention of causing her distress. My client reacted, and very constructively, lambasted the female barrister concluding with, 'I doubt very much that you have children, madam, and sincerely hope, for their sakes, that you never do!' Normally I would intervene in such a scenario – on this occasion, I did not.

As the case progressed before the Lord Justices the female barrister, and those (solicitors) instructing her, committed a very basic faux pas in that they produced a letter from my client to her former husband that had not been disclosed to us. However, Lord Justice Karminski, though not impressed, asked to see it with a view to establishing whether it should be disclosed and deemed an exhibit. The handwritten letter was handed to the court Usher who in turn handed up, the not insubstantial height, to Ld Justice Karminski, who immediately enquired of counsel for the Appellant whether copies were available for those sitting with him. Now, if as a lawyer you choose to practice in the realms of contentious work then you learn during initiation some basic rules, and one of those is that you never ever produce a hand written document without a typed copy for the judge or judges. Accordingly, Lord Justice Karminski simply held the letter in his outstretched hand and let it fall very slowly to the floor of the court. It would not, needless to say, be deemed an exhibit.

As in many cases, our case had a weakness in that for a period of time my client had left her two younger children (aged six and eight) with their father until such time as they could be better housed and accommodated. Meantime the eldest daughter (ten) lived with her mother.

After much deliberation the Lords decided that the children should be split between mother and father, the two younger children staying with their father and the eldest child staying with her mother.

Lord J Karminski said that it was, '...*one of the most difficult cases I have come across.*' Lord Megaw concurred, but Lord Davies, while not dissenting, agreed with the decision of the County Court Judge, and said, '*If possible the three children should be together, and also they should be with a whole- time mother at home rather than a part-time father, however well he did his parental duties.*'

The case received much national newspaper coverage. The Guardian: 'Appeal Judges Split A Family.' Daily Express:

'Judges Split Up Children In 'Tug Of Love' Battle.' The Daily Telegraph: 'Judges Decide Children Must Be Split.' The Daily Mirror: 'A Knife-Edge Ruling On Family.' And The East Anglian Daily Times: 'Children Split In Difficult Case.'

Needless to say my client was extremely saddened and anxious as a result of the verdict but had at all times acknowledged that by leaving the two younger children with their father, the status quo could be upheld. I'm bound to say, however, that I shared Lord Justice Davies's opinion that the children should not be split. It was a decision that I would not, thankfully, encounter in the many years to follow.

It was around this time that another of my cases received media interest, simply because of the somewhat satirical content, in that the husband's wife had left him for the milkman.

Chapter Eleven

DIVORCE REFORM

The Act was introduced in 1969, with a view to simplifying divorce due to the increasing numbers of failed marriages. It was also designed to encourage reconciliation, an aim and objective that I viewed, despite only having practised divorce law for about seven years, with some scepticism – a view that would not diminish with time.

In my opinion – based on *my* findings – once a wife or husband crossed the divorce lawyer's threshold, the marriage was at an end. Reconciliation was often attempted, but I do not recall a single case where the parties successfully reconciled their differences.

If a client instructed me that it was his or her intention to attempt reconciliation, I would merely advise that, given their circumstances, a reconciliation was unlikely to prove beneficial, but always stressing that if I was wrong then I'd be genuinely pleased for them, especially if there was a child or children of their union.

The Act also provided that the 'irretrievable breakdown' of the marriage be the sole ground for divorce. However, it would still be necessary to show proof/cause of the breakdown and so the previous grounds, as alluded to earlier i.e. adultery, desertion etc, would now form the cause of breakdown. However, in an effort to inject a conciliatory approach, adultery would provide proof so long as the petitioner also found it intolerable to live with the husband/wife. Cruelty was replaced with unreasonable behaviour, the nature, or severity, of such, made it impossible for the petitioner to continue living with the respondent. The period for desertion was reduced to two years, but the most important change was the provision for divorce in the event of the parties having lived apart for a continuous period of two years and the respondent *consented* to the divorce, and a divorce, without the respondent's consent, if the parties had lived apart for five years.

***

I should perhaps mention/emphasise that much of my early references herein to cases, the law and my experiences, relate to the nineteen sixties and seventies during which I was still in my late teens or in my early twenties. Further I think it perhaps sensible to stress – perhaps a statement of the obvious – that as a divorce lawyer I'd represented vast numbers of clients during 38 years, but have obviously alluded to only a handful.

Chapter Twelve

CHILDHOOD / POST WAR BRITAIN

Born to Henry Bainey and Rose May (Tyson) on the 23rd May 1944 in Colchester, my parents, to escape the blitz, having moved from London with my six year old sister, Sylvia, following my conception.

My father's age and occupation – he was 34, and an engineer – categorised him, when attempting enlistment, as 'Reserved Occupation,' thus resulting in him, like many others, joining 'Dad's Army,' working by day, and defending the realm by night.

Having decided to escape the Blitz, Colchester was (and still is) a Garrison town, so we were not apparently excused the occasional bombing e.g. windows shattered. Having apparently survived various air raids, including a couple of near-by Doodlebug explosions, the cessation of war, for me, was followed by a fate worse than death – SCHOOL!

I found it incomprehensible the necessity of having to commence school, since I was very happy being at home, particularly as I adored watching the regular, and countless, array of aircraft, armoured vehicles, and soldiers – with guns!

Most Saturdays, Mr Mason called with his horse and cart to sell vegetables. He fascinated me due to his size – he was a dwarf. Despite this, he was very strong and impressed me by lifting items as if weightless. Some occasions he'd let me take the reins and drive his horse and cart to conclude his rounds.

Horses were still common-place during these great times not least a huge horse, Bess, which pulled a large wagon carrying hardware, including paraffin and vinegar etc. Sometimes I was allowed to help connect the horse's feed bag/sack, not that I was much help given that I couldn't reach the horse's head.

A large imposing, and foreboding, Victorian building was to be my place of education, and mental torture, for the next six years – then called Canterbury Road CP School, later to change to, St George's.

My initiation was horrific. Most of these wretched children were scared and crying. One boy, screaming and struggling aimlessly, was grasped by his wrist and ankles, and carried by two teachers to a classroom. He, like other children, wet himself.

It must have also been traumatic for my mother, and as she waved goodbye through a small window in the classroom door, I began to cry, but was promptly threatened by a female teacher.

Due to financial constraints, as experienced by most families, it was necessary for me, that first day, to walk about a mile to a bus stop, and catch a number seven home. My parents simply could not afford the bus fare to collect me. I was just five years of age, and my parents drummed into me where I should alight, namely, 'Berechurch Hall Road'.

I hated school, and longed for weekends and holidays. Not least, as life was good during post war childhood in Colchester. Free to roam and cycle without fear. Accordingly (save for Primary School) life was undeniably GOOD. Oh, chilblains, frosty windows (wonderful patterns) and no central heating, with one small open fire to share in the sitting room, were challenging during Essex winters.

With the exception of English, and some aspects of History,

I was, to all intents and purposes, close to achieving dunce status. I could not comprehend arithmetic, and while the rest of the class appeared to grasp the difference between odd and even numbers, it took an evening with my father to comprehend this simple task. The following day, with much confidence, I awaited the maths lesson in readiness to show my expertise, only to discover that the teacher, and class, had progressed to the next phase. This was to be the format for much of my education!

I discovered during, indeed to this day, that if the subject matter was/is of little interest to me then I was unlikely to succeed, so much so that when attending Hamilton Road School in Colchester one morning, I was unaware that we were to sit an examination. I had, apparently, sat the 'eleven plus', and had difficulty in spelling my middle name – Crista, Christafer, Christerphor – still can't spell it, and failed.

My junior education showed no signs of minimal academia. However, I did spend much time laughing, which often got me into trouble, not least in the company of the maths teacher, Mr Balfour, a short angry Scot (boasted 40 press-ups every morning) who disliked me due to my inability to comprehend the subject. During one maths lesson (aged nine) I was, as usual, crying with concealed laughter behind my exercise book, with my best mate, Roger Williams, when a yardstick cracked me on the head with some deliberate and meaningful force. Looking up, with tears of laughter running down my face, 'I hate your face boy!' I recall thinking, 'I'm not so fond of yours, either.'

It occurred to me in later years that in addition to my slow comprehension of maths, I must have annoyed Balfour immeasurably, since he was completely devoid of any humour.

During one morning – having successfully persuaded ('swinging the lead') my parents that I was unwell – I decided, in their absence, to attempt some cooking. I was particularly fond of my mother's cheese scones, so armed with what I presumed were the ingredients, I formulated a mix of flour (lots everywhere, kitchen and outside path leading to a generously covered garden rockery) eggs, cheese and insufficient water, resulting in a thick pastry mix. Having rolled, and utilising pastry cutters, the scones were placed on a tray in the very old gas oven, which, very surprisingly, I was able to operate.

Constant checking and removal during baking resulted in unidentifiable objects that were, when chef-tested, wholly unsuitable for human consumption (not a chef-d'oeuvre!). That is, until my sister arrived home and scoffed three.

That evening my parents summoned Dr Clendon to attend my sister who was unwell. She was diagnosed with chronic indigestion!

My childhood included regular trips to West Kensington with my parents and sister, to visit, and stay with, (no bathroom, one outside loo, and strip-wash in the scullery) my maternal grandparents, Alice and Tommy Tyson.

Tommy was, from his shaven head to his baggy trousers and boots, straight out of the 'Alf Garnett' mould, save that Tommy, from the East End, was tougher, and in his youth an Army Physical Training Instructor. However, Tommy was also a bit of a geezer and apparently often stole money from his daughters, culminating in my father having words with Tommy and a fight ensued. Henry won!

Although apprehensive, Tommy fascinated me. He also took me dog racing at White City Stadium, and taught me how to drink hot tea from a saucer in Lyons Corner teashops. He also taught me ditties i.e. *'Old Mother Riley had a cow and how to milk it she didn't know how. She pulled its tail instead of its tits, and all she got was a bucket of....'* And, every Christmas, *'It was Christmas day in the workhouse. The walls were grim and bare. They brought around Christmas pudding for all the Paupers there. One Pauper got excited. With face as bold as brass. We don't want yer Christmas puddin'. Stick it up yer....* (He would say 'lookin' glass').

Unlike my granddad my grandma (Nan) came from good stock i.e. her father, Thomas Frederick Nash, possibly the last Handsome Cab driver in London, owned his Hansome Cab business (detailed later) and she paid the price of her early infatuation for Tommy, who had apparently been violent towards her culminating in her losing their expected sixth child, when he pushed her down the stairs. Suffice it to say, I loved her dearly, and even this short reference has resulted in a tear or two.

During one trip, when four years of age, my parents took me to a cinema (my first film) but did not check the content. The black and white film had started and there, for my entertainment, was an operation in progress with surgeons and theatre nurses fully gowned and masked. I burst into tears and was carried to safety. That film probably caused me a degree of irreparable harm in that for many years I had a fear of hospitals and anyone dressed as nurses. Indeed every time my parents drove me through the East End, I was aware of a hospital (The Royal London) that, unknowingly to them, freaked me out.

Crossing the road to school, one morning, (I was six) I was hit by a cyclist. The metal mudguard cut into my leg, but my anxiety was increased considerably on seeing an ambulance pass at the end of the road. 'Please don't stop.' I silently pleaded. It didn't, and I was tended first aid by a teacher. Despite my fear of hospitals (in later years my fears would be severely tested) I adored our trips to London, and it still galls me that Hitler's antics resulted in my being deprived of, 'Londoner, born and bred mate,' status.

Although London is only about forty-five miles from Colchester, my parents were not well received by some, in particular their immediate neighbours on the Mersea Road, simply because they were from London. While my father was more than capable of dealing with any neighbour problems, sadly my mother was not, and she suffered two mental breakdowns when I was pre-school age; resulting in my having to stay with elderly neighbours which was quite frightening and confusing for a little boy.

My parents' home was a two bedroom semi-detached property, built in the 1930's, and the adjoining property was rented by the offending neighbours, the Goldings. I think that Mrs Golding took exception to my parents for reasons that never became clear, save that they were from London. Neither parent had strong London accents, and both simply sought peaceable enjoyment of their home and children. Mr Golding was clearly pressured by his wife to complain about – well, basically, anything/nothing.

As a young child I shared my parents' very small bedroom and one Sunday morning I was singing a song, 'Domino' (a popular song written in 1950 that I'd heard on the wireless) and Joe Golding confronted my father. On hearing him complaining to my dad about my singing (it wasn't that bad) I ran downstairs. At the back door my father was attempting to diffuse the situation, but was not succeeding so he gently stroked Joe Golding's chin and told him, 'run along home' – which he did!

One morning (dad was at work) I was in the upstairs bedroom at the rear of our home with my mother, who, while cleaning, opened the window and was immediately (from the Golding's back garden) verbally abused by them and their adult son who picked up, and threatened to throw, a flowerpot at my mother. She told them to clear off. However, these totally unprovoked events clearly proved detrimental to her mental health.

A few years later, when I was about eight, my mother

appeared to be eating mostly Shredded Wheat that would be placed in the oven until virtually burnt and then returned to the box to be eaten later. I recall her taking a good supply when we travelled to London (in my father's converted, and very old, Bradford van). It transpired that my mother had been pregnant, but given the small accommodation at number 26 Blackheath, Mersea Road, it was decided, I subsequently learnt, much to my father's distress, that my brother or sister should be aborted.

I learned, when older, that during that very trip to my Nan's in London, the abortion was performed by a guy (a 'back-street abortionist') recommended by my father's brother, Albert.

It's little wonder that my mother would be denied mental well-being and stability for the remainder of her life. However, despite adversity, she provided love, care, and stability during my childhood.

Like most post war families, my parents had little, or no, disposable income. While Christmas and birthday presents were always minimal, they were of maximum appreciation to me; not least a toy cowboy pistol when I was eight. I adored cowboy films, particularly those featuring Roy Rogers and his horse Trigger. However, Roy had two revolvers and twin holsters. I could not believe Christmas morning when unwrapping my present from Nan Tyson; twin holsters and an extra pistol, not matching, but the best, the very best.

One trip to Nan's during the summer of 1951 my Dad took me to the Festival of Britain. I was only seven and was overwhelmed by the structural displays and the vast amount of people that were, unbeknown to me, in high spirits due to the cessation of war – a time to celebrate. Sadly I don't remember all that happened for me during that very exciting day save for watching a fairground attraction/game that (mostly) adults paid for to fire three shots at a target with a type of bazooka/tank buster. Sadly, I was far too young to have a go, but as I stood watching, the ammo, a bouncy rubber ball, rebounded from the target and hit me in the stomach, resulting in concerned voices, not least from the guy running the stall and my Dad. Fortunately, I was just a bit shocked and winded.

Chapter Thirteen

PARENTAL MISFORTUNE

My father was intelligent and extremely hard working. He did all that he could to provide a secure and stable upbringing for my sister and I, and despite financial constraints, he was a generous man. However, his kindly disposition and generosity would later be severely tested.

Some Saturday afternoons, during my time at junior school, he'd take me to afternoon pictures at the Empire Cinema (known as the local flea-pit) in Colchester. If a child, or children, were hanging around the entrance looking at the photo excerpts of the film to be shown, he'd invariably ask them if they wanted to see the film and would pay for them. A child or children would often be very pleased and we'd never see them again. However, on one occasion, in addition to a couple of lads, a girl of about twelve accepted Henry's kindness and like most of these kids we didn't see her after she'd entered the cinema.

Sadly my father became the subject of a police investigation following a complaint from the girl's parents who alleged that she'd been enticed by my father, culminating in he having to seek legal advice.

Though only nine years old I wanted to help my parents as I was present with my father during the film and at no time did he leave me and neither did I see the girl again. However, the simple fact remained that by going to the cinema the girl apparently arrived home late, her parents demanded to know why, so she told them that a man had taken her to the cinema.

The case did not proceed; the kids, however, needless to say, received no further free tickets from Henry.

The irony of this scenario is that my father really couldn't afford to provide free entry for kids.

My Aunt Betty (my father's sister) was an artist, and she gave me a painting showing a young Henry, selling ice creams to children, during his very short employment with Walls Ice Cream in Chiswick. He was sacked for giving children free ice creams!

One Saturday, prior to our visit to the cinema, my mother, who was working part-time for M&S, left instructions for Henry to load the week's laundry in the copper for washing and mangling that evening. On arriving home, my mother discovered that Henry had loaded, and lit, the gas copper, but had failed to fill it with water, thus burning and destroying the laundry. Henry was in the doghouse.

Perhaps 'inspired' by my old man, when aged nine, I became momentarily, and unintentionally, an Arsonist.

One summer Sunday evening, I offered to light a bonfire for my father. I decided en route to enter the garden shed where I lit a discarded oily rag. Prompt ignition was achieved necessitating prompt action, as I smacked the flames with a large metal file. Confident that I'd successfully smothered the flames, I left the shed and lit the bonfire that was soon ablaze. Later, as the fire smouldered, I adjourned indoors.

Soon, several parishioners, leaving the Baptist Church opposite my parents' home, were staring in our direction. 'What are those nosey blighters looking at?' enquired my mother, promptly followed by. 'The bloody shed's on fire!' from my father, who was up stairs having a bath.

His next words, as he eyeballed me, while rushing soaking wet to fill a bucket of water were, 'Bloody kids.' Clearly, and fortunately for me, there was no time for retribution, so I helped by passing buckets of water from my mother to my father. Several buckets and galvanised baths of water, the fire was out, leaving a skeleton of black twisted metal that had been our bicycles. The very old, and very full, garden shed, had been razed to the ground. Fortuitously, the shed was insured, resulting in a replacement, including a second-hand bike for me.

Save for singed eyebrows, when messing around with fireworks, or my junior chemistry set, major or minor fires were eliminated. Well almost, I've just remembered two further incidents during 'swinging the lead'. It was winter and my parents had lit a fire in the sitting room prior to going to work. I'd seen how they held newspaper across the open fire to draw and accelerate the flames, so I proceeded to emulate this procedure, whereupon the sheets of newspaper promptly ignited. Clutching the flaming newspaper, I ran to the kitchen sink and doused the flames as the net curtains above burned as if soaked in petrol. No secondary degree burns, not even a blister.

On returning home my mother was washing her hands at the kitchen sink. 'What the hell's happened here?' It might have been beneficial had I trimmed or removed the dangling remains that were, until then, the nets.

The second incident involved the making and firing of a tiny homemade cannon that I'd made, and which required Swan Vesta matches. Safety matches were useless. A much lesser incident, when positioned outside the back door, and my target promptly burst into flames. 'Where's my newspaper?' Dad enquired.

Dad, like many hard working pre and post war parents was

of the opinion that if you wanted something, you had to work for it e.g. pea and fruit picking during the junior school summer holidays. In addition I was asked/told to pick lavender that grew in abundance in our back garden. The lavender was then tied in small bundles, a 'Lavender For Sale' crudely painted and placed just outside the front garden where I waited for passing vehicles that occasionally stopped and a purchase secured.

My father also arranged delivery (probably through Uncle Albert) of nylon stockings, which meant, when just ten years of age, I was introduced to the realms of a travelling salesman, in that most Saturdays I was driven (by dad)) to various villages in Essex and given the unenviable task of attempting to sell nylons to housewives and elderly ladies – the nine denier to younger ladies and the crepe to elderly ladies. I think my age, and profuse blushing, left the ladies with little alternative – they had to buy.

Subsequently when eleven I was instructed – dad having increased his workload to include being an agent for Vernons' Football Pools – to deliver football coupons to residents on the Monkwick Council Estate, for those who wished weekly to 'do the pools', (complete the football coupon in the hope of a win). Every Thursday I cycled around the estate to collect their coupons, plus a betting fee. Most were regulars that unfortunately included a few that preferred their accommodation to be uninhabitable. The front door would open and the indescribable smell would hit me, followed by, 'Come in, you must be frozen.' For this I received pocket money of two shillings and sixpence.

My father was of the view that life was, and would remain, no picnic, so he expected me (and rightly so) as a male species to show, among other things, respect and courage. As a child, showing respect was not difficult for me as my persona basically reflected this so being taught, among other basics, that you always gave a seat to a lady on a bus, and to walk on the outside when accompanying a female, were natural respectful gestures. [In later years when escorting a young lady colleague she asked, 'What the hell are you doing?'] However, courage was severely tested when Dad asked me (I was nine) to enter a very dark and somewhat foreboding property, and to climb some stairs to establish whether it was occupied. While he waited outside, I entered and commenced slowly climbing the stairs. Half way up I decided to rapidly descend and told Dad that no one was there. He then entered the property and made contact with someone. Angrily he said to me, 'In life you have to have courage.' And then, repeated twice, 'You must always have pluck.'

My father was predominantly of an affable disposition with a good helping of humour. However, I did encounter his wrath on a couple of occasions i.e. a 'good hiding'. One in particular mentally scarred me due to my infancy, I was about six years of age and sharing a bedroom with my parents; it was a Sunday morning and I'd just woken-up. My parents were in their bed and awake. My mother left the room and my father told me to stay in my bed. I didn't want to and attempted to get out of my bed, whereupon he angrily and forcefully placed me in my parents' bed. I continued to complain and was quite severely punished. My father's face was distorted with anger. I was very frightened and pleaded with him to stop, which he eventually did. Given my parents' circumstances I assumed, in later years, that my father and mother were hoping for some marital action and I'd vetoed it.

Chapter Fourteen

A week before our usual summer trip to my Nan's (I was about 11) I decided one evening that an empty coke bottle was a suitable target for my air rifle. Being a 177 (as opposed to a more powerful point 22) the pellets simply chipped the thick glass, so having tired of this uneventful pursuit, I decided to hit the bottle with a brick thus achieving the removal of the neck of the bottle. Having disposed of the neck I proceeded to throw remaining part that promptly sliced off the top of my right index finger. A trail of blood followed my path, and with my finger bound with various bandages, I was taken by dad to the local surgery down the road. Given the amount of blood seeping through the bandages, those gathered in the waiting room appeared anxious to let me jump the queue. Dr Paros attended me but could not stitch the wound since it was a slice as opposed to a cut.

I attended school the following day in absolute agony. A few days later while in London at Nan's I removed the dressing, as I'd done several times to have it redressed, but when placing my hand in a bowl, as usual the wound began to bleed, but this time it looked like red smoke rising, whereupon I attempted to walk to the dining room and walked into the door surround as I was passing out. Henry was NOT impressed.

Following the death of my granddad in 1956 (I was often reminded, fortunately in jest, that Tommy had died within a week of me provoking him into chasing me around the paddling pool in Brightlingsea) my Nan often travelled by coach to Colchester to stay for a few days with my parents. One Sunday afternoon my father requested a cup of tea. Surprisingly, my Nan and mother didn't want tea (were they ill?) and I refused to participate; I had an ulterior motive that my Nan would appreciate. My father reluctantly went to the kitchen and while there I blew, and over-inflated, a 'whoopee cushion' which I carefully placed under Henry's sofa cushion. The sofa was a small very low two-seater, and Henry overweight. He entered with cup and saucer, and sat. As the novelty cushion slowly farted, Henry began to roll in various directions while depositing the tea in various directions. Finally the novelty cushion was flat, and Henry, clearly not amused, threw the cup and saucer as it smashed to the floor. Nan laughed – job done.

It was normal for men and women (including my mother) to be grafters e.g. spending most free time gardening a lengthy plot in our back garden, primarily to provide vegetables.

Henry's childhood was spent with his parents, and brother Albert and sisters at British Grove in Chiswick, London.

Two anecdotes, related me by my father, warrant inclusion:

1   When about nine years old, Henry, with the aid of his older brother Albert, made a cannon, utilising lead pipe. They acquired some gunpowder and successfully - their first attempt - fired the cannon in the back garden. The cannon was reloaded but failed to fire, so they added more gunpowder and shot, but the cannon failed to ignite so the lead tubing was sealed at each end and discarded behind the garden shed. Some years later Henry heard of a hobby pursued by other lads that involved making castings out of molten lead. He prepared a work surface at the rear of the

house and after some searching found the lead pipe. However, despite apparently being of above average intelligence he failed to question why it was there, or to remember what it contained. The fire in the sitting room included a suspended cauldron into which he placed the tube and returned to the back of the house while his father sat by the fire reading his newspaper. Henry told me that he actually felt the house shake when the pipe exploded. On entering the sitting room his father, and previously white beard, were engulfed in soot. Henry swiftly left the house, returning much later when he knew his mother was home. She apparently adored him and ensured that he was spared retribution.

2 A year or so later my father and brother Albert were asked by their father to take a revolver and ammunition to a pawnshop. This they managed without incident but decided to keep two of the point 38 calibre bullets, which they placed in a small tin on the mantelpiece in the sitting room. A few months later, while their father sat in front of the fire reading his newspaper, and Henry and Albert were out, their cat apparently walked along the mantelpiece knocking the tin containing the bullets into the fire. Henry's father retrieved the tin but was unaware of the contents. He returned to his seat, with newspaper, as one bullet hit the ceiling, the other narrowly missing him, as it passed through his newspaper!

At 18 years of age, Henry was instrumental, with a colleague, in designing a Hovercraft. My father had related this to me when a boy and drew pictures. He told me that he and his older colleague (who was financing materials) had built the craft with a view to promoting the venture, and securing finance, for the construction in the USA. The plan was for his colleague to book a passage on a liner carrying the prototype with Henry stowed therein. Henry apparently waited dockside but his colleague and hovercraft did not. Never to be seen again.

Needless to say, given the era (early 1920's) the Hovercraft was very basic in design and very different to the technically advanced crafts of today. That said this was an innovation.

In later years, he painted a picture that I have now, which reveals a conventional winged aircraft with enclosed cockpit. Two engines and propellers positioned beneath each wing. However, each propeller consisted of four blades with rear square extensions of possibly eighteen to twenty four inches, and above each propeller an oval cover of the same depth of the propeller. The objective was to create sufficient downdraught to raise the aircraft thus achieving, Hover. My understanding was that forward flight would be possible with facility for retractable parts to the rear of the blades.

In his twenties, Henry designed and made a small adjustable (sliding mechanism) spanner that was subsequently produced in small quantity for sale, sadly with little profit.

Suffice it to say that my father was a 'Schemer', a clever chap who could turn his hand to practically anything – which succinctly leads me to his daughter, my sister, Sylvia, but more particularly to the man she married, my brother in law, Ken.

First, my sister: During childhood we really didn't get on too well which I assume could simply be the result of age (six years) difference or perhaps her preference for a sister rather than a masculine child. We were, and still are, very different, but that said time and age have resulted in an acceptable and lasting relationship.

Ken: He is a fellow that I have time and respect for. He's simply a nice guy, but also a nice guy with a brain, a brain that I would have welcomed in half its capacity. His work: technically challenging, and included his contribution to fiber optic cable. Like my father, Ken could/can also turn his hand to practically anything but 'practically' is not an acceptable measure of achievement for Ken.

I alluded earlier to Thomas Frederick Nash, my Nan's father – my Great Grandfather – and his Hansom Cab business. It is thought that he may possibly have been the last Hansom Cab driver in London. I have a newspaper cutting, the Evening News dated 3rd August 1928 written by a journalist who'd interviewed Thomas (known as George), and showing two photographs of him, one with cab and horse. As with all Hansom Cabs, the driver sat elevated outside at the rear while using lengthy reins and whips to direct and control a single horse.

The Headlines:

'STORIES FROM SOME OF THE
DOZEN HANSOM CABBIES OF LONDON'

A Vanishing Race: "Londons All Dead Now" says George of Barons Court: Real Ladies Didn't Ride in Hansoms............

"ONE of the last thirteen hansom-cab drivers in London" the solicitor said at poor "Sneak the Pie's" inquest last Saturday, but even that is an overstatement. "Teddy Oysters" has had an accident and is in hospital, and Walter Franklin gives up his hansom this week for a 'Growler'. The ranks of the hansom cabbies are very thin.

George, of Baron's Court, is still going strong. He is a young man of 72, with white hair and moustaches, and a fine healthy colour, who sports a swagger horse-shoe of brilliants in his tie; and his name is really T. F. Nash. I hailed him and asked to be driven to a quiet place where we could talk; and as we went along with that gentle rocking motion of hansoms, to the clip-clop of hoofs and jingling of bells, the whip lash occasionally flipping the window beside my head, I had it in my heart to wish there were still many Georges. We stopped in Bruggelsmith – Kipling readers will understand – where a passing growler's driver waved a salutation with his whip.

No Night Life Now!

"Well, I've been at it fifty-three years," said George "and I've always worked round these parts. I helped to lay the first tramline on the Uxbridge road, a single track a mile and a quarter long it was from the station to Askew Crescent; and then I drove the horse tramcar. It was all brickfields and open country there in those days. The tramcar was oval-shaped, with a dicky seat on top at each end for the driver, and it could hold forty-six passengers."

The venture was not a success at first – in fact, it 'went bust,' George told me, four times and finally he gave up tram driving and took to hansoms, which he has driven ever since.

One of the ?? fares he remembers was a man he took from Addison road to Westminster early in the morning of the Queen's Jubilee. "I got ?? for that" he said "It was a long day but I did it.

"It's dead now," said George contemptuously. "There ain't no night life anymore and you don't get the same class of people you used to. Why, in those days the young fellers used to come into cab shelters in their evening dress and order steak dinners all round for the cabbies. And they'd start an argument, the young feller would, when you'd driven 'em just to get up fight. I didn't like that much – usually got the worst of it. I remember one of 'em picking a quarrel with me in Piccadilly by the Ritz and a rare hiding he gave me. They did it for the fun of it, you know there was never any bad blood – they paid up handsome afterwards – and the police never interfered in those days.

I asked George how the ladies managed to get their crinolines into his hansom. "I don't know how they did it" he said" They made a bit of a fuss about it but they managed somehow. But ladies don't take hansoms, you know not real ladies.

"It's all different now. Gentlemen always wore top-hats then; you can't have a gentleman without one, not to my way of thinking. And how many do you see about nowadays?"

***

I recall my Nan saying that working as a cabbie meant that her father was out in all weathers – it was an extremely demanding job.

A 'Growler' (first paragraph of press cutting) like the Hansom Cab, was horse drawn but unlike the Hansom, with two wheels, the Growler had four and often two horses. Its real name was a Clarence but due to the noise of four wheels on cobble-stoned streets, it was known as the 'Growler'.

My great grandfather married Mary Anne Emar, a White Russian Jew, in March 1887, she having been born in St Petersburg. It is believed that when five years of age she fled to London from St Petersburg with her parents during a conflict in the 1800's.

Chapter Fifteen

SHORT TO LONG TROUSERS

In 1955 I attended a large modern designed comprehensive school namely, Alderman Blaxill, where I commenced just above the bottom stream, but inexplicably was soon promoted to a slightly higher stream, where I remained until cessation at the age of fifteen. However, it's fair to say that I preferred my secondary experience to my junior torture, not least as my interest in music and drumming had been duly noted, and girls were in abundance.

Within a short time, I met a lad who not only attended the same school, but also lived about a mile from my parents' home. Peter Streete ('Streetey') was a good mate, and was part of a hilarious, yet precarious, event that took place in our early teens.

Streetey and his father were keen to see a war film at the Playhouse cinema in Colchester, and suggested that I join them.

We entered the foyer and Mr Streete (Maurice) purchased circle tickets for 'Streetey' and himself, leaving me with insufficient money to buy circle tickets, by which time my mate, and his father, (could be a bit overbearing) had gone.

Not to be beaten, I entered the circle in the darkness, the film having begun, and persuaded the usherette to allow me in with stall tickets.

I began larking about i.e. pushing Streetey's elbow off the arm of his seat, messing his hair up, and making various frivolous remarks about the film. He remained quiet throughout, and though I found this strange, simply thought it was because his father was present. The film finished, and as the lights slowly illuminated, I spotted Streetey looking around to find me – he was with his father, four rows in front! I was stricken with silence, as the young man, a total stranger, rose cautiously, and without a word, left his seat, never to return.

I was to discover, during a routine foot-nurse inspection at school, that my big toe was (and still is) apparently very large. The nurse simply observing, 'Oh, that's where it ends.'

A few weeks later, during an indoor five-a-side football match, when bare feet were compulsory, having missed the ball, and kicking an opposing player in the shins, I broke my big toe.

Despite much swelling and pain I rode home and later decided to ride to and attend our local youth club in the church hall where *some* of the girls from school were likely to attend. On arrival some children were finishing their early evening recreational games that required my help by lifting kids quickly to help their team win. As I crouched down the seam in the rear of my jeans (purchased by Henry from a newspaper ad) came completely apart thus exposing my backside (with underpants). Reversing through a door, I mounted my bike and, in much pain, pedalled home. However, I then had to seek help from my mother as my opened jeans had wrapped around my saddle preventing dismounting.

I did much cycling during secondary education, often cycling to West Mersea (an Island off the east coast about five miles from Colchester) during the summer months for a swim despite having cycled 6 miles to and from school on a bike that had no gears. This appeared to enhance my ability to run and being chosen for the four by one hundred yards relay. We won and were awarded medals by the headmaster that we never received!

However, the headmaster always remembered to administer corporal punishment, but it's fair to say that on the one occasion I was caned, I deserved it. A new lady teacher in her early twenties was attempting to give a history lesson during which six lads continued to comb their hair and pick up pieces of paper with the static generated. Pathetically, and apprehensively, I joined them. Given the then hairstyles (Elvis) like me, most lads carried a comb. Following the lesson we were reported to the headmaster, each boy receiving two of the (very) best. I liken it to having been cut. Dent, the headmaster, was of height and build to administer punishment on a scale that most would prefer to avoid i.e. a repeat performance.

A somewhat surreal episode, involving Dent, would follow. We heard that someone had written something on a blackboard. The second, third and fourth year pupils were (it was assumed, I presume, that a first year pupil could neither write nor spell!) ordered to write a short text that included the offending letters within two minutes, thus eliminating any attempt to improve the culprit's handwriting. I finished well within the two minutes. During next morning's assembly Dent angrily indicated that he was onto them (having studied the written evidence) and that the guilty party would be expelled. However, while expressing his wrath he was looking in my direction towards the back (third year) of the large assembly hall. I glanced round thinking he must be looking at the boy behind me – there was no boy. 'Oh shit', has my appalling handwriting left no room for negotiation?

Within five minutes I was ordered to see the headmaster. 'Take this paper, place it on this door and write the words, 'Dent is a bugler.' This I did but indicated that:

I would never consider, let alone actually, doing such a

pathetic thing.

I would confess, and not beat about the bush.

He left the room and shortly returned, 'I believe you boy – dismissed.' The following day a lad was apprehended by a teacher, as he, (the lad) was putting the finishing touches to, 'Dent is a bastard' on the blackboard. I received no apology, and the episode, not surprisingly, resulted in my opinion of Dent – irreparably 'Dented'.

Save for running – as mentioned earlier – my sporting achievements were minimal. However, I was a fit and strong chap (or so I thought) not least my ability to lift the garden roller at home or walk a few steps while carrying three lads, all to impress the girls. In later years I would pay for such frivolity with regular back problems.

For field sports I spent much time practicing the shot-put, principally as the area was close to the sixth form girl's typing domain. I also, on one occasion, implemented my showpiece head-stand, that successfully attracted the attention of some of the girls, only to subsequently discover that my shorts, were not my shorts – my shorts did not have a large crotch split, and underpants were not permitted! Probably, a 'nothing to see here,' moment.

Earlier I described my broken toe ordeal following my attendance at the local church hall. During an earlier visit to the hall, while waiting with a couple of school mates, I was excitedly relating a fight scene I'd seen in a recent film, and was showing how the guy cleverly blocked a punch and followed with a left hook. Unfortunately *my* left hook connected with my mate's mouth resulting in his temporary concussion as I, and my other mate, held him from collapsing. I checked his open mouth to discover a very loose tooth. Later that week I couldn't resist in saying that it was lucky that it had not been my *right* hook! Pathetic, us lads!

Drumming and music took precedence over the rest of my secondary education, except that during my last year (1959) I determined that I should attempt to achieve reasonable end of term exam results. Though still difficult to comprehend, I actually received an impressive (for me) final report.

At the end of term, prior to the summer break, I had intended to return to school for a final year, since I'd decided to explore the possibility of joining the Police Cadets, in which case I would require some paper proof that I was not completely useless. However, circumstances (mother) prevailed on me to get a job.

Subsequently I learnt that the Head Mistress, of my former school, had asked my mother why I had not returned as previously planned. Apparently it was her intention to make me Head Boy! One could be forgiven for doubting her judgement, so I should explain.

Her judgement (reasoning) lay within the boundaries of Blackheath, Mersea (Oysters) Road, Colchester where she lived, and I down the road at number 26. During the summer of 1959 there were long intervals of hot dry weather that resulted in many heath-land fires, which I enjoyed assisting the local fire brigade in extinguishing. However, one evening I noticed flames and smoke rising from a neighbour's garden, and ran to their aid, only to discover that it was the Head Mistress's home and garden. Once there, I quickly connected a garden hose and extinguished the fire that was about to engulf her garden shed.

A few days later I received a box of chocolates that she had delivered. There you have it, a concise briefing on how to become Head Boy.

Coincidentally, Gareth also achieved the heady heights of Head Boy while at junior school, the honour having been bestowed him by the Head Master, David Holman, thus ensuring the continuance of Gareth's unwavering vigilance in the pursuit of his and Jim's (his younger brother) safety and welfare, given the conduct of Holman, as particularised later.

Chapter Sixteen

WHAT A JOB

Earlier I referred to, '...circumstances (mother) prevailed on me to get a job', which perhaps gives the impression that I was given an ultimatum. This was **not** the case. Given the prevailing circumstances, it was simply the type of scenario that **most** post-war kids expected to experience i.e. school's over – get a job!

Given the obvious austerity experienced by many families following the War most children recognised the hard work of their parents, and that they, the children, were fortunate to have their parents' love and a home to live in.

I acknowledged during junior and secondary school that independence was fundamental to one's future and one's acquisition of possessions e.g. drums, motorcycle etc, and that this could only be achieved if you had a job.

Immediately following commencement of school holidays in 1959 I attended a Youth Employment Office and was given details of a job vacancy.

I started work with an old established ironmonger's shop in Colchester, where I worked five and a half days a week, for which I received £2.10s. My mother received £1.00, and I saved as much of the residue to buy records, but primarily, to buy a motorcycle prior to my sixteenth birthday.

I was employed to cut and sell wood in a cellar beneath the shop that provided just one area where I could stand upright and, needless to say, no heating. Much regular cleaning of the entire shop was also part of my work, including polishing the lino shop floor on my knees. Not at all therapeutic, especially when customers were obliged to enter when wet outside.

George Farmer, the owner, was a pleasant fellow, but this could not be said of his manager. Mr T, a tyrant, who could also be sickly-slimy if seeking a favour. On one occasion he ordered me to carry out a task that I explained could not then be achieved. 'Would you like to step outside?' he enquired. 'Yes' I said, with much eagerness. 'With your cards?' he responded.

Two of my mates were working as juniors for a local firm of solicitors, which meant that they did not work Saturdays. This, combined with fourteen months working in a cellar, convinced me to find other employment. Answering an advertisement resulted, very surprisingly, in securing the post of Office Junior with a firm of solicitors.

Indisputably, a good time while in the employ of Marshall & Sutton, well, with the exception of Maureen, then receptionist, whose boyfriend had allegedly been embezzling the firm! Maureen was a bubbly pleasant natured (well, to me she was) young lady who one afternoon assaulted a motorcyclist in the mistaken belief that the guy astride his motor bike was me. Red in the face she described how the fellow was sitting on his motorbike with helmet and goggles covering his face, and she grabbed him from behind. Eventually the young man was able to remove his goggles and...'oh my god, it was so embarrassing!'

One of the senior partners was of interesting lineage but appeared to have frozen in time. If entering a room, having knocked, I would apologise for interrupting him, assuming he was interviewing a client, only to discover that he was talking to himself. He was, I was told, single and occupied a remote dwelling. I often wondered if he'd encountered a traumatic experience when younger, perhaps the loss of a loved one. He seldom spoke to me, save that on one occasion I'd attempted to fit a replacement ceramic lampshade in the typing pool. Unbeknown to me the wires were frayed thus resulting in a large flash and bang as the new lampshade crashed to the floor in pieces. 'In future, leave all electrical matters to me,' he muttered.

Chapter Seventeen

MUSIC/DRUMMING

My interest in music manifested itself at an early stage of my life, probably as the result of my home being situated about five hundred yards from Cherry Tree Army Camp, which provided the regular sound of marching bands. I absolutely adored the drums – how those guys must have loved this kid running beside them with an empty paint tin strung round his neck, and two pieces of kindling for drum sticks.

I drooled over a glass cabinet in the infants' school hall that contained two small drums. Once a fortnight, together with umpteen triangles, the drums were distributed to us kids to accompany the teacher on the piano. One occasion the teacher handed me a drum and sticks. Delighted, I started to play a basic marching rhythm. 'Did I ask you to play that, boy?' The drum and sticks were snatched from me, never to return.

Encouraging or harnessing possible potential of a six year old, was not on the agenda. It occurred to me (not many years later) that signs of early musical development would have been differently assessed in America.

My interest in drumming was severely handicapped as I had no drums, and with the exception of a very old 78rpm record of 'St Louis Blues', a wind-up gramophone, and my parents' wireless, I had limited knowledge of, and limited access to, music. However, aged ten, I was to experience the true meaning of euphoria while listening to the wireless, when I heard 'Rock Around The Clock' by Bill Haley and His Comets.

My pocket money was saved and the record bought from Mann's Music in the High Street, Colchester.

A space was cleared in the garden shed, and I commenced playing along to Bill with the wind-up gramophone and using tin cans and old baking tins for cymbals, advancing subsequently to a fragile toy drum. I then used a discarded pedal bin as hi-hats i.e. a pair of cymbals that close together when the pedal is pressed – wholly useless given that a pedal bin obviously opens when pressed.

Bill Haley and Little Richard were followed by the 'King' ELVIS.

The neighbours' suffered hours of practice without complaint. One neighbour's budgerigar actually enjoying the noise emanating from the garden shed.

One tin of gramophone needles later, and I'd mastered 'Rock Around The Clock.' Just as well, as a groove had worn into part of the record thus rendering it impossible to play same without a pause while I lifted the arm and needle over the groove – HAPPY DAYS!

My father had dimly viewed my obsession with drumming, even introducing me to a piano accordion, but much to his credit he eventually conceded, and while in London for Christmas 1956 he took me to a music shop, 'Birdland Music Box', in Shepherds Bush, and after some haggling, bought me a second-hand Premier snare drum. A few months later Dad arrived home with a bass drum, no ordinary bass drum, but a huge one from the 1930's with 'The Cavaliers Dance Band' on the front head, and inside an electrical socket for a bulb to illuminate the interior. Given that Elvis and others were providing the unmistakable and breathtaking sound of Rock 'n' Roll, the ageing bass drum was sadly obsolete and very, very un-cool, not least as it provided a sound akin to a cannon. That said, I much appreciated Dad's attempt to encourage my drumming, and I spent time dismantling the drum and painting it. Sadly, however, save for shed use, it never gigged.

During commencement at Alderman Blaxill Secondary School, when eleven, my interest in music and drumming had been noted. This involved a somewhat scary encounter with one of the known third year tough guys, Kenny Long.

One morning while walking through one of the corridors I noticed Kenny looking, and coming towards me. As I didn't know him to speak to, I ignored him. 'Are you John Ledbetter?' He forcefully enquired. Cautiously confirming my ID, I was much relieved when he asked if I would be interested in joining his Skiffle Group.

For the uninitiated, a 'Skiffle Group' usually comprised of four to six members playing acoustic guitars, tea-chest bass(es), and often, a washboard. The bass, invariably brightly coloured, bearing the band's name – in this case, 'The Blackzillions' – together with a broomstick to which cord is tied at the top and the other end secured through the centre of upturned tea-chest. As the player plucks the string, and moves the broomstick back and forth, various bass notes are achieved.

The washboard player was equipped, and played same, with thimbles attached to fingers and thumbs. My enlistment soon became apparent, in that, immediately following our first few gigs, mostly at a local cinema supporting Saturday morning pictures for kids, the washboard player was politely asked to leave. You didn't argue with Ken. However, I had to agree that the sound left a lot to be desired, and this, combined with the player's repeated inability to avoid dropping his thimbles, effectively sealed his demise.

Subsequently, Mr Tripp, science and music teacher, who was extremely supportive and let the band practise in the science lab, bought the piano accordion, thus enabling me to return to Shepherds Bush, and purchase second hand hi hat cymbals and pedal. I was on cloud nine, the lads were impressed, and we played a Christmas gig at Paxman Engineering Social Club, Colchester in January 1957. Thanks Dad.

The Backzillions proved quite successful, given that we were all under sixteen years of age. The then manager of the Regal Cinema in Colchester arranged more Saturday morning slots for the appreciative kids, plus a couple of gigs at the Gaumont Cinema in Ipswich, resulting in press interest and photos in the East Anglian Daily Times, and Essex County Standard.

Given my age, my means of transport was my bike, so Henry made a carrier that fitted behind the saddle thus providing for my snare drum. However, the acquisition of the hi-hat stand and cymbals meant that the carrier was too small, resulting in dad buying an old trades bike that not only provided carrying facility but also much fun when transporting my mates over bouncy tracks situated in and around the Wick military (mentioned later) shooting range.

My mother made a cover for my snare drum out of a pair of my father's pyjamas. I was assured by mum that Henry needed a new pair, Henry disputed this, but it was too late. Needless to say, the drum cover was not weatherproof.

During this time a new television pop/rock programme '6.5 Special' commenced featuring the likes of Lonnie Donegan (skiffle & blue grass) Tommy Steele, Cliff Richard etc. I was informed that another skiffle group, who'd appeared on the show, were based in Colchester and were auditioning for a drummer. Having established when and where, and booked a slot, I parked my trade's bike, entered the hall with drum and hi-hats (plus new 'Jim Jam' cover) and introduced myself. I'd seen them on '6.5 Special' but had failed to observe their ages or, more importantly, that these were professional musicians and I was (13) still at school. However, despite these obstacles the audition went well and they were suitably impressed. 'Well done, but...' They couldn't even utilise the customary dismissal, 'please don't ring us, we'll ring you.' No phone at home.

A former schoolmate asked me to checkout some young lads that were rehearsing for an audition. Immediately it was apparent that the drummer was in need of some basic lessons – he was dreadful. (Lessons, however, seldom result in timing, or provide a natural aptitude for rhythm). I said nothing but was asked to accompany their version of Elvis's, 'That's Alright Mama'. As a result, I was asked to travel there and then to Lowestoft and to perform with the group. There was no time for me to collect my snare drum, no time for a rehearsal, so I performed two numbers on stage with a bass drum and a snare drum (a beginner level red Mastro Eric Delaney [later reference] drum available then in some music shops) that also had a small holder and cymbal attached. The lead singer, slightly older, handsome, with Elvis hairstyle and suitably attired, resulted in girls screaming and, 'In first place...' Not us! However, for my part this had been an extraordinary experience not least as the next band to follow was, 'Peter Jay & The Jaywalkers', thus enabling me to watch Peter Jay, professional drummer, from the wings. Prior to the fifties, drumming was mostly jazz and shuffle, so to see this guy playing 'straight eights' on a ride cymbal at speed with a fabulous drum kit, was unimaginable. No time to waste, off to my mate's with snare drum and cymbal to listen on his tape recorder and to play to the Ventures's, 'Perfidia' and 'Walk Don't Run', until I'd mastered 'straight eights'.

Thereafter we played for some well-received gigs but disbanded a year later.

My father, having had enough of engineering, secured the post of Area Manager with Vernon's Football Pools. This involved driving his very old Morris Minor. The engine was knackered, and the brakes virtually useless, due to the fact that extreme foot pressure was required, merely to slow the car.

Dad was anxious that I learn to drive so he gave me lessons that commenced two days after my seventeenth birthday. Often I awoke from a nightmare, my feet pressing hard, and painfully, onto the footboard at the end of my bed, having fought frantically to stop the 'Moggie' that was out of control, due to failing brakes.

Shortly after commencing lessons, I noticed an advertisement in the 'Musicians Wanted' column of the Melody Maker. *Young drummer wanted urgently for guitar band with management, tours and contract.'* On telephoning I was informed that auditions would take place the following Tuesday at 'Old Mac's Rehearsal Rooms' in Soho.

My father suggested, as part of my learning, that I drive him to Mile End Road, where I could Tube it on the central line to Holborn, and from there to Piccadilly Circus. While driving (near Romford) I was following a brand new Jaguar – gun-metallic finish. 'Lovely, but concentrate on your driving,' observed Henry, which was fortuitous given that a lady driver waiting to turn right towards us, inexplicably drove and collided with the Jag thus effectively re-shaping its off-side. Fortunately I was travelling a safe distance behind the Jag, since slamming the brakes on merely slowed the Moggie but not sufficiently to avoid having to swerve around the accident. Classic response from Henry, 'Well done, but you should have stopped.'

With my pair of old odd drumsticks (couldn't afford matching) in hand, I eventually found 'Old Mac's' which was situated at the rear of a strip-club. I entered a large smoked-filled room where the band had commenced auditioning one of about twenty hopefuls. I was reassured as the first and second were not too good, one attempting a marching beat to a Rock instrumental. The guys requested a drum split (solo) that was well received, and keenly enquired where I was based. Colchester was too far away – passed yet failed.

While in the employ of Marshall & Sutton, the younger son (later to be a QC) of the senior partner, played guitar and we formed a group, 'The Sabres.'

Subsequently, Maureen, receptionist at Marshall & Sutton solicitors, suggested – I think she thought I was bogus – that I contact another musician living in Tollesbury, Essex, who she knew had a band and he'd mentioned that they needed a drummer. Subsequently I successfully auditioned with them, and as a result the Deltas were formed, a Rock/Pop combo: Brian, lead guitar, Johnny O'Halloran, rhythm guitar, Ken Winger, bass, and yours truly, on drums. All, with the exception of me, sang. The band was subsequently managed by Mick Walby.

Chapter Eighteen

Very soon the Deltas were regularly gigging, mostly Fridays and Saturdays in various venues in Essex and Suffolk, and occasionally in London. It was following a gig (Nuffield Centre?) in London that an offer of a World Tour was made by an agent, culminating in Press interest and interviews, plus an evening TV appearance. However, aerial pick-up at Glenys's home denied her viewing but her girlfriend's viewed and merely said that I was frantically chewing gum!

The press release of the Colchester Gazette reads:
Meet the Deltas – a group of amateur musicians, already well-known to Colchester, who have at last got their big chance. Playing in London last week they were heard by an agent who arranges overseas tours, and offered them six tours of British bases in the Middle East and Far East. These would include three weeks in Cyprus and a similar period in Kenya and Japan. In the group are Johnny Ledbetter of Mersea Road; John O'Halloron, of Collingwood Road; Kenny Winger, of Tiptree; and Brian, of Layer Road.

How times have changed: Home addresses disclosed!

And in the Essex County Standard:

'World tour for TV men?
Amateurs find success after all.'

'A Colchester musical group who missed an audition with Anglia Television on Tuesday because two of the players could not get time off from work had an even bigger chance offered them on Wednesday.

They are the Deltas – a group formed by five [four actually!] young men about a year ago.

On Wednesday they were playing at an engagement in London when they were heard by an agent who arranges overseas tours. They were offered six tours of British bases in the Middle and Far East.

CYPRUS, KENYA & JAPAN

These would include three weeks in Cyprus, four-and-a-half weeks in Kenya and similar period in Japan.

Manager of the group is Michael Walbley [Walby] of 19 Belle Vue Road, Wivenhoe, [Colchester] Lead Guitarist is Brian Newton, a salesman of 134 Layer Road Colchester; John O'Halloran of Collingwood Road, is rhythm guitar; Ken Winger of Tiptree is base [bass!] guitar and main singer – although all members of the band sing; Johnny Leadbetter [no 'a' in Ledbetter] of Mersea Road is drummer.

Accepting the tours would mean turning full-time professional musicians and they are making their decision today.

MISSED OPPORTUNITY

On Tuesday, the group thought they had missed the chance of fame and fortune. They were to have been auditioned by Anglian Television with the possibility of appearing in a series of programmes but Johnny Leadbetter and John O'Halloran are both employed by Woods of Colchester Ltd, who have a rule that no leave of absence is granted for sport, games or entertainment.

The group has spent a year working on their performance and nearly £1,000 on instruments and equipment.'

In addition to errors bracketed, 'Johnny' was not my choice and was eventually replaced with my birth-name, 'John'. I was not employed by Woods of Colchester Ltd but John O'Halloran was. Quite where the Journalist got his notes from will remain a mystery since in addition to very basic errors there was no 'MISSED OPPORTUNITY' as we appeared during a local TV programme in Norwich, playing two instrumental covers.

Prior to the TV appearance I had to concede that my vintage drum kit would have to be replaced, so off to Chas E Foote (drum store) in Soho with Mick our manager. I fancied a black Premier kit; fortunately a three piece (toms and bass) was available. However, given my age, and very low income, it was necessary for Mick to act as guarantor for the HP agreement.

An interesting trip home with my new cased drum kit followed. Mick, having left his car in East London, meant that we, and drums, were to return courtesy of the Underground on a Saturday afternoon. Fortunately youth, strength – particularly on the escalators – resulted in success.

Subsequently it also proved necessary to replace my Ajax snare drum which failed to provide for guitars and vocal amplification. A black Trixon snare drum, as advertised in the Melody Maker, was for sale at the same drum store i.e. Chas E Footes. However, I simply did not have the time to travel to London to view it and wrote to Foote's explaining my dilemma. Two days later the drum arrived with a covering letter inviting me to purchase same, if satisfied, or return it them. An incredible gesture – purchase secured.

Brian (lead guitar and vocals) was an Army Corporal [the Press release shows 'salesman] that appeared not to interfere with gigging. He was a likeable fellow, married with two young daughters. Most rehearsals took place in Brian's sitting room, his very pleasant wife providing endless cups of tea. I have to confess that I often felt extremely uncomfortable when his daughters were encouraged to run around the house naked. I simply thought it wrong. However, my misgivings would be raised irreconcilably when I learnt that Brian would be leaving the band, and that he was being prosecuted for sexually abusing his eldest daughter, then ten years of age.

Given the circumstances, it's essential that I provide some clarity in regard to Brian's offence.

I was just sixteen years of age when I successfully auditioned with the Deltas and, accordingly, when I first met Brian.

His departure from the Deltas took place within a year or so of my joining the band, and it may sound bizarre, **now**, but I was completely unaware that his offence categorised him as a paedophile, indeed, neither I nor Glenys were aware of the existence of paedophiles, or the crime of paedophilia.

The remaining members of the band were shocked, but Brian's offence was hardly mentioned, and the local Press allotted a small back page reference to Brian's Magistrate's Court hearing date, and that the family intended to move to Hampshire.

Glenys and I realised that what Brian had done was very bad, and we were concerned for the child, her younger sister, and her mother, but our ages, education and circumstances excluded the actuality of certain aspects of life which today would probably be included in the dialogue of nine to eleven year old children.

Oblivion was a circumstance (to follow) that would remain comatose until the arrest and subsequent trial of David Holman, former Head Master of Charlestown Primary School, and who died of Aids while in prison.

This nightmare scenario – as is sometimes the case – was

replaced with the good news that lead guitarist, and vocalist, Len Dally, would be joining the band. Len was an accomplished musician. Many years later I would discover that Len (recently departed) was an extremely accomplished Artist.

It was decided that the band needed sixties style clothing, so off to London. However, I decided not to join them in London, preferring to spend time with Glenys, it being the first gig-free Saturday for many, many months. Slightly, ever so gutted, to learn that the rest of the band, while having lunch in a café, had met, and chatted with, John Lennon – smartly attired in his brown sixties suit, he gladly joined them for a photograph! Sadly I did not bother to get a copy.

On another occasion when returning to Colchester from London, Mick was driving us in his Jag on the A12 and decided to overtake just as another driver decided the same manoeuvre, resulting in a quite massive collision and a total reshape of Mick's beautiful gleaming 3 litre Jag – well the front end, that is. No seat belts, and no injuries!

The band was popular, particularly in the Colchester area, sometimes even achieving screaming females, particularly in response to Beatle covers. However, often the finale resulted in spontaneous cheering and screaming during our loud but meaningful version of Elvis's (Len's) 'One Night'.

I think that in the absence of secure relationships and jobs, the four members of the band would have accepted the contract. Our cautious approach to the unpredictable and fickle world of music was significantly highlighted when occasionally supporting a 'name' band, not least the Mersey Beats at the Clacton Town Hall in January 1966. Their single 'I Think of You,' had just hit the number one slot of the top ten UK singles chart.

'We're H.A.P.P.Y.' – not particularly! They were tired and all looked as if they could do with a square meal, and a good night's kip. I grabbed a moment to chat with the drummer, an affable chap, who let me borrow his hi-hat stand that was heavier than mine thus minimising 'creeping' (slipping away from the kit), but clearly he was not a happy bunny. He explained that they had spent three nights touring, during which much time was spent sleeping in a transit van with their equipment. He also explained that at the end of that evening's gig they were to travel north in time for another gig the following day. Their amplifiers and instruments had seen better days, indeed my drum kit, despite much use, was in far better nick than his, and reading between the lines, I got the distinct impression that money was in short supply. I think it is fair to say that the Deltas unanimously agreed that, all in all, we were better off on the semi-professional circuit. That, of course, was then – I could not imagine a band or artiste at No.1 in the charts today, experiencing the same situation.

That said, The Mersey Beats survived and remained very much a part of the Liverpool Beat era.

Mentioning the problem of a drum kit moving (creeping) while performing reminds me that during a 1960's gig in a large concert hall in Southend on Sea (Palace Theatre?) my drum kit was positioned in an elevated position about six feet above the centre of the stage. During a rock number, before a capacity audience, my bass drum plus first tom and attached 'ride' cymbal began to creep. My attempt to grab it failed, resulting in said kit crashing to the floor! Fortunately no damage and I think the appreciative audience thought it was part of the performance and were further entertained when repositioning the kit and hammering some large metal staples – that I always carried with me, plus a wooden cosh – into the elevated stage thus preventing the bass drum from moving. By this time the audience was a mix of cheering, screaming and whistling.

Chapter Nineteen

'BRASS MONKEYS'

During the winter of 1962-63 we experienced the 'Big Freeze'. Despite this the band managed to fulfil all bookings, that is, until about the end of January. A gig on the Friday preceded a booking at Little Oakley in Essex, close to the Suffolk border. I collected Glenys from Tollesbury and immediately encountered snow. It was obvious from the outset that this was to be no ordinary snowfall, so in anticipation we parked and watched as Mick Walby (manager) drove past thus indicating that despite the forecast he was going to attempt to drag The Deltas to Lt Oakley. Eventually I drove to my parents assuming that he had aborted the trip, particularly as a blizzard and drifting had commenced. No, he arrived in his Jag with the remaining Deltas plus amps and guitars in his boot. My concerns fell on deaf ears, and I was persuaded to travel in the Jag, which somehow, accommodated my drum kit. Within a few miles, driving became extremely difficult, followed by 'white-out' thus necessitating the use of a spotlight that was fixed next to the windscreen, and which swivelled when operated by hand, by the driver! By this time the roads were thick with snow. However, a left turn from our main road route brought our slow passage to an abrupt halt. The beam from the spotlight focused on a sight that was temporarily impossible to comprehend. Venturing outside, we were confronted with a wall of snow approximately fifteen feet high. 'Right,' says I, 'let's get the hell out of here, Mick, you fucking imbecile!' (I rarely swore in those days!) Back in the front passenger's seat, I sat frozen, but was forced to look once more at the wall of snow. 'Stop!' I pleaded. Through the blinding blizzard I thought I could see an object at the foot of the snow-wall. Leaving the car, once more, we discovered the rear end of a vehicle and immediately commenced removing snow with our bare hands and discovered a guy attempting to open the driver's door. 'I thought I was a gonna,' he exclaimed. With the aid of a tow-rope, the car was pulled from the snow and he proceeded on his treacherous journey, obviously in the opposite direction.

The Deltas and manager were frozen, not least as sixties fashion, and a lack of disposable income, provided no suitable winter clothing, e.g. in my case, a summer lightweight (not even shower-proof, but fashionable!) raincoat.

Johnny O'Halloran (rhythm guitarist) began to laugh. 'Look at your face, John.' With the aid of the rear-view mirror, I could see an extraordinary sight. I was adorned with icicles attached to my hair (I had lots in those days, hair, not icicles) that ran in lines to my cheeks.

A somewhat precarious ride home, but we made it. We discovered that Little Oakley would remain snow-bound, without transport, for a week. Any observation on my part would be a statement of the bleedin' obvious.

A few years later, during another snowstorm, our peace was interrupted by a knock on the door. A not so welcoming police Sergeant attired in helmet and (in those days) black cape, and covered in snow. 'Mr O'Halloran wants to know if you're going to attend the hotel in Frinton-on-Sea tonight?' I explained that I knew nothing of this gig, but would be there, snowstorm permitting. He left muttering to himself, but confirmed he would telephone the hotel. Needless to say, we didn't then have a telephone at our disposal, simply relying, like many others, on the local red telephone box.

Despite her concerns, Glenys conceded. (She was quite used to my travelling to and from gigs during bad weather) So with drums loaded, I set forth.

The A12 was passable, and haste possible. However, on leaving the A12, and joining the A120, snow had impacted culminating in my driving too fast, losing control and eventually resting on the middle reservation of the dual carriageway. Fortunately no crash barriers (or collisions!) thus enabling me to cross to the adjoining carriageway, reach a roundabout, and try again, this time successfully.

Chapter Twenty

Our popularity resulted in having to decline bookings that often culminated in advance bookings, sometimes a year ahead. One booking that was repeated immediately following a gig, was an engagement at Stansted Hall in Essex, the home of Lord Butler MP (known as RAB Butler). We performed in a large barn in the grounds of Stansted Hall where we were very well received, and RAB, a quiet and personable chap, always chatted and thanked us for the evening's entertainment.

We also entertained the Cobbolds (of Tolly Cobbold brewers in Ipswich) at their spacious abode when we were forced to drink Champagne owing to a delivery error – there was no beer left!

The Army Officer's Club in Colchester was also a regular fixture. Needless to say, catering was at its best. However, during the interval of one gig, (transport having been provided) I was taught a salutary lesson. Large army catering bins were filled with Champagne and strawberries. I jokingly requested less strawberries and more juice. My drumming provided highly suspect patterns.

Another fixture that was repeated each time a multi millionaire's daughter attained twenty-one i.e. three daughters, three very decent gigs. I regret not having a camera to hand each time I arrived and parked my Morris Minor between Rollers,

Ferrari, Aston Martins, Porsche and Jags.

Follow that? Very simply, we also (once only) performed with female strippers at a club in Colchester. The lead stripper ran through her routine and stressed that when she and her two colleagues turned to face us for the finale (completely starkers) we should finish. As young males this proved difficult resulting in a somewhat prolonged finale!

The Deltas were also well received at Wethersfield USAF base in Essex where we regularly performed.

One Friday evening, following our sound check, a black American guy approached me and explained that his routine was predominantly tap-dance and asked if I would provide him with some backing brushwork. Brushwork entails the use of wire brushes that are specifically designed to provide a distinctive sound when stroked across, or struck upon, a snare drum. This type of playing is perhaps more commonly associated with *bluesy* jazz tracks, skiffle, rockabilly, and so on.

I accompanied this guy, who was a brilliant exponent of tap, but it was not until he was part way through his act that I experienced a '*déjà vu*', rapidly followed by a realisation that I'd seen him (Will Gaines) perform on, 'Sunday Night At The London Palladium,' six days earlier, then accompanied by Eric Delaney, a big time show drummer. On entering the venue I'd seen various notices of forthcoming entertainment and some mention of the London Palladium but the penny had not dropped. He thanked and congratulated me, culminating in a short press release in the Essex County Standard.

Some may recall Eric Delaney. He was a flamboyant drummer, mostly playing Premier six to seven piece kit, including double bass drums, and backed by a band of a dozen or so musicians. His aim, up-tempo dance music, but his piece de resistance was his drum solo, which sometimes included a quite spectacular piece of entertainment. Positioned on one side of the stage, his drum kit, and on the other side, a set of four tymps (tympani or kettledrums). A unique, and always impressive, performance as he sprinted back and forth.

Occasionally I received a phone call from an entertainment's Agent in the hope that I was available to deputise for a drummer or, as in this instance, to accompany a radio 4 Organist at the Copdock Hotel near Ipswich, where he hastily ran through his gig-list. I positioned my drum kit on stage close to where he would perform. Commencement was soon interrupted by the leader of a seven-piece dance band, who complained to the organist (upon discovering) that I did not belong to the Musician's Union. I was urged to continue, which I did, whereupon the dance band threatened to refuse to perform. However, we persevered, and more importantly, I got paid.

The elderly Organist/Musician was of pleasant disposition, and he (a Londoner) kindly invited me for drinks and to meet a close friend of his, an East Ender – a wealthy East End scrap metal dealer, it transpired. I was made to feel very welcome and was also introduced to two women who accompanied him, one of perhaps similar age to himself, and the other younger and very attractive – escort ladies? (Who knows, could have been his wife and daughter!) As the evening progressed the Krays were alluded to and I got the distinct impression that the Organist had been part of the entertainment provided during that era. When indicating that it was time for me to leave, the very likeable and wealthy East End scrap dealer was disappointed, but also surprised – I think he assumed that booked rooms would include my desire to entertain the very attractive young lady. Or more likely, my imagination ran away with me! Who knows, perhaps an East End connection may have resulted in this young drummer deputising, or regularly gigging, during those Kray days.

Regular gigging, resulted in, 'The Tax Man Cometh!' Clearly

someone (I think he's dead now) took exception to this drummer's drumming and 'dobbed' me in. Luckily I'd retained lists of gigs and receipts but obviously band earnings were thereafter declared. (This scenario would be repeated some years later when gigging with another band in Cornwall.)

An earlier song penned by Johnny O'Halloran and Len Dally, titled 'She's A Wildcat' plus our version of Elvis's 'One Night' on the B-side, was recorded and vinyl cut in Colchester as a 45 single that sold in some otherwise unlikely retail outlets e.g. Curry's.

More media interest followed a further offer during the mid sixties from a London agent who was present at a gig at the Wethersfield USAF base in Essex. He offered The Deltas a contract to play London clubs three nights a week, supporting such acts as the Rolling Stones and The Animals. It would have meant packing in our jobs, and although tempting, we unanimously decided to decline the offer. I'm confident when I say that had either offer to turn professional coincided with different circumstances, not least my love for Glenys, I would have accepted the offer. It's fair to say, however, that had we accepted the offer, then our lives would have been quite different; for better or worse, we'll never know, but if we'd achieved an eighth of what the Stone's made, then this would have reflected significantly in our wealth and disposable incomes – for better or for worse!

It reads:

'For the second time within three years a Colchester pop group has turned down an offer of turning professional. They are the Deltas – a group of four local boys who started about three years ago.
Manager of the group is Michael Walby, of 19 Belle Vue Road,

Colchester. Lead guitarist is L.G. Dalli of 30 Queen Elizabeth Way, Colchester, and John O'Hallaron of 114 Collingwood Road Colchester plays rythmn guitar. Ken Winger of 11Paternoster Row, Tiptree, plays the bass guitar and the drummer is Johnny Leadbetter of 23 Blackheath [Ledbetter and 26!] Colchester.

SUPPORTING THE STONES
The group were playing at the Wethersfield air base when a London agent heard them. He offered them a contract to play at London clubs three nights a week, supporting such groups as the Rolling Stones and The Animals.
Accepting the contract would have meant becoming full-time musicians and giving up their jobs and it was the unanimous decision of the group to decline the offer.
"We all have good jobs that offer security and giving them up to enter show business seemed a bit too risky." said John O'Hallaron.

£1000 EQUIPMENT
M Walby added that the money offered would not have covered all the expenses involved. "Equipment, clothes and travel mount up to a great deal. At the moment we have over a £1000 worth of equipment in the group," he said.
The previous offer of turning professional came in 1962, when the group had the opportunity of playing on six tours of the Middle and Far East.'

Subsequently it became abundantly clear that Mick Walby was failing in his duties as Manager. The rest of the guys adopted a period of complaining/moaning, but not to Mick. During an unexpected appearance by Mick at the Affair Club in Colchester, where we were gigging, I decided that it was time for Mick to depart and made this abundantly clear to him, which was a difficult stance to adopt, since I bore him no malice – I liked the guy, but when a drummer's got to do, what a drummer's got to do..........

Further press coverage followed The Deltas demise in 1969. The end of an era, and the end of a fascinating (and often exhausting) period of my life. The Deltas were primarily a successful covers band that lasted ten years and provided an inexhaustible and versatile repertoire including dance, pop and rock. It also (sadly) included some country music – suffice it to say that I'm a 'Rocker' at heart.

Subsequently Johnny O'Halloran, (sadly no longer with us) a mate of his on bass, and yours truly formed a Pop/Rock trio, The Hallmarks. We were soon capitalising on the Deltas' demise, and regularly gigging.

The salutary lesson, mentioned earlier, remained indelibly printed in my mindset; that is, until a gig in Braintree when, once again, transport was provided. During the interval Les, the bass player, won a bottle of Scotch that he shared with me. Suffice to say that at close of play, my drum kit was packed for me having apparently attempted to place the bass drum in a square case. A few days later I learnt that Les had collapsed in the loo and had to be rescued by the police, the staff (including the band!) having vacated, completely unaware of Les's plight!

With the exception of regular gigging with a three piece covers band, Proudfoot, in the 1980's, and a few deputising roles, I've long since ceased to gig. I secured my seat/stool with Proudfoot, simply by chance, when Vernon (lead guitar and vocals) sought my advice with a view to divorce. During initial instructions he mentioned that in addition to his regular job he also performed in a band, but that their drummer had left. Say no more, save that he appeared to fully accept my word, and without rehearsal or details of their repertoire, we played our first gig four days later in Bodmin!

Chapter Twenty One

LET'S TALK GENETICS

Whether it be our surname (Ledbetter), or another alternative, 'Leadbeater', the desire to beat something is clearly apparent, and is defined thus: *English: occupational name for worker in lead, Middle English ledbetere, from Old English lead 'lead' + the agent noun from beatan '**to beat**'*.

Gareth played drums while at school and although his eventual, and extremely important, career in the Home Office was perhaps inevitable, he adores heavy metal music and 'air-drums' with purposeful and accurate definition.

His brother, Jim, began playing drums when nine, and I provided very basic tuition, having never had tuition myself. What I was able to provide was encouragement (and a second hand kit!) but Jim was a natural born drummer and disciplined in that every day after junior school he'd don his head phones and play to Rock tracks that I'd recorded to tape from vinyl.

Absolutely steadfast, a brilliant, and I mean brilliant, drummer who had the courage, at the age of seventeen, to abandon Cornwall for London to pursue his dream, with little financial assistance from his parents, culminating in his living in a squat.

Prior to his departure from Cornwall I spent much time

scanning the Melody Maker in an endeavour to find a suitable band in London that required a drummer. Phone calls were abruptly brought to an end with the understandable – 'He's far too young.' Jim was then sixteen and my attempts to convince the recipient of my call that he was an extraordinary drummer fell on deaf ears. That is until a female lead vocalist with a band called Zue agreed to an audition in Old Ford in Bow (Tower Hamlets). However, given that this was a Hard Rock band, she stressed that ability to play double bass drums was essential. I'd recently purchased a second bass drum pedal and beater that's specifically designed to attach to the existing pedal thus enabling a drummer to achieve the sound of two bass drums with effectively only one bass drum. Jim spent a day or two attempting to provide the patterns sought in their demo tape – it was hard work.

We (Jim, Glenys and I) arrived at the rehearsal rooms and were greeted by Trixie who in turn introduced Jim to the band, when it was immediately apparent that these guys were much, much older than Jim. The lead guitarist left us in no doubt that he saw Trixie's kindness to provide Jim a slot as a waste of time.

Jim set up his drums and he played two heavy rock numbers utilising double bass drum pedals. Immediately the lead guitarist left the stage and with a grim face approached us and demanded, 'How the fuck does a sixteen year old play like that?' We've been auditioning for weeks, some professional drummers, one from Whitesnake, and he (Jim) turns up ....'

Following rehearsals, Zue played the Legendary Marquee and we, unbeknown to Jim, travelled to London to see the gig. We met him outside the dressing room and we all shared an emotional moment.

Given the age difference and the fact that Jim had no means, at that stage, to earn a living, Zue and Jim were forced to part.

A later audition in London was arranged with a Hard Rock

band, but similarly there was a huge age gap. However, it occurred to me that the audition was to take place not far from where my cousin Tony then lived with his wife and two young boys. He and his wife kindly agreed to our staying overnight.

During early evening Tony suggested that we eat at an Italian Restaurant and that we should travel in his works van; Jim, I and the kids in the back. Tony explained as we fell around inside that he didn't hang about these days and seldom stopped at roundabouts! Shaken but not stirred we entered the restaurant and were greeted by (supposedly) Italian waiters.

Now, what I should have explained is that prior to leaving their home his wife had clearly been drinking, so much so that her words were slurring.

It was apparent to the trained eye (one's parent) that Jim, at sixteen, was quiet and a little concerned, and that concern would gradually intensify. Suffice it to say that (now) in his forties, he recalls the evening clearly as having been 'freaked out.'

The waiters having provided wine and soft drinks was followed mostly by very nice pizzas. In the middle of the table were two large lit candles placed in stick holders. Tony's wife made a grab for a very large bottle of white wine thus knocking the lit candles over which immediately set fire to six large used paper napkins/serviettes. Jim remained quiet, the children looked concerned, Tony looked as if he was accustomed to a scenario like this, while his wife picked up the very large bottle and attempted to attack the flames with said bottle by bashing it upon the table. Jim still remained quiet and I think I'd closed my mouth by which time the waiters managed to drag the burning items into a large bin. Signs of a fire in the centre of the table top were evident – thank goodness there was no table cloth to consider!

The next morning Jim played a 'blinder' at the audition having learnt five of the band's composed and complex hard rock numbers. He was offered the job but as semi professionals they couldn't assist him with very basic needs if he joined them in London, not least accommodation.

Tony? Well, Tony is basically a nice chap, and a very clever guy to boot, who worked extremely hard and eventually achieved his own printing business. He loves his boxing, and boxed at amateur level during his youth, and while Tony is not forthcoming, I understand that having defeated various opponents he was asked if he would consider going professional!

He divorced, and subsequently remarried Lynne, a lovely lady. I was honoured to be Tony's best man.

Jim's anecdotal references to 17 years in London as a musician (playing, recording and touring with various bands, including a BMG contract) plus often an essential full time job, are indisputably the stuff of autobiography.

During this time Jim met Aki, a bass player from Japan – another story – his story.

In 1998 SUCKER[p]UNCH, an Alternative Metal four piece, was formed with Jim on drums and Gareth lead vocals. All songs and arrangements were penned by the members of the band.

SUCKER[p]UNCH was eventually signed, and achieved the Heavy Metal section of some major outlets.

In March 2018 Jim and Gareth performed rock covers in Brighton with Nick (bass) from SUCKER[p]UNCH and Mark (lead guitar) from The Rays, to celebrate Gareth's 50th birthday. It/they 'Rocked' and it was an extraordinary achievement (out together via email and three rehearsals) not least as Jim was still recovering from a back injury sustained at work in December 2016 and spent the entire gig with pain killers and an ice pack; plus obviously *some* alcohol!

Much to my sister's dismay her son Richard, when about ten, caused his parents' concern due to his incessant knife and fork drumming at meal times. Perhaps predictable, but what should a drumming Uncle do? Buy his nephew a pair of drumsticks. Suffice it to say, Richard is an accomplished drum tutor.

Gareth's son, Stanley Albert, now sisteen, is an awesome drummer having commenced playing when nine years of age. His ability to emulate complex drum patterns and fills, is simply amazing. Further, he is an accomplished bass and guitar player. A quite extraordinary talent, not least his incredible ability to learn and play lead guitar within eighteen months at a standard almost beyond comprehension – I wish him every success.

And then, grandson Victor Bainey – yes, you've guessed it – drumming, having achieved distinctions in Grades 1&2. Will the gene pool survive? Probably!

Chapter Twenty Two

'MOL'

Molly Leigh is the youngest of four children of close friends and following her birth in June 1999 Glenys and I spent many enjoyable hours looking after her for four years, Jo and Sally having asked if we would provide care since they were still working. Given my/our circumstances, not least my premature retirement (facts to follow) at just fifty five years of age, the introduction of one, Molly Leigh, provided the impetus which was so essential in reshaping our lives. Molly was, and remains, very simply, a lovely human being – we love her dearly.

During Molly's infancy it became apparent that she liked music, and very soon she was playing the piano, swiftly followed by the flute and violin – not to mention her singing – all of which provided her natural ability to achieve ***perfect pitch*** (in my humble opinion she was born with this gift) culminating in her now (2020) attending Bristol University where she performs as lead violinist. Her extraordinary talent must eventually result in being snapped-up by a name orchestra. I acknowledge my obvious bias but this young lady has much to offer, not least her modesty and wonderful personality – audiences will adore her!

Paul (Francis) is a drummer and tutor, but unlike me, he is

a professional musician and has been so since the age of 14. His big break commenced in the 1960's when he successfully auditioned with Tony Jackson, lead singer, till then, with The Searchers. Thereafter, Paul played and recorded with various name bands, including Maggie Bell, Bill Wyman, Steve Harley, Jack Bruce and many others and played great venues like Carnegie Hall. Paul completed, and published, his autobiography, 'Drumming Up Vibrations'. www.orchardpercussionstudio.co.uk

It would be inexcusable not to recount Paul's experience, some years ago, that he subsequently imparted to Glenys and me on a beach in the Algarve.

It involved organised swimming with Dolphins, and Paul explained that while other participants waited in the pool, attired in wetsuits, Paul encountered problems with his wetsuit, having to remove same. Eventually suited, he joined the instructor and enjoyed the activity. Later the instructor informed Paul that he should not contemplate pursuing the activity on a professional basis as he was wearing his wetsuit (in some discomfort!) back to front! This, not surprisingly, culminated in guffaws of laughter, and Glenys pleading with Paul to stop since she needed a pee-break. 'Please stop him, John', *too* late, since Paul had eagerly announced, 'It's all captured on video!'

We much appreciate Paul and Goldie's longstanding friendship that included five holidays with them staying in their apartment in the Algarve.

On one such occasion Paul decided to drive us to see, what would be best described, as a mountain. Suffice it to say that it was high, very high, with a summit point. Now, I should explain that while Paul is a very careful driver, his gear changing could be a bit crunchy.

As we approached, I felt confident that we'd view the mountain from the ground – 'He surely will not attempt to ascend by car?' I thought, 'oh yes he will!'

We commenced climbing a circular single rough terrain track that slowly became quite treacherous, not least because of the shear drop to the left that eventually became a thousand feet and advancing. Eventually we reached the top, a dead end, which required driver and vehicle to turn around for exiting. 'Please ensure you've got the right gear, Paul', was followed by crunching gears and the car reversing towards certain death, but not immediately since the car had to fall a considerable distance. However, I have to confess to cowardice on my part as I leapt from the car leaving my wife (having recently celebrated our Golden Wedding Anniversary) in the back of the car! Meantime Paul, Goldie, and Glenys laughed, as first gear was engaged and car and occupants successfully turned around. 'Let's have some lunch', exclaimed Paul. I attempted to eat but my appetite was adversely affected since we of course had to soon negotiate the descent! The entire scenario was not enhanced by the weather, which had changed from blue skies and uninterrupted sunshine to an electric storm that hissed around the various transmission aerials that adorned the summit. Obviously we survived, and I think, indeed hope, my wife forgave me my act of self preservation.

While still within the confines of entertainment it is perhaps pertinent to mention that my good friend Bill Price – who enjoys investigating one's ancestral lineage – discovered that a cousin, one Nellie Ledbetter, was married to Randolph Sutton, a well known concert/music hall entertainer who was best known for his song, 'On Mother Kelly's Doorstep'.

Chapter Twenty Three

FAMILY AND LAW

In 1969 Glenys, Gareth and I moved from Somersham to Capel St Mary, a small village about six miles south of Ipswich, which had been considerably enlarged, due to the expanded development of modern dwellings. We had carefully done our sums and reckoned that we could just about afford to live there so long as I continued to supplement my income with band earnings.

We bought a three bedroom detached house, which for a limited time caused us some concern, due to the fact that two or three Ipswich Town football players* resided on the estate, and while they were not in receipt of the phenomenal salaries now paid professional soccer players, they were clearly earning far more than me. In fact, the then manager, Bobby Robson, lived in a property, obviously somewhat more palatial than ours, on the eastern boundary of the development.

*I acted for one of the Ipswich players and while walking with him in Princes Street we were apparently spotted by a friend of my secretary who had much pleasure in telling me that her friend had questioned my being a lawyer and had assumed that being seen with the Ipswich player meant that I too was an Ipswich player! I played football, and my position was mostly left back – in the changing room!

Accordingly, we wondered if we could truly afford to live there, not least as Glenys was, at my insistence, no longer a wage earner.

I firmly believe that babies, and pre-school children, need the undivided attention of their mother, and the divided attention of their father. I will doubtless be defined as out of touch, but in my opinion, there is no substitute for a mother who can provide, love, security and stability. Such provisions are indisputably imperative for any child's present and future welfare.

I fully appreciate that provision of these basics may often be easier said than done, because of prevailing circumstances e.g. mental instability of one or both parents, environmental problems, or the most common, a cessation of the marriage or relationship. I'm obviously aware, these days, of the critical impact of what I say, most adopting the, 'how on earth would we manage if we didn't both work?' To which, I respond, 'how on earth did my parents manage?' How on earth did my wife and I manage?' We *had* to manage without most of what is now defined as *essential*.

Children are the principal consideration for all family lawyers and since there are children of most failed marriages, or relationships, it is imperative that that consideration be paramount, and seen to be paramount, by not only the lawyers but also the Courts. That, sadly, has not always been my finding. However, that said, while I have had occasion during my lengthy career, to be critical of legislation, the Judiciary, and fellow lawyers, my principal criticism lay with the parties themselves, in particular, fathers. I stress that what I say is a generalisation, and is simply based on my findings during a period of almost forty years. Of course there have been times when the parents have been infinitely sensible and reasonable in regard to their children; of course there have been times when a father has been infinitely sensible and reasonable in regard to his child or children, indeed I have acted for fathers who have retained custody and care and control, and provided an extremely stable environment for their children.

Sadly, however, this has been the exception, rather than the rule, given that I have been involved in umpteen cases where a party's dislike, indeed hatred, for the other, has severely clouded their ability to adopt a small degree of common sense or consideration for a child or children of their union.

Fathers have invariably been difficult in regard to access (now called contact) and have often erroneously alleged that the child's (or children's) mother has denied them regular access/contact, simply using the child as an excuse to have a 'pop' at mum. Of course there have been cases where mum has denied the father contact, but mostly that denial has been justifiable due to the father's conduct.

Often I represented a very concerned mother in contact proceedings involving various attendances at court as the result of the father's insistence that contact was not working, only to discover subsequently, sometimes years later, that he had not bothered, following the proceedings, to see his child or children.

My genuine concern for the welfare of children, is perhaps suitably highlighted in a case when I breached my client's confidence. I received a message from the lawyer representing my client's wife, and he explained that the two young children of the marriage had told their mother that their father (my client) had asked them to, 'hold his willy'.

In the company of his father I questioned my client and he admitted the offence. Given that he worked part time at the local swimming pool, I was obviously concerned for the safety of kids and therefore decided to reveal the offence to a senior Court Welfare Officer which culminated in my client being suspended, only to be subsequently reinstated! During this time I was regularly playing squash with a dentist mate at the local sports and swimming centre, and was aware that his two children regularly swam while dad played squash. Avoiding any breach of confidence (or inference that I may be involved professionally), I merely stressed to my mate that I personally didn't like, or trust, the guy. Two days later I received a phone call, 'John, that guy at the swimming pool has just interfered with both my kids.'

Chapter Twenty Four

SYMBOL – FEMALE

I swung the lead (my father's saying when I faked illness) while attending infant and junior school, but sadly not as often as I would have preferred.

However, I did have one overriding feature that helped me through, in fact my entire education, without faking ailing health – GIRLS! I cannot recall a period when I was not infatuated with one or more females. The various girls would, with few exceptions, have been unaware of my feelings. Perhaps, however, my profuse blushing gave the game away. I think that the lyrics of the song often associated with Maurice Chevalier, 'Thank Heaven For Little Girls', (or to be precise, 'Sank 'eaven For Leeetle Girls') suitably describes my then (and thereafter) adoration for the female species, not least the second verse of the song, 'They Grow Up In The Most Delightful Way.'

During junior school, Cherry Dart had an overwhelming effect. She was an extremely pretty blue-eyed blonde with ponytail, who often chose me to be her dancing partner. I hated Country Dancing, but it clearly had its rewards.

One teacher, a keen Morris Dancer, taught the class a simple routine, to be presented in the grounds of Colchester Castle. I arrived, promptly got lost and began to cry, only to be caused insurmountable embarrassment when Cherry found me and asked if I'd been crying.

I appeared to be the only child who was unaware that we were to dance our routine at the Colchester Carnival in the presence of a few thousand people in the grounds of the oldest recorded Castle.

About this time a school trip was planned – Whipsnade Zoo, no less. We were advised that some parents were to be allocated as carers and that we would learn who would accompany us. During morning assembly the list was read out, 'Cherry Dart's mother will accompany John Ledbetter and Roger Williams.' Perhaps, despite her overwhelming existence, she did like me, even if only a little. However, I was subsequently to be mortified when Cherry told me that her mother had said that she liked my mate Roger very much.

When ten, it was time for the class of forty-two kids to have a (school) group photograph. I was to experience immeasurable sadness when Cherry arrived that morning, minus the ponytail!

Kaye Parker ran a close second to Cherry but a new kid, tall, good looking, and a rival, culminated, during unparalleled desperation, in my theft of sixpence from my sister (her pocket money in a drawer at home) to finance sweets from the corner shop for Kaye. Also I gave her the remaining part of a stationary set, a gift I'd received the previous Christmas.

Age dictated my departure from Junior school, and farewell to Cherry and Kaye as I was living in a different catchment area.

Having completed secondary school, and in the employ of Marshall and Sutton, I spotted Cherry working as a ladies' hairdresser in Pelham's Lane in Colchester. Whether she ever noticed me while often, (but not as often as I would have liked) walking past, I don't know. She had blossomed into a stunningly beautiful young lady, but I still considered her to be out of my league, and never attempted to speak to her. However, while that situation would persist, I did see her one final time while I was playing drums with the Deltas. The stage was elevated thus enabling me to see people entering the hall, and I noticed her. She was looking in my direction but left before we'd finished our set. I think she'd simply showed an interest following the World Tour offer.

I think I should clarify that while girls played a significant role during my infant, junior and secondary education, I lacked confidence and contact therefore, was minimal. Very simply, I had, and continue to very much appreciate, and *respect* the female form, and its femininity. I guess I'm not unique!

Prior to cessation of secondary school, I again became somewhat infatuated with various young ladies including Hazel, a particularly pretty girl, but sadly very mature for her age, so I had to accept that even my Skiffle drummer status would be insufficient to attract her attentions.

My mate, Streetey, and I always chose to ride early morning (through all weathers), in particular, via the Monkwick Council Estate, where some of the girls, including Hazel, from our class, were regularly waiting at their bus stop. One morning while negotiating a corner in thick snow, and while attempting to overtake Streetey, opposite *the* bus stop, I fell, and slid at speed on my backside landing at the very feet of Hazel. 'What the hell are you doing, Ledbetter?' Well, at least she knew who I was!

A new arrival at school prompted immediate attention; Pat MacClean who for a short time was clearly impressed when I emulated a part in a film where the drummer on seeing a young lady immediately interrupted the band by playing a drum solo. The Blackzillions were rehearsing in the Science Lab when I saw her, and – works every time! I jest, but it's fair to say that during a gig with the Blackzillions, Pat climbed the stage, and with clear intention, kissed me, thus stunning the band and audience.

With the exception of another kiss at a school party, for reasons best known to her, those stolen moments were to abruptly end. Pat was, despite being in her very early teens, of extreme maturity and exuded much femininity, an aspect of apparent interest to the Daily Mirror when they published her scantily clad photograph – which I missed!

With the exception of the band, some school gigs, and the impression this made on some of the girls, there were few high points, save that during one morning assembly, in the presence of a thousand plus pupils, the police, myself and only one other, a fourth year 'Ted' (Teddy Boy) with flick knife suitably concealed, were presented with second, and quite rare, Cycling Proficiency badges. Surely, Hazel and Pat must have been impressed!

Another percussive solo at a mate's house party proved beneficial when Mary (just post school days, I was fifteen) a lovely petite girl, again of much femininity, and older, provided me a lengthy session of simple petting (kissing and cuddling) culminating in my uncontrollable shaking. Some years later Johnny Kidd And The Pirates (featuring Clem Cattini on drums) recorded 'Shakin' All Over'. Those lyrics proved descriptively accurate. Given my then age, this would probably be considered by most kids today as 'old hat'. Suffice it to say that my fondness for action movies is on par with my fondness for a good love story, save that I'm easily, very easily, and very embarrassingly, reduced to tears.

While in the employ of Marshall & Sutton I experienced a definite response from some of the girls, but have to confess that again my lack of confidence meant that it took some time for the 'penny to drop'. However, during an office coach trip, Maureen 'snogged' my face off, Pam showed much positive interest/ action (nice girl), and a very shapely and mature (name escapes me) young lady enjoyed showing me a photograph of her and her best friend in their bra and panties, simply to monitor my reaction – not difficult! On a subsequent office outing I sensed a degree of hostility in the female ranks when I sat with Pam. All the girls were slim and attractive – no obesity in those days.

Had I been of roguish persona, (dodgy geezer) then my stay with M&S may well have resulted in a 'beyond the call of duty', scenario, not least in so far as Barbara was concerned. Barbara was a year younger than I, and had recently joined the firm as a trainee typist. Her extremely good looks were immediately noted by the senior partner's son, and a courtship commenced. However, Barbara often sought my advice, (silly girl) solace and comfort, during lunch breaks when she confided her relationship problems, culminating in much embracing and eventually kissing. I think she was confused, which was nice!

Cessation, however, would shortly follow.

Chapter Twenty Five

I knew that Maureen (receptionist at Marshall & Sutton) would be at a Co-operative employees' social dance with 'Bob Miller And His Millermen' (brilliant big band) at the Corn Exchange in Colchester (March 1960) with girlfriends from Tollesbury, so Geoff (a good mate) and I, dressed rather pathetically like twins, soon found six girls seated at a table in the bar area. Maureen introduced us and revealed that each girl was courting, until, 'This is Glenys, she's not courting.' I recall an immediate coronary response, how on earth was this extremely attractive girl not courting? 'Hello.' I said. She smiled. Her eyes penetrated, her hair Mediterranean, her face, beauty personified, her stature diminutive, and Geoff confident and quicker, and soon successfully dating her!

I licked my wounds as he gleefully related details of their first intended date. However, not all was lost, since Geoff was with the Army Catering Corp, stationed in Aldershot, thus limiting his ability to further pursue their courtship. What followed could be misconstrued as a blatant piece of skulduggery. In fact with the exception of a misdemeanour on my part, which I attempted to redress, the scenario was devoid of any premeditated or malicious intent.

One Saturday evening, when unusually the band had no gig, I met up with the bass player and he and I went to the Astoria

Dance Hall in Tiptree (the purveyors of highest quality conserves). I was looking forward to seeing a Colchester based band, 'Jimmy Pilgrim and the Strangers', as the drummer had been a mate of mine during our 'Skiffle' days, while at different schools.

I had no idea that Glenys would be there but since she was, I asked her to dance. I immediately sensed that my feelings towards her were being reciprocated, so much so that we kissed, and spent most of the evening repeating this process – which was nice, *very* nice.

Though obviously dangerous, motorcycles are by far the most exhilarating form of transport, and the ride home that night was, despite the rider's guilt, akin to floating on air.

Being aware that Geoff would be home on leave the following Friday, I decided I would take him for a drink and tell him of my indiscretion. Very reluctantly, I also decided, in an effort to diffuse any possible acrimony, to attempt to get Glenys and he back on track.

Geoff's reaction confirmed my earlier analysis that he wasn't as keen as I was, given that he assured me that it was not a problem. Nevertheless, I told him that I'd arrange for him to see Glenys the following evening, having first established with Maureen that Glenys would be at the Astoria.

During Saturday afternoon I rehearsed with the band and recall having difficulty in concentrating, culminating in it taking most of the afternoon to achieve a satisfactory cover of 'Frightened City' by the Shadows.

That evening, while Geoff waited outside, I entered the Astoria, soon found Glenys, and explained that I was not proud of my previous conduct, and that Geoff was waiting outside. 'Well, I don't want to see him – in fact I don't want to go out with him again.'

I was perplexed, but in truth, pleased, and was impressed

when Glenys made it crystal clear that despite her decision, I should feel no obligation towards her.

I conveyed her decision to Geoff, who departed, and rode into the darkness leaving Glenys and John to resurrect what they'd previously experienced...

Chapter Twenty Six

Despite her dislike for motorcycles, Glenys rode pillion on a few occasions, including a trip to Bradwell, Essex – suggested by her mother – to visit and view Tom Driberg's (MP) country home that was open to the public. We arrived, entered his home, viewed various rooms, including a bedroom with an unmade bed, which seemed odd, and on descending the stairs were met by a gentleman who introduced himself as Tom Driberg. He then asked what we were doing there. It transpired that his home was open to the public but only designated days, and this was not one of them!

My father kindly loaned me his 'clapped out' Morris Minor to take my driving test, which happened to be a *Test* in every sense of the word as the Examiner asked if I would object to a trainee examiner accompanying him. Naively, I agreed, rendering the handbrake hill-start impossible, given the state of the engine (combustion practically nil) and the extra weight of the portly trainee in the back of the car. After three attempts, combined with clouds of exhaust smoke in the foot-well, the Examiner asked the trainee to vacate, which he did, thus enabling me to complete the manoeuvre, and the remainder of the test – I failed.

Subsequently, using a replacement vehicle, I passed, and immediately bought a 1949 Hillman Minx for £45.00.

Glenys had mentioned that she'd never had a holiday, so I offered to take her to the New Forest (six days after passing my test) and she accepted.

Needless to say, I'd not driven far during driving lessons, so Colchester to the New Forest, represented a challenge. Despite a minor collision (bent bumper), a blocked main jet in the carburettor, continuous flapping from rubber tread lifting from two of the tyres, Glenys and I had a brilliant week's holiday, on a joint weekly income of £11.00!

Subsequently, my father kindly gave me his 'clapped out' Morris Minor, Nan Tyson loaned me £35 to buy a Gold Seal reconditioned engine, and Henry and I fitted it, thus improving my chances of travelling to Glenys, gigs and work.

During the early stages of our courtship Glenys and I encountered the locally based police officer, PC Light, who was soon categorised as 'Pervy Constable Light'. Passion within my 1949 Hillman Minx and subsequent Morris Minor, at night, was regularly interrupted by this ageing Copper who maintained that he was doing his duty by keeping an eye on visiting lads thus protecting the local village girls! NO, Lighty, you were pursuing a blatant and perverse activity, and had I been older, and wiser, a formal complaint would have been appropriately lodged with a view to disciplinary action.

With time, and in anticipation of his regular visits, Glenys and I would park up and sit in the back of the car and await his arrival. Without fail he'd light us up with his torch, and we smiled politely in response. One night, well past midnight, I was convinced that he was lurking about 20 yards from our car. I had acquired a good torch for use during much night driving following gigs. I eased out of the car, aimed the torch where I thought he was lurking and succeeded in lighting him, his bike, his helmet and cape. Following this we had few encounters with PC Light.

I continued gigging with the band and Glenys often came with me. Little did she know how many she would attend during our courtship. Suffice it to say that she displayed admirable fortitude.

Glenys and I were engaged with a view to marrying when both twenty-one. I was insistent that we should avoid renting and save sufficient money to provide a deposit to secure a mortgage.. Each week Glenys handed me half of her £6 income, and often more, which combined with part of my £10, and band earnings, was paid into a Building Society account. A date was fixed for the marriage and we began house hunting in Suffolk. Immediately we found a two-bedroom semi bungalow in Somersham, about six miles from Ipswich. The price was £2625, of which we had saved a pretty impressive £425. This, however, had taken its toll on us, not least me, as I had supplemented my income by playing, not only with my regular band, but any other band requiring a drummer, culminating in performing every weekend, plus most weekday evenings at holiday parks in Clacton-on-Sea. At most, I managed 5 hours sleep each night, and travelled a minimum of a hundred miles a day.

The Building Society, that had previously assured us that investing a reasonable sum to be utilised as a deposit, would guarantee a mortgage, but subsequently requested a further £75.00, which amounted to a deposit of almost 20% of the asking price! With Eric's (my boss) help, we secured a mortgage with another Building Society utilising the £425.

During the fortnight preceding our wedding I worked day and night, including the Friday night before, when the band played a regular fixture at USAF base Wethersfield in Essex.

The following day saw Glenys and I tie the knot at the local church in Tollesbury. The photo call was, perhaps predictable, given that, unbeknown to me, my mother had arranged for the rest of the band to provide an archway of guitars outside the entrance to the church. Soon we were *en route*, in another Morris Minor, to Devon, stopping the first night in a somewhat seedy hotel in Earl's Court. A week at a chalet park in Dawlish Warren and we were on our way back. The first, and absolutely essential, port of call being Tolleshunt D'Arcy, (twenty years later made infamous due to the so-called Whitehouse Farm Murders) to collect some hard earned wages owed me by a fellow musician.

The Essex County Standard carried a large photo of Glenys and I underneath the archway of guitars, plus the predictable: 'Local Drummer Weds.'

Back to work, and my little room frivolously adorned, including a little ditty prepared by the secretaries, 'Early to bed, and early to rise, makes Glenys sore, but satisfied!'

Shortly before our wedding, Glenys was successfully interviewed by the Manageress of M&S in Ipswich, and on our return, she commenced work there as a sales assistant. Financially, this was to prove probably our best period, not least as it was frequently possible for staff to purchase food at the close of business, at ridiculously low prices. After only three and a half months, Glenys received a Christmas bonus of £30!

A holiday in June 1967 in the Highlands was followed by confirmation that Glenys was pregnant.

Chapter Twenty Seven

LEARNING CURVE

As my career progressed I became increasingly aware that there was indeed no substitute for experience. Virtually every case I dealt with gave rise to something new, and rather like my school days, no sooner had I thought that a point or aspect (legal or procedural) had been grasped, then I realised that I'd merely scratched the surface. Equally this would apply to the circumstances of each and every case, since all were similar but different, and while there were often similarities, no single case was the same.

Another of Judge Drabble's cases proceeded on the grounds of the husband's cruelty. I represented the wife and as her husband failed to sign and return his acknowledgement of service of the copy divorce petition, it proved necessary for me to effect personal service of the documents upon him. The Judge enquired as to the means of identity of the respondent when I served him with the papers. Erstwhile confidence that this case would be problem free was immediately, and quite severely, dented. I had merely asked the respondent if he was Mr H, and he confirmed that he was. This was insufficient for the purposes of personal service at that time, and an aspect I was well aware of but was overlooked, mostly due to an increasing caseload.

The Judge indicated that he was prepared to either adjourn the case or place it at the end of the afternoon's list. A quick chat with my client revealed that she had a fairly recent photograph of her husband at home so the Judge was asked to implement the second option. I had about an hour in which to obtain the photograph and achieve a sequel that would satisfy the Judge that the Respondent was indeed the man who had accepted service of the papers.

I sped to the other side of Ipswich with my client and having collected the photograph we drove to the Respondent's home and as luck would have it, he was just arriving home from work. My client confirmed it was her husband and the photo verified this. Back to Court in the nick of time where the Judge noted the sequence of events and granted my lady a decree nisi. An example of the essential procedural measures that are not always readily apparent, but always part of the learning curve.

It was in the same courtroom in the Ipswich Assizes Court some weeks later that my fitness and strength was put to the test.

On collecting a barrister from Ipswich train station, he indicated that it was essential for him to return to London post haste, as his wife was about to go into labour. It was his first child and he was clearly anxious. Unfortunately Judge Drabble was not sitting that day and the much younger Recorder was clearly intent on seeking clarification and verification of otherwise normally acknowledged simplicities. As my Counsel, who was clearly becoming more and more agitated, attempted to satisfy the Judge's query relating to a specific point of law he, the Judge, persisted to doubt Counsel's interpretation and reached for the *Bible* (a large heavy book of some 2000 pages containing the law, case law, and procedural measures) namely 'Rayden on Divorce', which for some inexplicable reason was not available. Counsel, with an indisputable sign of displeasure bellowed at the Judge, 'Here have mine!' And rammed 'Rayden', into the hands of the Court clerk who eased the book up to the Judge who turned the pages to the index at the back. Eventually he found what he was looking for and, with a smile, confirmed that Counsel's understanding of the law was indeed correct.

The Judge indicated that he was satisfied on the evidence before him and granted my client a decree nisi, with costs against the husband. As Counsel attempted, with due haste, to leave the Courtroom he caught part of his gown on a piece of the ancient wooden bench-seat, tearing a sizeable stretch of the fabric.

In the small corridor outside the courtroom he politely let me know what he thought of the Recorder while heading in the direction of the exit. 'Oh bugger, the bloody Recorder has got my Rayden.' As explained earlier, the Ipswich Assize Court was an extremely old building. The corridor, with low ceiling and poor light, was of panelled wood design and comprised of three doors, one of which was almost concealed within the panelling and led to the Court clerk who sat in a raised position at the front of the courtroom with the Judge elevated above him. With much haste I entered, by which time another case was in progress. I was prevented from explaining to the startled clerk the purpose of my being there. I could not see the Recorder and he could not see me crouching below. Immediately I spied Rayden above. My clasp was simultaneously emulated by the Recorder and the voluminous book was pulled back and forth two or three times. My strength prevailed and I hastily left with 'Rayden', while the Judge exclaimed, 'Oh it's gone!' and the courtroom dissolved into laughter.

During much of the sixties I continued playing as a semi professional musician with the band, but as my full time work as a divorce lawyer progressed it was merely going to be a matter of time before the inevitable happened. Whilst playing a gig in

Felixstowe I looked up from the drums (like many drummers I too performed with head down and cocked to one side) to see one of my female clients 'twisting' (a popular dance of that era) the night away. She, almost simultaneously, recognised the guy on the drums, and her response, not surprisingly, was complete and utter astonishment. 'Of all the people, in all the places.......' During our break I spoke with her and reassured her. Why 'reassure' her? Well, she'd instructed me that since her husband had left her she seldom ventured out and that there was no one else in her life. Not only had she ventured out that evening but a replacement male, like the proverbial rash, was all over her.

This type of scenario was thereafter often repeated and I cannot recall any client taking exception, on the contrary they were often complimentary and I'm certain that many were reassured that the guy who was entrusted with their problems and the resolution thereof, was just a normal regular, sort of chap, who was more than capable of relating to their problems. Some may seek qualification of the adjectival reference to 'normal'.

I previously referred to 'instructing' and 'briefing' Counsel. I said this because it is, strictly speaking, correct, in that if one sought Counsel's Advice in the form of a written opinion or asked him/her to settle a pleading e.g. a divorce petition, one would prepare detailed instructions that would contain all documents relevant to a client's case. If Counsel was to appear in Court to represent one's client then he would be sent a Brief, which was often far from 'brief', and contained all papers pertaining to a client's case. Like the instructions, the Brief would be bound with pink fabric tape, tied securely around the Brief and accompanying documents.

The young lady secretaries who occupied the office with Michael and I, having succeeded twice in locking us in our small room, attempted, when we confiscated the key, to bind the door handle with the pink tape and tie it – unbeknown to us – to the top drawer of a filing cabinet. Brute force resulted in the door being opened, the filing cabinet crashing to the floor, and a complaint from the business tenant in premises below to our boss.

Chapter Twenty Eight

CARS/BIKES/BOATS/ACCIDENTS

When 4 years of age, I began riding an old two wheeled pedal cycle that had one brake which, when operated, simply pushed a piece of shaped metal down upon the solid rubber tyre. Needless to say, stopping was difficult, collisions were not.

When six I had a Post Office savings account that, I presume, was the result of my parents, and kind relatives, paying into it, and totalling £5.00, which was utilised in the purchase of a second-hand Raleigh bicycle.

Despite shouts from my father (during my first ride) to stop, I actually rode through crossroads and thereafter, rode through various incidents requiring first aid. I thoroughly enjoyed my Raleigh bike, of which, incidentally, I attempted (stopped by dad) to modify/cut the traditional shaped handlebars to provide straight handlebars – far cooler!

When thirteen I secured a Saturday morning job, on the Monkwick Council Estate, riding the CO-OP trades-bike, which mostly avoided gigging (Skiffle) problems.

I always attempted to load maximum boxes of groceries, necessitating the use of one hand to support the boxes, and riding like a maniac! On two occasions, while riding through snow, bike and I parted company together with the groceries. A hasty attempt to repack resulted in many complaints from customers, to the manager, that they'd not received what they'd ordered.

My personal means of transport was an ageing bicycle (cow-horn handlebars and 'The Flying Drummer' crudely painted on the frame) that I used for travelling – about six miles – to and from school – featured earlier following the shed fire.

I also alluded earlier to my desire to buy a motorcycle, so with a weekly income of £2.10s I somehow saved sufficient to buy a 1939 Francis Barnett Cruiser with Villiers 250cc engine (saw one, in later years, in Beaulieu Motor Museum) from a former school-mate for £6.00. However, riding the bike was limited to my parents' back garden path, since I was still fifteen. However, on the Monday 23rd May 1960, having obtained a Provisional Licence, I rode to the town (Colchester) lent the bike against a fence close to the entrance to the Castle and continued my day's work in the Ironmongers shop which appeared interminable – I couldn't wait to get back on my bike. Later I rode to Colchester Civic College where, each Monday, I attended a night school course for English, which must have indicated my wish to achieve something............ .

The motorcycle required some fundamental maintenance, not least, the brakes; the rear merely slowed the bike, the front did not, thus preventing me from achieving an Emergency Stop, and almost colliding with the Examiner, during my Test. He was not impressed, and failed me.

Subsequently while attempting to avoid a stationary bus at the top of Colchester's aptly named Cemetery Hill, bike and I were abruptly separated. After remounting her I took a trip to A&E (stressed as essential by work colleagues) for an X-Ray – sprained ankle!

For my second Test I borrowed a guy's 1959 250cc C12 BSA, which was a huge transformation given the smoothness and performance compared with the Francis Barnett, particularly as the BSA had telescopic front suspension forks and rear sprung absorbers, unlike the FB's solid front (and no rear) suspension that provided shock-waves sufficient to knock your teeth out when merely connecting with a minor blemish in the road. More importantly, the BSA had brakes, and I passed.

It would be remiss of me not to mention the kindness of the guy who loaned, and subsequently sold, the BSA to me. While working in the Ironmongers I occasionally had lunch in Nan's Café in Queen's Street, where I got to know him and his lovely wife. They were aware of my need to replace the Vintage motorcycle and on discovering my disposable income, offered me the bike for £75.00, to be repaid at just £1.00 a week.

One wet afternoon, while travelling *up* Cemetery Hill, I passed a former schoolmate, struggling on his pedal-cycle, at the foot of the hill. I raised my hand as I passed him and proceeded to display (showing off!) my expertise in negotiating, at speed, a right-hand bend, with adverse camber. Unsurprisingly I fell off, leaving the , BSA to precede me with sparks flying from the end of the exhaust pipe, as it gouged its way through the tarmac. I followed at speed, initially on my back, and then my backside propelling me to a sitting position. I attempted to stand, but fell over. By this time my former schoolmate had reached me and without stopping proceeded to cycle past, and merely enquired, 'Alright?'

During a Friday afternoon I left the office in Colchester to ride – about sixty miles – to Great Yarmouth where my parents were staying the week in a caravan. Very soon, the heaven's opened. Brakes applied (to retrieve waterproof leggings from the rear of the bike) and the rear wheel locked sending me in to a lengthy skid. Miraculously while controlling same and avoiding other oncoming vehicles, I spotted a small lay-by and stopped. In my haste to retrieve waterproofs, the base of my right trouser leg caught in the kick-start culminating in the bike and me falling to the muddy ground.

Another trip to Gt Yarmouth, again to stay the weekend with my parents, but this time with my mate, also riding a C12 250 BSA. It was during a March Easter and the weather when we arrived was good. Subsequently we learnt from my mother that as we left, two girls were hoping to link up – perhaps best described as 'Sod's Law'. The trip home was punctuated with rain, most of it sleet and treacherous road conditions. We chose not to stop and on arrival at my mate's parents in Colchester, both of us were so frozen that removal from our bikes was initially impossible. Fitness, youth, and motorcycles, however, provide for regular bouts of hypothermia!

In the late 1970's I bought an old 250cc Villiers trials bike and enjoyed some 'off road' in the Cornish countryside. The front suspension was of 'swinging arm' design.

The next, and final, motorcycle I acquired as the result of a young wife I was representing in her divorce, she having retained her husband's motorbike, he having retained the couple's car. This bike rated the indisputable winner of the few bikes acquired – a TRIBSA. (Some enthusiasts will recall the TRITON) The TRIBSA I purchased consisted of BSA 1950's frame, front and rear suspension, and tank with Shooting Star badge. The engine: The Triumph 650 Thunderbird, a Speed Twin capable of exceeding 100 mph. A real eye catcher – well, most of the time, sadly mine was not always a reliable runner, and quite heavy to push. Nevertheless, a motorcycle engine steeped in history.

When eight years of age my father was keen to show me something in the neighbour's garden. He'd obviously sought permission to hide his acquisition in anticipation of my very pleasurable surprise – he was not mistaken, since parked at the rear of the Powell's bungalow was a motorcycle and sidecar. The motorbike, a late 1930's 350cc single cylinder Panther with manual gearshift positioned on the right of the petrol tank. My first ride in the sidecar was, needless to say, euphoric, and the following trips were always very special, not least as I was allowed to stand with the roof opened while wearing goggles.

Prior to acquiring the Panther the only means of transport for dad was his bicycle, which enabled him to travel to and from work, some ten miles each day. Our trips to London were with Grey Green coaches and later with a very cheap hire car from Kelvedon, a few miles from home.

Henry's aim was to eventually build a new sidecar, so for a few months the old sidecar was removed and a sack of heavy objects was placed on the chassis as ballast.

Dad bought wood, to make a frame, and sheet aluminium. Having built the frame he cut and attached various pieces of the aluminium, and the finished sidecar, resembling a small boat, was secured to the chassis. No small achievement – a clever fellow.

In a second hand shop in Colchester, Henry purchased a leather RAF flying helmet (crash helmets were not compulsory) with two protruding rubber pieces originally provided for headphones. This amusing sight was to be suitably enhanced by a pair of goggles, but not, however, RAF issue, but what one would have expected a Kamikaze pilot to have worn, i.e. the protective glass which protruded, was tinted yellow and the frame of the goggles lined with fir!

Off to London for Christmas, with my singularly unimpressed sister riding pillion, and mum and I in the sidecar. On reaching the Berechurch Hall Road, approximately half a mile from home (commencement of journey) a chap was riding his bicycle with his dog running beside him *without* a lead. A rabbit ran across the road swiftly followed by the dog, which was promptly run over by the Panther. Everybody out, while the injured/dead (can't remember) dog was removed from between the Panther and the sidecar. Not a good start, but we nevertheless had a Merry Christmas at Nan's.

During the Suez crisis in 1956 my father bought an Excelsior motorbike with a 125cc engine to economise on dwindling fuel supplies. During that period I would often see Henry riding to and from work while smoking a cigarette!

My father told me that during the 1930's he bought a Harley Davidson motorcycle with sidecar. I found this of much interest not least as the Harley, despite its early production, had both hand and foot clutch control. Dad also told me that during a trip, with his mother in the sidecar, he lost control tipping bike and sidecar and ejecting his mother.

Having passed my driving test, as particularised earlier (Symbol Female), I purchased a black 1949 Hillman Minx with running boards (a 'Mafia Staff Car'). The tread, as previously mentioned, was lifting from two tyres thus providing the sound of clapping whilst driving.

My father's clapped out 1951 'Moggie' followed, culminating in several attempts to cure big end knocking. This involved my lying beneath the car in my parents' drive while removing the oil sump and disconnecting the piston conrods and inserting (Henry's suggestion) tinfoil between the big end shells and crankshaft. It didn't work, so dad and I installed the reconditioned Goldseal engine.

With the passing of time, people (neighbours previously from hell) change with age e.g. Mr Golding offering to sell me his 1956 Morris Minor (split windscreen) with a small deposit and £10.00 a month. Each month, without fail, I ran next door, paid the tenner that was acknowledged by a receipt. On one occasion the Goldings were out and when next visiting them and checking my envelope the ten pounds – a week's wage – was missing, With little optimism, and much distress, I phoned the police, 'Yes Sir, a lady handed in £10 she'd found right outside your home.' A large box of chocolates and my heartfelt thanks were her reward.

The 'Moggie' was immaculate but was high mileage, eventually requiring a cylinder re-bore (courtesy of Mr King, a neighbour and engineer), new crankshaft, pistons and reground valves. A pause during my dismantling the engine proved stressful when unbeknown to me Henry completed the job, but not with the degree of care I would have hoped for i.e. engine parts scattered around the floor of the garage, not least eight push rods that one would normally prefer to replace in numerical order!

A second-hand Morris 1100 would replace the 'Moggie'. Without doubt the worst car I would ever purchase. A new sub-frame section was required within a few months of purchase, and the first attempt to use maximum revs was promptly followed by a ticking sound from the engine. 'Could this be a small end?' I enquired of dad and a neighbour, both engineers. Their attempts to reassure me were very soon replaced with, 'Dad, on returning home from a gig last night the engine lost power, followed by a dreadful sound.' Yes, it was a 'dreadful sound', it was the sound of number two piston breaking in two and scoring the cylinder. Yet another Goldseal reconditioned engine for dad and I to fit, and then – with care – back on the road for work and gigging.

Chapter Twenty Nine

During the afternoon of Tuesday 13th February 1968 I was attending a half-day release Crime and Tort law degree level course at Ipswich Civic College in readiness for exams in May of that year. I recall a humorous moment with the crime lecturer being interrupted by a woman who entered the room and asked if Mr Ledbetter was present. I accompanied her, and as we walked the corridors she explained that my mother had telephoned and informed her that my father had been involved in a serious motor accident. I recall saying that there must be some mistake. I needed a safety net, and adopted a simple reasoning that enabled me to consider the chances of my father, who was in his sixties, and had driven all manner of motorcycles, and other automobiles since the age of fifteen, (apparently earlier), having an accident, was wholly inconceivable, indeed, impossible. A 'safety net' of self-denial, that permitted a moment of simple naivety.

The BMC Goldseal re-conditioned engine was just two weeks old, which in those days, unlike modern engines, required at least 500 miles of careful driving i.e. no labouring or fast acceleration, to 'run in' the engine. Some motorists would exhibit a sign in the rear window of their vehicle, 'RUNNING IN PLEASE PASS'. Accordingly the drive from Ipswich to my mother's in Colchester, about 20 miles, did little to enhance the 'running in' process. From my mother's to Chelmsford where we found Henry close to death, indeed we discovered, on arrival at the hospital, that he'd been tagged for the mortuary until someone noticed signs of life. We were told that a lorry had hit his patrol van. Given that in the sixties, RAC vans were Mini's, the chances of survival were remote.

We were advised to go home and phone later. My mother, needless to say, was in a state of shock, which bore a twist of irony given that for some time she had been close to another mental breakdown and had just been advised by her psychiatrist that she should consider shock treatment.

My mother urged me to return home to Glenys. I have to confess to some concern in this regard since she was over eight months pregnant and I had spent much time during the afternoon worrying about how she would react to the bad news. She took it on the chin and did her level best to console me and provide much needed support, and rational thinking.

Details of the accident began to emerge, enhanced significantly by a motorist who witnessed the actual impact and instead of stopping, drove to the nearest telephone box, and dialled 999. His cool head and prompt action was doubtless a major contributory factor in Henry's survival. He was travelling on the A12 dual carriageway, had overtaken an articulated lorry and had noticed an RAC van parked off the road on the verge. In his rear view mirror he then saw the lorry veer off the road and collide with the rear of the mini van.

It subsequently transpired that my father had stopped to retrieve a hank of rope from the road, considering it to be a hazard to other motorists! The driver of the lorry refused to concede that he'd fallen asleep, was fined and had his licence endorsed for careless driving. My boss sensibly persuaded me not to attend the Magistrates' Court hearing for fear of my possible, or indeed probable, reaction.

Meantime I had arranged to view, and photograph, the wrecked RAC mini van, which was, of course, traumatic, not least as it was inconceivable that anyone could have survived such an impact, given that only part of the cabin of the van could be vaguely recognised as forming part of the vehicle. I retrieved Henry's portable typewriter and various pages of script from the van. He was a keen writer and spent his breaks compiling short stories.

After some weeks in traction my father was transferred in a removal lorry (a necessary, but somewhat unique method of transport, attracting local media interest) from Chelmsford City Hospital to Broomfield Hospital, where he remained in traction for several weeks in the hope that the severe injury to his vertebrae would mend.

The traction consisted of a clamp similar to the claws of the crane that one could then find in an amusement arcade game.

The claws were embedded in his skull. Cord was attached to a pulley above his head and, from there, to weights that hung below at the rear of his bed. This ensured that movement was, for most of the time, virtually impossible so Henry remained static for two to three months – it must have been hell.

Prior to his move to Broomfield it was apparent that Henry was unable to speak coherently given that words were few and often incomprehensible. At first we thought it was the effects of concussion but it soon transpired that a far more serious problem was causing his inability to converse. A blood clot had formed on part of his brain. It was inoperable and could not therefore be dispersed. The prognosis was grim.

During the afternoon of Wednesday the 6th March 1968, Glenys went into labour and was admitted to Brook Street Maternity Hospital in Ipswich. I naturally visited her several times and on each visit our conversations were punctuated by contractions that required much puffing and blowing (mostly from me) which continued until about 3AM on Friday the 8th March, when with much perseverance and fortitude on the part of Glenys, a pair of forceps and the expertise of our then GP, Gareth John Ledbetter arrived, weighing in at 7lbs 12ozs, which on the face of it was an average sort of weight, but not when mum was your original 'Miss Petite'. Prior to Henry's accident, he often attempted to reassure Glenys by saying, 'It'll be like shucking peas'. Some pea Henry, and it would not take 48 hours to shuck a pea!

Within a few days of his arrival, Gareth was en route to Broomfield Hospital to visit granddad. Broomfield was then of modern open plan design with large windows and as we approached from the car park we could see Henry on the second floor, so I lifted the bundle that was Gareth for him to see. Henry raised his hands to his eyes in an attempt to stem the freely flowing tears of joy.

During this difficult period I continued to drum, dissolve marriages and study for law exams, which, due to some indisputable miracle, I passed.

Subsequently Henry's Consultant advised us that the traction had proved unsuccessful and that it would be necessary to operate. The day before the operation, my father, who had been a smoker, but had stopped some years earlier, requested a cigarette. He, like us, had accepted, having survived such a horrendous accident, that the chances of surviving a major operation were slim, and like the guy facing the firing squad, he made one last request.

The operation took eight hours, during which time the surgeon grafted bone from Henry's thigh onto his vertebrae. Henry survived this ordeal only to be immediately hit by a lengthy dose of pneumonia necessitating another tracheotomy i.e. a puncturing of the trachea at the front of the throat to enhance breathing. He eventually recovered and was discharged from hospital some eighteen weeks after admission. The prognosis was two to three years depending on the stability of the blood clot to the brain – but he lasted twenty-five!

Although unable to speak coherently, Henry was capable of some words and although often frustrated, his sense of humour invariably saved the day. However, he was able to comprehend most, if not all, of what was said to him and this could, depending on the content, give rise to an angry response e.g. having to explain to him that his late brother's, acutely estranged wife, would probably receive Albert's estate in its entirety!

It became clear during Henry's convalescence that while his vocabulary was limited, his ability to swear was unlimited. This was due to the effects of his brain injury, since prior to his accident he disliked swearing.

While standing in a queue for ice cream with Henry during the summer of 1969 at West Mersea, (an island off the east coast, approximately seven miles from Colchester) he decided to let me know what he thought of Albert's estranged wife. This, while naturally embarrassing, did at least achieve a gradual, but noticeable, shortening of the queue.

By this time a writ had been issued and served upon the lorry driver's employers and following a conference with Queen's Counsel in London, and the disclosure of the content of Counsel's opinion to lawyers for the Insurers, my father's claim was settled, thus enabling my parents, to buy a modern bungalow a few miles from where they had lived since 1943.

Chapter 30

'HAPPY DAYS'

My father, having recuperated following his horrendous accident, for reasons best known to him, and without word to his family, purchased a boat that was advertised in the Essex County Standard. Henry was not in good fettle, but would not accept any advice, or factual comment, not least that neither he, nor I (nor anyone else for that matter) had any experience of boats, or the sailing thereof. To make matters worse, Henry purchased an old boat, a two and a half ton Gaff Rig, with no mooring.

The bill of sale, and accompanying nautical log book, made interesting reading given that the boat had played a part in the repatriation of troops at Dunkirk, and we also subsequently learnt that 'Happy Days,' was alluded to on a gravestone in Maldon cemetery in Essex.

The vessel was wholly inappropriate for a guy in his mid sixties, who had just recovered from serious trauma and was now living with a brain injury.

A mooring was found for 'Happy Days' in Tollesbury (Glenys's home prior to marriage) a small village on the East Coast that terminates abruptly on the northern side of the Blackwater Estuary, about a nautical mile or so from Mersea

Island. I'm convinced that the name, not the boat, was Henry's downfall given that 'Happy Days' were words often uttered by him to define his feelings during good times and adversity.

Henry normally drove to Tollesbury where he would board 'Happy Days' and sit for hours enjoying the solace and tranquillity of the marshes and saltings. However, one day, during the summer, he decided to venture forth into the River Blackwater. The ageing motor, which had been tested (H.D. in static mode) by me only once since its acquisition, must have functioned, since Henry managed to manoeuvre the boat from its mooring, and from there to just beyond the entrance to the southern side of the Estuary, where the engine failed and could not be restarted. Fortunately Henry and Happy Days were close to the sea wall and coastal footpath, so he dropped anchor, rowed the accompanying dinghy to the sea wall, and made his way back on foot. No small achievement, given his state of physical health.

I received a phone call from my father-in-law. Apparently Henry had arrived there, and although initially having some difficulty in explaining what had happened, Joe and Alona Bowman (my in-laws) soon comprehended what he was attempting to communicate to them. I agreed to collect Henry the following day from Colchester and drive him to Tollesbury. Time was of the essence, since spring tides were imminent and, as such, were essential to re-float 'Happy Days', which was high 'n' dry on the mud flats.

Next day, fortunately a warm and fairly calm summer's day, having checked the tide times, and armed with the dinghy oars, I walked with Henry and Glenys's younger brother along the sea wall to where the boat was anchored. It rested about one hundred yards from the sea wall and already the spring tide was lapping at her underside. Soon the tide had reached the sea wall, thus enabling me to lower the dinghy into the water. It immediately became apparent that this incredibly small light vessel was extremely difficult to manoeuvre, particularly with Henry weighing in at about 15 stone. Perseverance paid off and I boarded 'Happy Days', and then, reminiscent of Laurel & Hardy, hampered by the collective (nervous) giggles, I hauled Henry on board.

As I cranked the engine, which did not immediately respond, I heard the unmistakable and plaintive tones of Joe Bowman, who was striding along the sea wall. "You'll never bleedin' start that!" he yelled. (Joe was a Londoner, born and bred – trained with Brentford Town in his youth), and had decided that his knowledge of boats and seamanship, like mine – nil, would be advantageous. "Get the bleedin' dinghy over 'ere!"

The tide was almost high and the wind was creating a few small waves as I made my way towards the sea wall. Joe, inappropriately attired, attempted a quick entry into the dinghy, resulting in the rear of same sinking, followed swiftly by the front, and him and me sitting in the submerged dinghy looking at each other as the water lapped around our waists. "You bloody fool, what d'yer do that for?" I began to laugh – he did not!

We tipped the water from the dinghy and I rowed in small circles to the boat. Joe enquired several times, "Why yer goin' round in bleedin' circles?" Eventually we arrived at, and boarded, 'Happy Days.' My father – dressed for the occasion in grey flannel trousers, shirt, tie and his favourite charcoal grey, double breasted, wide lapelled suit jacket, that he wore for my sister's wedding some twelve years earlier – began to sing. Glenys's brother Paul was also aboard, but I have to confess that I cannot recall how he got there. He too, must have been rowed in circles!

Having secured the dinghy by tying it aft of the boat, I attempted to start the engine, and following some tinkering with the carburettor, the engine ignited. We weighed anchor, and with some force upon the gear-stick and objectionable sounds from the gears, the boat lurched forward. As it did so, I watched the dinghy, slowly but surely, disappear beneath the sea. "Call yerself a bleedin' sailor!" taunted Joe – not that I had!

It was immediately apparent, even to the un-initiated, that the rope securing the dinghy had wrapped around the boat's propeller. I stripped to my M&S under-pants (dreadful nylon and coloured striped) and with my trusty pen-knife secured between my teeth (I'd seen Lloyd Bridges do this), I dived in. Now, I mentioned earlier about the mud flats, so it's not difficult to deduce from this, that I was to see practically nothing in the murky depths of the River Blackwater. However, after surfacing and resurfacing for air a few times, punctuated by a repetitive, "Aint you bleedin' done that yet?" From Joe, I eventually freed the propeller.

The engine was restarted, and we headed out to sea with the intention of doing a 'U' turn and head back through an estuary, the River Blackwater, to Tollesbury. The engine, though willing, appeared to be hunting. Full marks to Joe, as he remarked, "This ain't bleedin right." He then pushed the gear lever forward with his foot and the engine responded with that slow thudding stroke of the piston. 'Happy Days' responded by raising her bow and displaying her strength and splendour. Unfortunately, part way into the River Blackwater, I decided that a bit of fine-tuning to the carburettor was in order. "Don't bleedin' touch that!" from Joe, resulted in a spontaneous cessation of the engine.

Now, I should have mentioned that Joe didn't like the water, and Paul could not swim, so they were not impressed with my moment of mechanical madness, and were even less inspired when the engine could not be restarted. By this time the tide was on the turn, and we were drifting in an Easterly direction, effectively in the direction we had just come from. Joe was concerned that we would drift as far as the North Sea. Henry sat at the stern of the boat, and while his brain injury severely limited his vocabulary, he was able to sing, so while I concealed laughter, and Joe and Paul quietly panicked, Henry sang, 'Why did I leave my little back room in Bloomsbury?'

Not all was lost, however, since this was a Gaff Rig, a sailing craft, and we proficient sea-faring folk. We would raise the heavy brown canvass sail and head for home.

The sail was stretched along a boom and could, we presumed, be raised up the central mast. It appeared not to have been raised, possibly since Dunkirk. Slowly, with much effort, and a song from Henry, the aft sail was raised. I moved Henry from the stern to portside to facilitate the unfastening of the boom. What was to follow was perhaps predictable to experienced seafarers, but not to this fundamental excuse for a crew. Suffice it to say that 'Laurel & Hardy' fans would have been impressed. The wind, that had increased to about force three, injected life into the sail and the boom flew round knocking Henry into the sea! I had just made my way to the foredeck cabin and rapidly retraced my steps, obviously with the intention of rescuing Henry. His legs were still in the boat and the boom was lying across his chest.

The image of my father, lying trapped beneath that boom, is as if it were only yesterday. He was holding onto the boom, and as I reached him he was coming up for air only to be immediately submerged as a result of the combined weight of the boom and passing waves. I can still see his face appearing and then disappearing, and those wide lapels on his suit jacket rising and falling with the ebb and flow.

With Joe's help I lifted the boom and hauled Henry from the murky waters. Unlike me, Henry was always cool in the face of adversity, and simply sat his sodden wet torso at the stern, and sang, "Why did I leave my little..............." which he continued to sing while Happy Days was towed by another vessel, the owner having witnessed our predicament and kindly offered assistance.

It was impossible for H.D. to be towed to her mooring, so a space was found, and the anchor lowered. Having never anchored a boat before, I surmised that sufficient slack should be provided to compensate for movement, particularly in view of spring tides.

The following day we returned for high tide with the intention of returning Happy Days to her mooring. The spring tide was so high that it engulfed the access road to the harbour, known as Woodrolfe. We scanned the area where she had been anchored, but could not initially see her due to other small vessels obscuring our view. As the tide subsided we were able to move slowly forward to improve our chances of spotting H.D. I was confident that one particular boat was in the way and that H.D. was behind it. My confidence was not misguided, since I was just able to see her mast. As I waded in, my confidence turned to despair. Yes the mast was indeed visible, but the rest of Happy Days, was not. Two and half ton Gaff Rig – sunk!

When eventually reaching H.D. her contents were mostly floating around her; plastic cups, Tupperware and Henry's waders, to mention but a few. We spent the day attempting to salvage anything worth salvaging, and as the tide went down we commenced pumping her out with a view to re-floating her on the next tide. Needless to say difficulty was encountered when trying to start the engine.

Thereafter, and fortuitously for us, Henry lost interest, and Happy Days was eventually given to Glenys's brother, who spent many hours converting her and rectifying an ongoing problem with the engine, which it transpired, was probably due to exhaust gas flow being obstructed by a cockle that had lodged itself in the exhaust pipe.

Following this episode, anyone inviting me to join them for a spot of sailing, would receive the response thus, "have I ever told you about the time..."

Chapter Thirty One

MORE COMBUSTION

During the early progress of the Deltas it was often possible for the equipment to be carried in two cars, one of which was an old Vauxhall saloon owned by Brian, the then lead guitarist. What we didn't know was that he suffered from night blindness, culminating in the Vauxhall leaving the road en-route to a gig, and hitting an unseen obstacle. I knelt and shone a torch under the front of the car and discovered that the oil sump had been completely removed thus exposing the crankshaft that began turning when Brian decided to attempt to restart the engine – surreal!

The Morris BMC 1100 alluded to earlier left no doubt whatsoever that if I was going to achieve regular high mileage and performance that could handle maximum revs then I was going to need another Morris – a Morris Mini 1275cc Cooper S (PPU935D). Would a drum kit fit in a Mini? Having found a 1965 Cooper S advertised locally I arranged a viewing somewhere in the Suffolk country side where I found, what I would describe as, a Ranch in acres of land with various vehicles including an E Type Jag, Aston Martin DB5, and a racing green Cooper S with white roof. The owner joked (I think he joked) that the Bank Manager had instructed him to sell some of his cars. I deduced that the Mini hadn't been used in months owing to the large cobweb running from the exhaust pipe to the ground. Recently I'd seen TV footage of a Cooper S rallying while filming from the passenger's seat, and this was exactly what I experienced when this guy (the owner) took me for a spin - I was smitten. I explained that I had to first establish whether my drum kit would fit and he very kindly, and without hesitation, agreed to my driving home to Somersham – well, he did of course have my Morris 1100 as surety!

With the bass drum in the front passenger's seat, the toms, comfortably in the rear, and snare and stands booted, I returned and clinched the deal. Fortunately Glenys seldom attended Deltas' gigs – she'd regularly attended seven years of my drumming!

A second-hand 1971 white 1300 GT Escort would follow – a very reliable car that coped with high mileage, not as fast as the Mini Cooper, well, not immediately, but a few hours removing the cylinder head, regrinding eight valves and polishing inlet chambers, plus a straight through exhaust silencer fitted with flexible pipe from Halfords, performance was noticeably improved. The flexible pipe enabled me to fit the tail-pipe to the offside of the car just in front of the rear wheel.

Having commenced driving lessons in the Cooper S, Glenys then recommenced lessons in the Escort GT, at which stage the driver's seat was not broken! It was not broken until I was exploring the possibility of reclining the back of the seat further by pushing in a seated position – seat broken! Thereafter Glenys drove with our garden spade wedged beneath the driver's seat, and the spade's handle resting against the rear seat. Glenys passed her driving test first time having been taught by me save for two driving school lessons when she was advised to slow down!

While driving this car (Escort GT) when returning from

Devon to Suffolk Glenys and I (Gareth was asleep in the car) would witness a horrendous motor accident. In those days I generally chose to drive through London. We arrived in London about 11PM and while on the Chiswick fly-over we were joined by a couple of young guys driving an open top Austin 'Frog Nose' Healey Sprite.

When driving in London I always chose the outside lane, but for some inexplicable reason, chose the middle lane when approaching the Cromwell Road. At traffic lights the guys in the Sprite, in the outside lane, were first away. It is difficult to describe what happened next; suffice it to say that I thought there'd been an explosion since there was smoke and bodies flying through the air. However, it very soon became clear that a vehicle (a Lotus Elan) travelling in the opposite direction had crossed the middle reservation, hitting pedestrians and then landing upside down on the guys in the Sprite.

With the help of others we lifted the Lotus off the Sprite. I was familiar with the construction of the Lotus, as my boss had one, and it was no surprise, given the bodywork is fibreglass, that much of it disintegrated as we lifted it.

The sight of the two guys, literally flattened, and presumably dead, gave immediate rise to irony, since the maniac who had been driving the Lotus lay beside the Sprite groaning, but obviously alive.

I attempted to speak with, or assist, the various injured pedestrians who were either lying or wandering aimlessly in a state of bloodied shock.

The incident was reported the following day in most national newspapers confirming that the Sprite guys had indeed died. It also reported that the driver of the Lotus had stolen the car!

The fact that I chose to drive in the middle lane and had not accelerated away from the traffic lights probably saved our lives, particularly our two year old son. It remains a mystery since my choice of car has always been one of performance, invariably resulting in quick getaways. Had I been a believer, I would surely have claimed divine intervention.

Being a musician obviously involved much travelling during the early hours of the morning when returning home, sometimes witnessing dreadful motor accidents. On one occasion, while negotiating an S-bend, I narrowly missed a car that was on its side and blocking part of the road. There was no street lighting so I drove my car into a position to provide light into the car. The engine of the upturned car was still running. Switching it off, I looked in and found two very badly injured guys. It was evident that the vehicle had hit the trunk of an enormous oak tree.

Now, I fully appreciate that those of the emergency services have to deal with these incidents on a daily basis, but for me, this was a very traumatic experience, particularly as the driver (pre seat-belt legislation) had the steering column firmly embedded in his chest. He, and his passenger, both covered in blood and semi-conscious.

Fortunately, despite the isolated location, it was possible to telephone for help from a near-by house. Meantime I heard a car approaching and flagged it down. I was obviously relieved to learn that the female occupant was a nurse. 'I'm very concerned about the driver, he's trapped and in a lot of pain....' was interrupted by the nurse who responded, 'Do you mind if I don't look?'

Eventually the rescue services arrived and I vividly recall the ambulance guy using a huge crow bar to release the steering column from the driver's chest.

Subsequently, I learnt that the driver had died.

My father's accident was obviously traumatic for our family, but the trauma then experienced was to be increased immeasurably one afternoon when a guy knocked on our door and frantically reported that Gareth (then twelve) had been knocked off his bicycle! My legs failed to respond to my head in that the fifty yard run appeared unending. A car had hit Gareth and he lay on the pavement, he was conscious, but cut and bruised. Glenys immediately phoned our close friend Jo Leigh, a doctor, who lived a short distance from our home. He rushed to Gareth's aid and considered him able to be taken to the local hospital (then situated about two miles from the accident) in his car. Gareth was coherent but obviously shaken, and in shock. Patched up and with a tetanus injection, he was allowed home. We, his parents, remained in shock, and considered the Ledbetter family *extremely* fortunate.

For my part I was not convinced that the male driver was completely blameless, but he, and his passenger, stressed that Gareth had turned in front of their vehicle. Either way, the Porthpean Road was not the race track it is today, and Gareth was not seriously injured.

Chapter Thirty Two

PETROLHEAD

I make no excuse whatsoever for being one (a petrolhead) and for those of similar persuasion, or with an interest in what are now mostly classic cars, read on.

Having seen an advertisement in Motor Sport I telephoned in regard to a full race 1600cc Ford Escort. I immediately, and bizarrely, recognised the guy's voice, and he confirmed that he was indeed a young clerk to a barrister's chambers in Lincolns Inn. The next Saturday I travelled to his home in Saffron Walden where I found a quite stunning fully modified Escort with engine conversion i.e. skimmed cylinder head and twin Webber Carburettors etc. The wheel archers had been professionally extended to cater for wider wheels, and the paint-job was to die for – silver fox top and Rolls Royce Regal Red below. The bad news – he'd just discovered oil in the cooling system when checking water level. Furthermore he was waiting for a new passenger's seat to arrive to match the driver's 'bucket' seat. Given that this transformation was primarily intended to race, all front springs and struts (suspension) were of race design and up-rated, and the rear shock absorbers, gas filled SPAX adjustables. A test drive revealed much performance and incredible road holding e.g. negotiating a chicane on a dual carriageway at 80 mph. However, despite the SPAX adjustment for road use it did not compensate for the up-rated front suspension resulting in much negotiating around uneven road surfaces – potholes designed to break your teeth! Despite all this, I was smitten and a deal was clinched when the vendor agreed a part exchange with my Escort GT. Glenys was far from smitten and thought, as she had many times before (and since), that I'd had leave of my senses. A few days later, having discovered that oil was still present in the cooling system (the cylinder head had been skimmed and I assume that in doing so the head was no longer flush with cylinder head gasket, thus allowing oil into the water). I had to acknowledge my wife's misgivings, and returned the car, the vendor having kindly agreed to accept its return and the release of the Escort GT back into my possession.

While a statement of the obvious, I nevertheless confess that I have been, and remain a, Petrolhead. NO DIESELS! That said, I acknowledge that petrol engines pollute, but not to the same extent of some diesels. I firmly believe, and have done so for many years, that diesel engines are injurious to health and are intrinsically linked to (the world's) pollution and some cancers.

A month later – the boss's son having acquired a V6 three litre Capri – and I'm off to Chelmsford to view a second-hand 1969 model in metallic deep green, when again the vendor agreed to take my Escort GT in part exchange. This car was powerful but smooth, and Glenys, though initially dubious, grew quickly to like the car due to its ability to cater for her regular (oversight) use of third gear when driving off!

The 3 litre Capri (GT3000) was often referred to as, 'The Poor Man's Ferrari.'

Three years later, and my regular perusal of Motor Sport culminated in a rail trip to Paddington to view a guy's 1971 Mini Cooper S; no ordinary 'S' however. I waited at the station where planned, and very soon 'S' arrived looking 'absolutely fabulous'. White, sitting slightly lowered at the front, with black sunroof and wide alloy wheels partially protruding the wheel archers. 'Hop in', he said, 'I'll take you to my home in Fulham.' I explained that I had to return by train if we couldn't strike a deal, and he said (music to my ears!) 'Oh, I have to sell, I'm moving to Australia in a week's time.'

Having negotiated a much-reduced asking price it was time to return home to Cornwall, which proved to be an interesting drive, a drive never experienced before, nor indeed since, for what he hadn't mentioned was that the car had also been fitted with a limited slip differential, which meant that when accelerating, the car responded with a desire to be driven in a straight line. Suffice it to say that following a few months driving the mini, Glenys reckoned she had muscles suitable for championship arm wrestling.

The mini had been professionally converted by, if I recall accurately, 'Sparrow Engineering'. The engine block had been re-bored, thus increasing its cubic capacity from 1275cc to 1340cc to facilitate larger pistons, new crankshaft and a 'Piper' high lift camshaft. Carburation remained unchanged i.e. 1½" twin SU's. Expensive front bucket seats had also been installed, plus a full, and quality, sunroof with green polarised front shade. Wheels were replaced with wider alloys.

We managed for three years, travelling mostly locally but also to and thro to Essex, with Gareth and James. Clothes were conveyed in bin liners and sometimes as a barrier between G&J, the boot having been significantly reduced in capacity due to twin fuel tanks. In the main our sons' dealt well with the confined space, uncomfortable rear seats and round trips of 700 miles. Call it character building.

When Jim was eight, and often keen to help dad with car maintenance, I enlisted his assistance in turning the engine over while spark plugs were removed from the engine. This involved a treatment whereby Redex was poured in measured amounts into each cylinder, a cloth positioned over the plugholes, and the engine turned-over for a minute or two. Jim sat in the driver's seat and turned the ignition key – sadly before I'd positioned the cloth! Eventually Jim heard my pleas to stop, but not before witnessing a very frightening episode i.e. dad's white tee shirt and face splattered with much (red) Redex!

A second-hand white Escort Mexico, with the customary red 'Mexico' stripes, would follow. This was not a particularly impressive motor and clearly needed some performance enhancing work that I could neither provide in time nor money. Given the extras e.g. quick release bonnet and boot clips, the car may have previously been rallied, albeit rarely, since the underneath showed no signs of serious pursuit.

A neighbouring petrolhead informed me that he'd seen, and tested, a second hand Escort RS 1600 that was for sale at a garage close to the A30, but was apprehensive about buying it. My test drive resulted in an immediate sale of the Mexico and the acquisition of the 1972 RS.

The 1600cc engine was BDA type (not dissimilar to the Lotus Cortina twin cam engine) with twin overhead camshafts and Dellorto twin 40 alloy carburettors. The four gear ratio was obviously designed with rallying in mind, and provided fast acceleration, which was ideal for Cornish roads. However, rides to Essex would have been significantly improved with fifth gear or overdrive facility. Suffice it to say that Glenys always travelled to Essex with cotton wool in her ears.

It was time to adjust tappets so armed with a workshop manual I commenced removing the twin camshaft carrier. I always preferred to refer to a manual if I hit a snag. Well, in this instance, not so much a 'snag' more a nightmare scenario. On lifting the cam carrier various pieces of metal fell to the garage floor. These, I discovered, were known as buckets, and the very small pieces, shims. I'd noticed that small magnets were suggested as aids to this procedure – I didn't have any – OBVIOUSLY.

The adjustment of tappets required removal of buckets and shims and calculating the depth of each small shim using a micrometer and replacing with one of suitable depth/thickness. A procedure that, with time, showed progress save that I overlooked the paramount importance of timing belt supervision, culminating in a very close call. Glenys had driven to visit friends, but was unable to start the RS when leaving. I arrived and attempted to jump start the car but could hear tapping from within. On inspection I discovered that three of the timing belt teeth were missing; the reason? Instead of removing the timing belt when performing the cam-carrier removal, I allowed the belt to be partly immersed in oil thus softening the rubber. Had this occurred while driving at speed the consequences could possibly have been terminal. Given that marks on the top of each piston were visible from contact with valves – need I say more? Well, like drumming, *timing's* essential!

In addition to tappet adjustment (and timing belt care) I also made good progress with tuning the twin carburettors, which required a short piece of garden hose placed in one ear and the other end in the air inlet trumpet, with the engine running. By listening to the hiss one could, in turn, adjust [gripping stuff this, you may need a tea break, or probably something stronger!] each of the four inlet trumpets.

Eventually it was time to sell, so off to the M5 and meet the prospective buyer at Taunton Services; he, having travelled from Birmingham, well to be precise 'he' and two of his mates. A bit of bartering and cash deal done. They then offered to take me to Exeter Station. Carrying the sizeable (for me) sum of cash with three strangers was a little perplexing, but they were honourable chaps and delivered me to the station. One of the lads already owned an RS1600 and I was congratulated by the purchaser who thought my tuning was better that his mate's attempts to tune the Dellortos.

For a short time a second hand 1600GT Capri was acquired but soon sold. It was sluggish and problematic e.g. about 100 miles into one of our journeys to Colchester from Cornwall, with Glenys, Gareth and James aboard, the car was overheating, culminating in obtaining a new radiator from a Ford garage, removing clogged rad' and fitting new one in bad light.

With the aid of a further advance on the mortgage (a joint mortgage, so Glenys must have agreed, albeit with under-standable concern) I approached Cornish Ford in St Austell and ordered a *new* Escort RS2000 (the first and the last *new* vehicle thereafter to be purchased). As soon as word reached colleagues I was, for a time, called Broadie, since in the series, 'The Professionals', Broadie and his side-kick, Doyle, often drove an RS2000.

The RS would be built in W. Germany and available in about a month's time, which posed an interim transport problem. Not so, a mechanic friend, Keith Wakeford, and his wife Pat, **very** kindly suggested that I use their ageing Morris Minor. Like my father's Moggie, Keith's was also lacking in the braking department in that much foot pressure was required in stopping. On returning from St Blazey with a Chinese takeaway I approached the traffic lights on red at Holmbush, braked and stopped five metres beyond the lights! Fortunately no car driving through the junction, and no police car!

During our (Glenys, Gareth and Jim) first trip to Plymouth in the Moggie I was in a hurry and overtook three vehicles on the A390, one of which was a 911 Porsche! The kids were very impressed.

Chapter Thirty Three

The 1979 RS2000 ('shovel nose') in midnight blue, proved to be worth the financial outlay and remained our family car until the late eighties when, sadly, rust became a burden, despite much cleaning and attempting to keep the car in very good order, a routine commenced when seventeen and continued today, save that I now have an excellent self-employed Ford mechanic, Chris Lofting. However, I'm still the washer and polisher!

Glenys and I sailed with the RS from Plymouth to Santander, staying in the Hotel Sardinero. While there we decided to drive through the Picos de Europa mountain range and head for Leon. During this period much of the roads were in need of repair and crash barriers were yet to be provided. On entering a small village with the intention of seeking refreshment, chickens ran for cover and I made the mistake of opening the car door before clouds of dust had settled. The scene was akin to a Spaghetti Western.

We travelled in the hope of meeting up with a Spanish friend, Francisco, who worked for the telecommunications office in Leon. About fifteen miles from Leon we were stopped by police who alleged that I committed a driving offence (clipped a white line when overtaking a lorry). These guys were out to get a Brit, and clearly had never seen an RS before. The same could be said of folks in Leon culminating in my stopping the car and checking under the bonnet and beneath the car as most were continually staring at the car. Francisco was not at work and a colleague suggested that he might be in Oviedo visiting his parents, so off to Oviedo. Having never previously visited Leon or Oviedo, we were fortunate, when parking our car, for the keenly offered assistance of a young student who spoke perfect English. He suggested that we accompany him to the local police station (the Civil Guard) having explained our attempt to contact Francisco. We were slightly concerned and confused as to this advice, but given the circumstances, we agreed. Our assistant explained our dilemma to a police officer. It is pertinent to mention that the interior of the station replicated something akin to a very dodgy Mexican film. However, our assistant explained the difficulty confronting the police officer. Apparently he had requested a photograph of Francisco. Immediately we realised a breakdown in communication, not least as we were aware that Francisco's parents resided somewhere in Oviedo. Our young assistant then explained that the photograph would enable the Officer to trace Francisco through Interpol! We thanked all concerned and returned to Santander – a significant and lengthy round trip in one day. We subsequently learnt that Francisco had been holidaying in the Canary Islands!

I'm often reminded that the Ford RS1600 and RS2000 are now quite rare and of significant value – one restored RS1600 recently selling for over 80k. Financial constraints dictated that keeping these vehicles was not a viable option.

The RS2000 was replaced with a S/H Orion 1600 Ghia with 'pepper pot' alloy wheels; not my preferred choice but was affordable and proved to be a reliable vehicle save for one electrical issue resulting in engine failure while on the fast lane of the M25. Fortunately the fast lane, and all remaining lanes were in keeping with normal M25 traffic, barely moving, thus enabling me to coast through traffic to the hard shoulder. I have to confess that 'coasting' was more luck than judgement – how this proved possible, remains a mystery. However, a breakdown recovery truck arrived but in accordance with what is, and always will be, 'Sod's Law', 300 metres ahead, a notice, 'FREE BREAKDOWN RECOVERY' Also in accordance with breakdowns, I assume (like us) that it's normal procedure for a vehicle to be taken to the most expensive garage available, in this instance a very large, but very clean, Mercedes workshop with adjoining luxury show room. We were, in fairness, provided with a good service, and a bill to match, a bill that should have reflected the fact that the part replaced was, we subsequently discovered, wholly unnecessary, since all that was required was a new chip!

Next a low mileage 1998 Ford Mondeo Duratec V6 24 valve 6 speed manual, purchased in 2003.

I was subsequently assured, when returning one day from Shoreham by Sea, and flashed by a mobile speed camera, that when contesting the three points and fine, that the road was dangerous. It didn't look dangerous then and when last passing through, it still didn't look dangerous. I also complained that a notice warning of their mobile unit should have been displayed as provided in the RTA. I paid up for the excessive speed of 10mph!

To Reading in April 2010 to purchase a 2005 Ford Mondeo ST220 (3 litre V6). A very nice model in silver with black leather Recaro seats and trim. Ten years on and its appeal never diminishes, it's a brilliant car.

It would, however, be remiss of me not to recount our journey to Reading and the transaction scenario. My mechanic Chris (previously mentioned) accompanied me and he suggested the aid of Sat Nav when leaving the M4 motorway. All went well until an instructed right turn into a narrow country road directed me to a Ford (no not a Mondeo, but a stream) with a steep cement entry and exit. Entry fine, exit, BANG, as the rear of my very good condition 1998 Mondeo hit the cement thus busting part of the bumper. Having arrived at our destination (with no thanks to Sat Nav!) the first priority was to gaffer tape the bumper.

I should mention that Chris Lofting, my mate mechanic, is a Ford man through and through and expects a Ford ST to have received the respect it deserves. It was clear on inspection that the car, if purchased, would be rescued just in time – it was in need (inter-alia) of much TLC and a major interior clean.

The vendor expressed his love for the car that he'd treated, 'as my baby', but that he had to sell due to, 'financial pressures'.

Some haggling but the sale was secured. Given that this was a cash transaction meant that we had to enter the vendor's house where we were invited into the kitchen. Touching anything other than money would be precarious and flirting with all that is Health & Safety. Sadly, however, both Chris and I needed to pee. I went first and was directed to an upstairs loo. What would normally be deemed as normal procedure was replaced by an interval that is indelibly imprinted on our respective brains. It is difficult, no impossible, to describe, in particular, the bathroom. Anyone remembering the sitcom, 'The Young Ones' will possibly recall the hellish student accommodation. What we experienced was factual and totally beyond comprehension – it was all adjectives listed under, 'filthy', in the Oxford Thesaurus.

Chapter Thirty Four

SUCCESSION

Where There's A Will, suitably befits this proverb, in that my father's accident, and resulting injuries, superseded the untimely death of his brother, Albert, in November 1967. What was to follow his demise would be a salutary lesson to anyone considering making a homemade will.

Albert was a Plumber by trade but eventually elected to make his living 'wheeling and dealing,' and spent many years as a stallholder in Shepherd's Bush Market where he sold second-hand tools, but anything he could lay his hands on. In addition he rented an engineering store in Shepherds Bush that contained lathes and other electrical tools that were available to hire on an hourly or daily basis.

Clearly a man of strong character who had – a according to his sister Betty – during his teens and beyond, achieved a reputation as a tough guy. As a child, and indeed in later years, I had much affection for Uncle Albert and was always extremely disappointed if a trip to London did not include a visit to him either at his very nice home in Acton, or to his stall in Shepherd's Bush.

May was Albert's partner, and had been so for many years. They were childless.

May was a pleasant lady but always appeared to distance herself from Albert's family. Occasionally when visiting my Uncle at his stall there would be an item, or items, of much interest to a young boy, not least a brilliant train set with American style locomotive. Invariably with a smile on his face, Albert would watch me drool over something, but any inclination to give me the item would be thwarted by the timely, stage entrance left, of Aunt May. Often when departing, my father would comment that had May not been there, Albert would have given me the item.

May predeceased Albert, and he coped with this by gambling exorbitant sums until his premature demise. My father then set about trying to establish the whereabouts of Albert's will, Albert having assured him only a few months earlier, that he had made, and indeed changed, same following the death of May, and had named my father as principal beneficiary. Enquiries of Albert's solicitors drew a blank culminating in my writing, to every solicitor's firm in Lincolns Inn and Lincolns Inn Fields, but sadly to no avail.

Much time was spent searching Albert's property and the store/workshop he rented from Boots in Shepherds Bush. Much joy and celebration followed the discovery of a handwritten will. Albert and Henry were not gifted in the art of calligraphy, despite the fact that Henry was capable of painting or drawing fine pictures. Sadly I inherited this frustrating, and often embarrassing, idiosyncrasy. Despite the scrawl, the will clearly provided for the bulk of his estate to pass to my father. This was indeed good news, not least as Albert's principal asset, the property in Acton, was of much value. As an illustration, the property would now be worth in the region of three, possibly, four million pounds.

By this time I had achieved minimal legal qualification, the equivalent of 'A' level, and was in the process of studying, while working, for a Law Fellowship. Accordingly, I had limited knowledge of Probate & Succession, but was nevertheless aware of the possible pitfalls connected with homemade wills, and stressed this to my father, but at least the will appeared to have been correctly attested.

However, what concerned me was the provision for a named woman, who, it transpired, was still his wife (of Irish descent and religiously alcoholic) of some thirty plus years who allegedly led him one hell of a life culminating in a separation within a relatively short period of the marriage being celebrated. What was to surface in regard to this was nothing short of a farce. Apparently tough-guy Albert was only tough on the exterior, but like his brother, and indeed the writer, the interior was soft. Not only had he refrained from divorcing her but had, without default, paid his estranged wife weekly maintenance for over thirty years.

Though my work was predominantly in the field of divorce, I had dealt with a few straightforward probate cases, so on my return to the office I set about obtaining a Grant of Probate. It was of course necessary in administering Albert's estate for all beneficiaries to be contacted, and this included Mary, Albert's estranged wife, who promptly consulted solicitors and they requested a copy of the will.

In January of the following year, 1968, I received a letter from Mary's solicitors indicating that as a result of their investigations the will was invalid as it had not been correctly attested, given that the witnesses had not both been present at the same time the will was signed.

For a will to be valid it is essential that the two witnesses are present when the Testator signs his or her will and that in the presence of the Testator they each sign the will.

First, it was for me to relate this staggering piece of news to my father who was just about coming to terms with the loss of his brother. Suffice it to say, he was not a happy bunny. Next, a trip to London to speak with the witnesses who respectively confirmed that they were not both present when Albert signed his will. Both indicated, once they were aware of the circumstances i.e. over thirty years separated etc, that they were disappointed that their evidence was to prove advantageous to Mary Ledbetter.

Detailed instructions were prepared by me to a senior barrister in London who advised that the law was against us. The 'Albert Frederick Ledbetter' file grew fat with the weight of a litigious suit in the High Court, and although devoid of optimism, it was hoped that the Judge may consider the circumstances to be such that so long as the estranged, and maintained, wife of exceptional duration, was adequately provided for from the estate, that under the Inheritance (Family Provision) Act, this would suffice, thus leaving a residue for Henry, who had some years earlier secured the job of RAC patrolman, to keep him going to retirement. Save for their modest home, my mother and father had no assets nor savings, so a few thousand quid, or indeed, a few hundred, would have been wonderful.

I duly attended the Royal Courts of Justice with Counsel, and while the Judge readily acknowledged the plight of my father, and that in principle Mary Ledbetter's entitlement was wrong, he was, as in any other case, intrinsically bound by the law, and decreed that Albert's will was invalid, and that therefore his estate should be duly administered as intestate i.e. no will, and pass in its entirety to his estranged wife.

Henry (as previously featured) had survived the horrendous motor accident, and was convalescing at home. Needless to say, he knew nothing of the court case but wanted to know when he was likely to receive his inheritance. It was down to me, with much apprehension, to attempt to explain the court's decision to a man who'd suffered a brain injury. Had he been in better fettle, I'm certain he would have hit me.

I firmly believe that, like the Ledbetters, most families and individuals achieve financial gain only through hard work. No prizes, winnings, inheritances or awards.

When I was twelve years of age, a good mate of my father, arrived on his gleaming 350cc BSA motorcycle. He allowed me to twist the throttle grip with the engine running thus creating a roar from the exhaust. Smiling, he looked me in the eye and, 'when you're a bit older, this'll be yours.' I couldn't sleep that night – and any subsequent dream would fail to materialise.

Around the same time, while in London with relatives, I was assured that two properties in West London would eventually be mine!

When my parents died (both in their eighties) my sister and I inherited their home in Colchester. The sale of their bungalow coincided with a recession, and a major drop in house values, culminating in the property, which had also been the subject of subsidence, eventually selling for much less than it was worth, and my sister and I receiving £30,000 each. Save for a couple of holidays in Florida with our sons, I invested the remainder in a reasonable capital growth fund provided by the Post Office. However, as will be explained later, an inheritance upon the death of parents does not guarantee future financial stability, and neither does it guarantee the normally accepted line of succession for children, particularly *rejected* daughters of the Bowman family!

I mentioned earlier, in this chapter, that Albert and May had no children. In or about 1987 I was at my desk when the office receptionist asked if I would speak to a Mrs May. Given my normal caseload I invariably asked for the call to be dealt with by my secretary, not least, as in this instance, the name 'May' did not register as a client. However, for some unknown reason

I eventually accepted the call.

"My name is May. Mr Ledbetter, you had an Uncle Albert who had no children." Having confirmed this, she then continued, "Well, Mr Ledbetter, he did, I'm his daughter."

She then provided the history at length in this regard which seemed to leave little doubt as to her legitimacy.

Jeanette May traced me via the Law Society's list of lawyers which, given my/our surname, was not too difficult.

A few weeks following the phone call, Glenys, Gareth, Jim and I are on the train to London to meet Jeanette May and husband Roy in their Edwardian four storey home in Wimpole Street! Suffice it to say that the handful of family relatives that I've remained in touch with, have all achieved wealth. A salutary lesson, John, 'divorcing and drumming – like crime, don't pay!'

Chapter Thirty Five

GUNS/WAR/AVIATION

As previously made clear, infant and primary school education was, for me, very much an intolerable period of my life, not least as it, in particular, disrupted my interest in aircraft, guns and armoury. Spitfires, Dakotas, Gloucester Meteors (some towing targets) Lancaster bombers, De Havilland Vampires, Mosquitos, and many others, were regular visitors to the skies over the Essex coast, often leaving masses of vapour trails.

During school holidays I enjoyed identifying aircraft, and this activity was subsequently enhanced as the result of my father joining the Royal Observer Corps, which allowed me to access cards showing silhouettes of primary listed aircraft in three positions. Later, photographs of aircraft were also provided. Unfortunately, as alluded to later, some of the ROC silhouette cards were often used by me for target practice thus reducing my collection of saved cards that are about to be given my grandson, Victor, who loves history, particularly WW2.

I was invited to attend an ROC operation one Sunday afternoon during which my father and two colleagues mostly chatted and drank tea. I interrupted twice, 'listen I hear something', simply to trick them into some action. However, the approaching low level flight of an American 'Shooting Star' fighter jet that twice 'buzzed' their post resulted in spilt tea and somewhat delayed action. Me? Well, I was an overwhelmed eight year old boy who loved aircraft and who couldn't get to sleep that night. I can still see that jet approaching.

'Health and Safety' was unheard-of e.g. entering Wick (Army) Firing Range and watching soldiers using rifles, light and medium machine guns/carbines (Lee-Enfield, Sten, Bren, Browning etc) without question or warning. A red flag was visible during firing but kids were assumed to have a good helping of common sense. My favourites were the light and medium machine gunners and the trained snipers using telescopic high-powered rifles shooting from much distance and hitting small targets.

Opposite the Cherry Tree army barracks was a polo field where I was able to regularly play with another mate, and occasionally we were treated to some army training activities/manoeuvres that included a Westland 'Lysander' Army Cooperation aircraft landing on the polo field while an injured (simulation) soldier was stretched aboard and flown a circuit while a second plane landed for a repeat performance. This lasted for hours during which time my mate and I lay, or stood close to the action, while watching with much excitement without any interruption or concerns of those in charge. The Westland Lysander, Army Cooperation Aircraft was actually utilised as a fighter during the early stages of the Second World War, but was described as, 'lethally slow' and was eventually replaced by Hurricanes and Spitfires. However, the Lysander was capable of short take-off and landings, hence its ability to operate on the Polo Field.

Aged ten I witnessed a mysterious and overwhelming airborne event. The back garden of our home was long, narrow and flat, and backed onto open fields. It was a summer afternoon, cloudy with no sunshine. Not a single neighbour to be seen.

I'd just joined my father in the garden when two Hawker Hunter jets flew low from behind us heading east. Immediately they climbed and then carried out a formation display for about five minutes, during which I was transfixed. Feining departure they subsequently went into steep dives flying very low at top speed and making me duck. As I turned both pilots tipped their wings and I wept with joy.

Given the circumstances I can surely be excused from thinking – 'that was for ME!' Could my father's role in the Royal Observer Corps have played any part? I think it possible.

In secondary school, I was to witness an even more extraordinary event while in the playground, and was able to record in the back of my Collins Pocket Dictionary – sixty three Canberra Jet Bombers and fifty two – what I believe to have been – Victor or Valliant Bombers – two of the three British V Bombers. I assume they were embarking on their final flights before the breakers yard.

My father was aware of my interest in the military, in particular guns. When ten years of age, Henry took me to town (Colchester) one Saturday by bus. Henry asked me to wait outside Markham's second hand shop. Shortly thereafter he handed me an item wrapped in brown paper; immediately I knew it was a gun. I sat with Dad on the bus holding tightly to the package and bursting with excitement. Arriving home I tore it open revealing a German 177 'Original' Air Rifle. He showed me how to use the sights and then in the lying position, on the garden path, I commenced shooting at a target drawn by dad. Fortunately our house had mostly open fields to the rear and the back garden long and narrow. Once supervised, dad gave instructions that I fire only at the target. Thinking he'd left I raised the gun in the direction of a flying crow - whack! A 'thick ear,' he called it!

About two years later I met up with some lads, all of whom had air rifles. Most were impressed as we exchanged guns and I hit the targets. However, as I left the field to hop over our boundary fence I heard pellets whistling past my head. Running for cover I returned fire narrowly missing the feet of one lad as dry dirt sprayed his shoes, and quickly reloading I fired making the enemy duck. For reasons best known to the enemy they (fortunately) declined to pursue the battle.

I spent many enjoyable hours shooting targets or cans, or balloons that had been hung in a neighbour's garden to scare birds, despite the fact that they were aware that this young lad had a gun!

It was, however, pretty fine shooting given that their garden was three plots away, and it's fair to say that I subsequently achieved some very reasonable scores when target (20 yards – group of 10 small targets) shooting with a borrowed sports .22 rifle at the Colchester Rifle Club, Henry having arranged this with a mate/member who allowed me weekly practice without formal membership.

Chapter Thirty Six

INDISPUTABLE HEROES

One of my cases was set down for hearing in Norwich, and as there were Barristers' Chambers in the City I telephoned and spoke with the Clerk to Counsel and he suggested one Raymond Chance, a senior barrister who had much family law experience. When subsequently meeting him I could not believe my luck, since Ray, as he liked to be called, was an extremely pleasant chap and an immediate rapport was achieved. Thereafter I instructed and briefed Ray on many occasions and despite a significant age gap, I like to think that a very friendly relationship developed. Indeed, he and his brilliantly down to earth wife, Jessie (a retired police officer) invited Glenys and I to dine out with them in Norwich on about three occasions and we occasionally visited them at their home. In addition, following a conversation with Ray about the 'Law of Theft', during the time when I was studying Criminal Law, a book arrived at my home, 'The Law of Theft' by JC Smith, a gift to assist with my studies. Also, when subsequently applying for student status with the Law Society, Ray provided me a glowing reference that he submitted the Law Society.

During a conversation with Ray's clerk I discovered that he (Ray) was a former RAF bomber pilot during World War II. Like most people who are unfortunate enough to experience the traumas of war, Ray made no reference to this. However, due to my genuine interest in the RAF, which has stayed with me since childhood, I tactfully raised the subject with him and he confirmed that he had indeed flown with Bomber Command during the war. He described his joy of flying but avoided any anecdotal reference to his role in the war but preferred instead to recount how upon being discharged from the RAF he was undecided as to what he should do to earn a crust and during this time of deliberation he, by chance (no pun intended) visited a local court where he sat in the public gallery and watched a barrister in action. He explained, "I thought to myself, I could do that", and 'that', following a period of study, exams and pupillage within Chambers, is precisely what he did.

During one evening in the company of Ray and his wife at a local hotel, Ray was in good spirits due to the effects of a relatively small amount of alcohol and I sensed that his wife was monitoring the situation. Ray made some comment that vaguely referred to the futility of war and immediately showed signs, albeit suppressed, of emotion, whereupon Jessie very tactfully suggested that it was getting late and that we should be making tracks. Ray went to the toilet and Jessie confided in us that during the war Ray had been shot down and had to ditch his plane in the sea and do what he could to save his crew. Some survived in an inflatable dingy but injuries and hypothermia resulted in Ray having to witness one of his crew die while waiting to be rescued. The fortitude and indisputable tolerance of the female species, which is often unsurpassed, was clearly evident in this instance, in that she informed us that the traumas experienced by Ray meant that virtually every night she would be woken as he attempted to scramble over her in an attempt to save his crew. A reoccurring nightmare, varying in content, for many who experience the gruesome reality of war.

Ray had been a Whitley pilot with 77 Squadron. The following is an extract from Ray's, 'Ditching in the North Sea' with the heading: *Personal Stories Dangers of War – RAF Bomber Command. www.rafbombercommand.com*

My Mae West shot me to the surface; I found the dinghy, pulled the cord, and it started to inflate. As it did the two who I understood couldn't swim started to climb in - think they had been hanging on the tail. We were joined by...the bomb-aimer, who I was told was now hanging on the other side of the dinghy. I didn't know then that I had a crushed ankle, a broken leg, and hair-line skull fracture.

It's appropriate that I mention that our friend and neighbour (mentioned later) had been a navigator with the RAF during World War II and would attempt, if leaving our home at night, to teach us how to navigate by the stars. He eventually confided in my wife that he'd been awarded the Distinguished Flying Cross, but preferred not to elaborate. We were privileged to have known Ernest Guest.

Glenys's father, a Sergeant, served with the Seaforth Highlanders Royal Artillery as a small arms instructor. Football played a large part for Joe during the War and was in charge of Searchlight operations, at one stage, in Tollesbury, Essex. As was (still is) one of the principal objectives while serving in the armed forces, Joe learnt a trade – building. Accordingly, once demobbed, he worked as a builder, subsequently becoming self employed – he loved it!

Having been born during the latter part of the war I was aware, during childhood and beyond, of various people who'd served their country, not least my Uncles' Jack and Gordon, brothers in law of my parents.

Jack served with the Royal Artillery and miraculously survived both Dunkirk and El Alamein. Apparently, there were few from his platoon that survived Dunkirk. However, my clear recollection, when visiting his home in London with my Aunt Phyllis, was that Jack was of a reticent nature, indeed very uncommunicative, so much so that it would be many years before I would have a conversation with him.

During a chat with Jack's son (my cousin Tony) he related one quite surreal episode i.e. while on the beaches of Dunkirk, an Officer of (it was assumed) high rank, and wearing, what appeared to be make-up, rode past on horseback and exclaimed, 'I'm with *you* lads.' 'He was the first to get on a boat!' said Jack.

Uncle Jack first enlisted (under age) in the latter part of the 1920's as a driver with the 1st Training Brigade, Royal Artillery based in Eastern Command, India. Having been discharged he subsequently re-enlisted with the Royal Artillery in 1939 and was awarded medals: Africa Star, Star, Italy Star, Defence and War Medals.

Jack's survival, however, did not exclude him from injury when, apparently and bizarrely, during commencement of the Dunkirk retreat and repatriation, he was kicked while attempting to milk a goat!

Uncle Gordon, on the other hand, was far more communicative; a very pleasant guy who survived having been shot when he was escorting a German prisoner following a robbery and who, unbeknown to Uncle Gordon, had a concealed revolver. A newspaper cutting reveals details and includes an interview with Gordon: 'I was lucky,' he told a Journal reporter who visited him in 94 British General Hospital in Hamburg. 'The bullet penetrated my greatcoat and then glanced off the buckle of my battledress blouse. Instead of going straight through and damaging me badly, all I got was a flesh-wound.' My cousins (Gordon's sons) observe, 'the scar looked far worse than a flesh wound........'

Gordon enlisted with the Grenadier Guards on the 5th April 1945, he having turned eighteen on the 13th March 1945 – VE Day was 8th May 1945.

Chapter Thirty Seven

IN THE AIR

Of essential inclusion is Rupert Leigh whom Glenys and I saw quite often. He was a very likeable fellow. The twinkle in his eye sometimes rendered one unable to establish whether or not he was being serious, or taking the 'mick'. On a personal level I consider myself privileged to have known Rupert, and to be able to recall the enjoyable times in his company. I recount just two: It was late afternoon in the office and I was in the process of preparing notes in a particularly difficult case, and needed a break. Leaving the office I walked briskly down Market Hill in St Austell and immediately spotted Rupert walking in the opposite direction. Despite being very pleased to see him, he observed, 'You're looking stressed, young man - you need a drink.' And that's exactly what I got, given that the 'Queen's Head' was just there! An hour later and yet another of Rupert's successful missions!

Another quite extraordinary anecdotal account was eagerly narrated by Rupert to Glenys and me following his trip from Algerciras (where he resided) through France to the UK. Approaching the French border the bonnet of his Citron 2CV flew up thus completely blocking his vision. 'It all went black,' he enthused, 'I thought I'd died!' Being a former pilot he continued to drive with head out the side window and entered the French border control where he attempted to explain, at first in Spanish and then in French what had happened. 'They thought I'd driven all the way from Spain with the bonnet up!'

As a Squadron Leader with 66 Squadron he'd flown Spitfires and Hurricanes during the war, including the Battle of Britain, and was instrumental in the reinstatement of Douglas Bader as a pilot following the loss of his legs in a flying accident.

It was considered by some an impossible mission but Air Commodore Rupert Leigh encouraged Bader to fly again, initially in a Harvard, an aircraft that was large enough to accommodate Rupert lying in the cockpit and operating the brake pedals for Bader. When subsequently flying Spitfires or Hurricanes, Bader had no problem since the brakes were operated by squeezing a hand lever on the control column.

Rupert's son (my longstanding best mate) told me that his father had occasionally alluded to, in particular the Battle of Britain, and considered himself fortunate to have been older and more experienced than many of his young pilots whom he led, believing that these factors contributed to his survival.

Rupert's undeniable character is perhaps best captured in various biographies written by fellow pilots, but on a personal level, the time he visited his family shortly after the opening of their swimming pool. His grandchildren called out on his arrival, eager for him to swim in the pool. (Our son James (Jim) spent many of his young years with Rupert's grandson, Matthew, and Jim recalls that he and Matt were changing very quickly into swimming trunks and racing to the pool – which was slowly being filled from just one narrow hose pipe – for the grand opening). On arrival at the pool they found the pool a third to about half full and Rupert swimming therein, fully clothed!

Jim and Matt were occasionally taken by Rupert to a local

shop to buy them Maltesers and often his (Rupert's) favourite Wall's bacon! Most return journeys, Jim and Matt were permitted to take turns as Rupert let them steer his car!

Clearly not a man to seek any recognition for his part in the war e.g. choosing not to attend the television programme, 'This Is Your Life' with Douglas Badar, maintaining that he (Rupert) could not afford a new suit!

On one occasion I raised the subject of flying, and my interest in aircraft, with Rupert, and he related his experience of flying a Gloucester Meteor Jet during the latter part of the war, when it was possible to catch, and tip the wing of, a flying bomb, thus causing it to miss its target, probably a city or town. Like many others, he epitomised all that represented the very reserved dispositions of those who had fought for their country.

"Rupert Leigh was a gentle, feeling man, who cared about his fellow men."

A quote from, 'Flying Colours.' 'The Epic Story of Douglas Bader' by Laddie Lucas.

In another biography, 'Battle for Britain,' H.R. 'Dizzy' Allen DFC recalls, with much affection, Rupert's friendship and his role as performed during the war. Given Rupert's persona it would have been readily accepted by those who knew him that he disliked any written reference to himself. Accordingly, Dizzy chose a 'nom de plume' i.e. Rupert became 'Jasper'.

There's much in Dizzy's account that so accurately epitomises Squadron Commander 'Jasper' Leigh, but I choose, if I may, the following excerpt:

'Jasper never showed any signs of fear, but this by no means implies that he was fearless; indeed he was far too sensitive not to know fear. But whatever his inner feelings he was on the face of it inevitably as calm as a statue of the Buddha. On one battle climb the controller rang up and informed him that a raid consisting of some three hundred bandits was crossing the coast in the Sandwich area. The controller then reported, 'Christ, I haven't seen reports of so many bandits since Michaelmas!' 'Understood, (Jasper replied, voice calm as a mother superior's confessing her sin to the local priest). The controller then reported, 'There must be at least 500 bandits crossing between Dover and Ramsgate!' 'Understood,' Jasper replied, 'We are just flying-over Lingfield racecourse – I wonder what won the 2.30?'

I recall an event that included a short discussion with Rupert, who was staying with his son, our then immediate neighbour.

As had been the case for most years, Gareth, Jim and I attended the annual RAF St Mawgan's Air Day. The following morning Glenys was in the garden, while the boys and I were lounging around. Glenys entered. 'Oh, very funny, did you get it from a stall at the Air Day?'

'Get what?' We enquired, 'The rubber snake you've placed with the Runner Beans – it's not very realistic, it's too big.'

Inspection revealed a lengthy, but motionless, snake lying among the Runner Beans. I approached with caution prompting movement and audible hiss.

Rupert, having heard us, popped his head above our fence. 'We have a snake, Rupert, just there.'

'I dislike snakes immensely.' And he beat a hasty retreat.

We discovered subsequently that while living in Spain, Rupert had experienced unpleasant encounters with snakes.

Glenys immediately sought assistance of Ernest, our ex-RAF neighbour, who very thoughtfully, brought a book detailing British snakes.

On further inspection, I discovered that the snake was stuck in plastic garden netting and had clearly swallowed something for breakfast thus restricting forward or reverse movement; so while I carefully attempted to cut the offending netting with nail-scissors, Ernest read passages from his reptile book which appeared to confirm that this rather formidable reptile, of some three feet in length, was a Grass snake. Nevertheless given the hissing and size I continued to seek reassurance from Ernest who recommenced reading, which revealed certain characteristics as experienced during my attempted rescue, namely feigning initial death and, more noticeably, the smell of garlic produced when threatened.

Eventually Sid slithered free and promptly regurgitated a mouse. A successful rescue, save that the following morning, while making tea, I glanced out of the kitchen window and witnessed a Buzzard swoop down and fly off with a snake grasped in its talons – the 'circle of life'.

Jack Gimblett also saw plenty of action while serving with the RAF. His daughter (and Rupert's daughter in law) Sally, is a close friend of ours and she has very kindly provided me with a fascinating account of her dad's service with the RAF. The content is such that it should – with the exception of one paragraph – which I consider personal to her and her dad – remain as written:

'Dear John

I have spent most of the day trying to find a bit more info on dad and at last have been successful. I hope you find the following useful:

Dad left school at 16 and did an apprenticeship in engineering at the Hawker Aircraft Co in 1938. He became a commissioned officer in 1942 and had too many postings to mention. In that time he flew between 60-65 different aircraft including singles, twins, jets and propellers totalling 7000 flying hours! He flew Typhoons in France for ground support in 1944 and when his 245 Squadron was disbanded he continued flying to police the peace in France, Malta and

Africa. From age 18-58 years all his postings were flying postings and only one was ground posting! This is quite unusual in the RAF.

In 1957 he had a 4 year posting to Malta flying Shackletons and did emergency patrols between Malta and RAF Cyprus. In 1963 he set up the RAF museum in Henlow. In 1966 he was posted to Zambia for 3 years and flew President Kaunda all over Africa and was in charge of training Zambian Air Force pilots. He flew Dakotas and Caribous (I used to go on many trips with dad!) distributing food and medicines to the Africans in the bush. In 1969 he had a posting to Odiham flying Chipmunks and during his time there he was in charge of all the arrangements for the Royal Visit by Princess Margaret. He was promoted to Squadron Leader in 1972.

Dad left the RAF in 1975 and became a volunteer reserve Flying Officer at Hamble. He was given a commendation for re-starting an engine failure mid-air whilst trining a student. He then moved to Bristol and was in charge of the University Flying Squadron flying Chipmunks.

He received an MBE for his flying contribution to the RAF, training pilots in the Zmabian Air Force and flying President Kaunda.

He also flew in the 633 Squadron film.

When he finally retired he became Selsey Parish Council Clerk and was a force to be reckoned with!

When he succumbed to lung cancer he said it was nothing compared to being shot at by enemy aircraft. He said his most memorable thing is his life during his tour in Africa, especially distributing food and medicine to those in need and his worst memory was 5 years of war.

Some of his planes: Hurricanes, Mosquitos, Typhoons, Shackletons, Dakotas, Chipmunks, Tiger Moths, Defiance, Bostons, Havocs, Neptunes, Caribous.

Not sure whether any of this is relevant but use whatever you like.

Hope to see you soon.

Love to Glenys,

Sal xx'

Similarly we were privileged to know Jack ('composed in the face of adversity') Gimblett. He was steadfast – unshakeable.

The plane featured in the 1964 film, '633 Squadron', was a Mosquito.

An unmistakeable trait of Jack, when speaking to me under the bonnet of a car, was his ability to substitute his strong and precise diction for that akin to Eastenders i.e. discussing the internal combustion engine.

Chapter Thirty Eight

George Albert Herbert was Glenys's grandmother's husband, and during the First World War he served as a Petty Officer with HMS Queen Elizabeth Super Dreadnought Battle Ship. His hands were scarred due to handling spent shell cases in one of the large gunnery sections of the ship. He also, perhaps not surprisingly, suffered tinnitus, a sensation of ringing, buzzing or hissing in the head or ears.

Following the end of conflict Mr Herbert was recruited by, and based at, the Tollesbury Coastguard Station. However, the persistent shelling had affected his mental well-being and on the 5th January 1920 George Albert Herbert took his own life.

A war grave was placed in St Mary's Churchyard, Tollesbury, Essex with Commonwealth War Graves Commission headstone appropriately inscribed and including his recent service with the Coastguard and, 'formerly HMS Queen Elizabeth, Royal Navy'. Inexplicably, and many years later, a person, possibly local to Tollesbury, considered the headstone to be incorrectly inscribed. This culminated in the War Graves Commission, without reference to any surviving relatives, destroying the headstone, and replacing it with a headstone merely recording George's service with the Coastguard.

It was clearly necessary, upon discovering this, to take

decisive action in the form of a letter from Glenys to the War Graves Commission, part of which reads:

My reason for writing this letter was prompted following my visit last year when I discovered that his headstone had been replaced.

For ninety years his headstone recorded his role, and rank, of Petty Officer with the Royal Navy, but to my distress, and indeed anger, his replacement solely records his service with H M Coastguard....

Petty Officer Herbert took his own life two years after the end of the First World War because, like many other servicemen, he was unable to recover from the traumas sustained during that War. His death, therefore, was intrinsically linked to the adverse and traumatic affects of War... Accordingly, in my opinion it is grossly wrong, indeed disrespectful, to reduce the significance of his role during his service with the Royal Navy which indisputably culminated in his death.

Fortunately the War Commission agreed to remove the headstone and replace it as originally inscribed.

Prior to George's death, his brother Private (Charles) Herbert, serving with The Queen's (Royal West Surrey) Regiment, was killed on the 25th September 1915 in France – his age, like so many, recorded as 'unknown'. The Regiment paid a high price (8000 dead) for its commitment in the First World War.

Chapter Thirty Nine

HENRIETTA

Henrietta Brown (know as Joan to friends and family) resided at number 1 and Glenys and I at number 10.

Joan, a sprightly senior citizen, lived alone having separated from her husband, a retired GP.

Joan had spent some years residing in Australia, often fondly recalling her visits to Moonee Ponds, situated in the inner suburbs of Melbourne. She also introduced us to what she described as the, 'equivalent of Australian plonk' i.e. Jacob's Creek; a Merlot, to be precise. As a result most Friday evenings, following a week of challenging matrimonial minefields, Glenys and I sampled the Australian 'plonk' that was always corked (for breathing) by Joan four hours earlier. A brisk walk from number 10 to number 1 invariably resulted in a giggling stagger on return, a second bottle having been consumed.

This quite incredible lady (sadly no longer) entertained us always with her memoirs, the content of which I've been able to recall, but often wished her extraordinary life could have been recorded by a better or more sober brain than mine.

She'd been a nurse during the 1930's, and having seen photos, she was indisputably, a very attractive lady. Henrietta had eyes for a professor whom she desired, and whom she subsequently married. However, it came to pass that the professor, tired of general practice within part of the matrimonial home, was desirous of returning to hospital to further pursue his role as (I believe) a gynaecologist, thus resulting in a Locum being secured for the GP practice, and Joan tiring of the regular absence of her husband, and seeking solace with the Locum, Geoffrey Brown. 'Solace', resulted in divorce, and while I'm uncertain as to when dissolution took place (probably 1930's) divorce was rare and severely frowned upon. However, it's fair to say, that knowing Joan, as we did, she would have dealt with this episode with dignity, drive and a good helping of humour. Following the divorce, Joan and Geoffrey were married.

Joan often spoke of their union, not least the fact that her father-in-law (Geoffrey's father) was Arthur Geoffrey Tillotson Brown, the Captain of RMS Maurentania who had also served in the Royal Navy during the First World War with HMS Seal. Tillotson Brown (see Wikipedia) Captained the Maurentania (following the end of conflict) for many years. He also Captained the second Maurentania, eventually dying on board, I believe in June 1939, while at sea in the Suez Canal.

During the Second World War Joan's husband served with the Army (Rank and regiment unknown) as a Doctor with the Medical Corps. Joan's memory in this regard was, not surprisingly, given the traumatic circumstances, very detailed in that she received a telegram informing her that Geoffrey was missing in action, presumed dead. This scenario continued for some time, until Geoffrey arrived home without prior notice. Joan always described her shock, his condition as unkempt, and in a very poor state of health.

Given the era (war, passion, divorce, sports cars, music, dancing etc) relevant to her memoirs, I'm confident that there was sufficient script material for radio, film or TV. Mention of sports cars reminds me that Joan's driving was such that she was known locally as Fangio Brown.

As is common with the ageing process, Joan's hearing and eyesight brought a cessation to driving. Glenys's many virtues include her ability to 'give' thus spending much time each week driving Joan here and there and often interrupting her routines to provide for Joan's needs. However, our Fridays, courtesy of Joan and Jacob's Creek, remained until age dictated a move closer to her son in Plymouth.

At about this time, but prior to her move, Glenys asked me to check on Joan who'd phoned asking if I could replace a light bulb. I'd just arrived home from work suited and booted, so I quickly changed into black jogging bottoms and black sweatshirt, leaving a white T-shirt beneath. On opening her door (poor eyesight) she stared with some concern, followed by a virtual order to enter. 'Joan, I understand you need a light bulb changing.' Whereupon she shrieked with laughter, 'Is that you John? I thought it was the bloody vicar!'

Chapter Forty

SCOTT

In September 1990 Glenys and I celebrated our 25th wedding anniversary by flying to Florida where we rented an apartment on Anna Maria Island.

While there we became friendly with the site gardener, one Scott Pender. Scott was a former Marine and it soon became clear that we were to discover another victim of conflict. Scott eventually confided in us that as a young man he'd existed on the margins and often got into fights. A criminal charge was brought against him, but he was given the option of a prison sentence or Vietnam – he chose Vietnam, trained with the Marines and survived the conflict. He told me that he had to shoot people, he didn't want to. Thereafter he had much trouble in holding down a relationship and would retaliate violently if offended. In addition he was relying heavily upon the demon drink. When visiting his modest home, humidity was high and the temperature even higher, and yet this extremely fit and handsome guy had a fire burning in a large hole in his back garden. His partner, Nancy, explained that this was something he'd done during the Vietnam War, and psychologically it still provided some form of security/stability, and which according to an immediate neighbour included random attempts by Scott to redesign the interior of his home – with a chainsaw!

He arrived one afternoon at our apartment, during his day-off and had been drinking given that he was holding - when he arrived in his truck – the remains of a six-pack. 'Drinking and driving, Scott?' 'Yeah, John, six-pack there, and six-pack back!'

Scott took us (as he called it) to a 'shit kicking' dance venue, but as further alcohol took affect, Nancy suggested that we leave. Sensible advice as I'd already sensed that Scott had taken exception to some guy and was about to display his combat skills. When arriving back at his home Scott opened the passenger door for Nancy to alight – he was still holding the top of the car door when Nancy slammed it shut. 'Fuck Honey you slammed the door on my fingers!' I assume his fingers weren't broken, but they looked broken!

Earlier that evening, when arriving at his house, I handed him a case of Budweiser, gratefully receiving same Scott lost his balance, reversed at speed and landed on his backside ('butt') while ensuring that the beer remained safe and secure. I assume that he was already suitably intoxicated, not least with the aid of marijuana which he grew in the back garden.

Scott was straight out of the silver screen right down to his macho image, good looks and large motorcycle – sadly not a Harley! However, this machine had been converted by Scott and resembled all that appeared to be a close relative. 'Take it John and ride through the Orange Groves with Glenys.' 'What if it breaks down, Scott?' I enquired, 'Chuck it in the ditch, John.' So early the next morning, wearing T-shirts and shorts, we set forth. Did I mention that Glenys dislikes motorbikes? However, all went well and we returned the bike in one piece. Riding a motorcycle in searing heat is something we'll never forget. Similarly, we'll never forget Scott Pender, a character, a little rough around the edges, but like many young men his courage came at a price.

Chapter Forty One

ACADEMIC ACHIEVEMENTS AND MATTERS ARISING

A year into my position with the small family legal practice in Ipswich, Eric (the boss) asked if I'd be interested in studying to become a Legal Executive (A Fellow of the Institute of Legal Executives – now Chartered). Eric suggested that I enrol with The Ipswich Civic College for half-day release to pursue the course. However, it would first be necessary to take (and obviously pass) an English O Level. I therefore recommended evening classes once a week, but by that time the course had commenced over a month before I enrolled. A minor miracle – I passed!

Before I could attempt the Fellowship examination (at Degree Level) it was necessary to attend College and study for part one of the Associateship ('A' level) Examination in law and procedure, and part two the following year. Needless to say, this involved home study, playing with the band, working as a lawyer, and later attempting to ensure that my role as father was performed fully and satisfactorily. These tasks, however, were only possible, and undeniably, due to the love and consistent support of my wife, culminating in my passing the Associateship exams.

My aim was to pass the various law examinations that would provide exemption from the Law Society's part one solicitor's qualifying examinations. I'm sure that I am not alone when I say that while my education and further education (one half day release) showed no signs of truly defined academia, my ability to absorb a particular subject was always substantially enhanced if the subject was interesting, or at least interesting to me e.g. coming top of the class in History during my final year at school, simply because we had advanced to the Second World War. Accordingly when it was time to progress to University grade exams, in particular Criminal Law and the Law of Tort (a civil wrong), I was able to absorb the subjects because they were interesting. That is not to say that they were easy subjects, on the contrary they demanded much study that included memorising innumerable cases. I'm informed (rightly or wrongly) that nowadays reference to a textbook during a law exam is permitted. Such a luxury was not afforded the law student of my day. However, I assume that the same standard is sought of the student and that the questions remain abstruse, or indeed, depending on the composer, often bizarre in the extreme. As an example of the type of question one could expect to test one's knowledge, comprehension and fortitude, I provide (having, as a hoarder, retained my copy) the following replication of question 5 of the Criminal Law paper for a Law Fellowship Examination on the 10th June 1970:

'Polly, intending her child to die, abandons it by the side of the road. Shortly afterwards, Greta, a passenger in a passing car, jumps out of the car to avoid being sexually assaulted by Rex. Greta lands on the baby, thereby killing it. Discuss the homicide liability of Polly, Greta and Rex'

It is clear from the notes made by me at the time on the examination paper, that I answered this one. As bizarre as the question appears, it is testing the student on their knowledge of criminal responsibility and sought reference to an early – possibly the earliest, or one of the earliest recorded cases – namely The Harlot's Case 1560 – in which a prostitute abandoned her child knowing that Kites, that were then common in England, would probably attack it, which is precisely what happened. It was clear that the woman either intended the death, or else was reckless whether it occurred or not.

It was necessary to establish that the accused had a 'guilty mind'. The ancient maxim: 'Actus non facit reum nisi mens sit rea' represented the normal test and requirement, and means, 'The mere doing of an act will not constitute guilt unless there be a guilty intention.' Which remains to this day i.e. to achieve a conviction it has to be proved that the accused intended (the 'mens rea') to commit the crime.

That exam is indelibly printed on my brain, simply because the 10th June 1970 was very hot and the examination room at the college in Ipswich was of modern design with low ceilings and no air conditioning. 'You may commence', prompted a young man to rise from his chair a few rows forward of me. He turned and began to walk slowly passed other students towards the back of the room; his face contorted and drained of life. About four feet from where I was sitting he vomited and by some extraordinary stroke of luck, the not insubstantial content of his stomach, hit the floor and not me. The stench – I need not elaborate. Suffice to say that the heat, lack of air and constant wiping of sweat from one's eyes, was hardly conducive to a successful and satisfactory examining environment. Another minor miracle – I passed!

The complete opposite scenario took place, a few years later, when taking a Law Society's exam in Birmingham. It was winter and as I entered the exam room I noticed students wearing scarves and gloves – the heating had failed and the large hall was, like me, freezing. My subsequent letter to the examiners seeking consideration due to the appalling conditions resulted, like the exam, in failure!

Having continued with my studies, including the half-day course in Ipswich, I took and passed the Law of Tort and Contract.

With my boss's blessing I was granted extended leave during part of 1971 to attend the College of Law at Lancaster Gate, London.

Having achieved a law Fellowship, I sought passes in Land law and Constitutional and Administrative law, thus providing me with the exemption, of those heads of the Law Societies' Solicitors' Qualifying Examination.

Previous study for exams had of course been done while in full time employment, so I was hopeful that a full time course of study would prove beneficial. The course would last for about three months i.e. a 'Sandwich Course'.

I chose to commute each day by train from Ipswich thus ensuring that my wife and three year old son saw me on a regular basis.

This was my first experience of student life and I enjoyed the company of other law students, mostly younger than I, but found Land Law and Constitutional Law quite boring, which was to prove of little benefit. That said there was much humour to savour, not least, as many of those attending the course were, like me, ardent fans of Monty Python's Flying Circus. Need I say more?

Often while waiting for the train at Ipswich station I noticed Sir Alf Ramsey on the platform. Eventually if I caught his eye, he would smile and nod in response. One morning he sat opposite me and like the day before, the train groaned to a standstill that would undoubtedly result in another delay. After about 15 minutes Sir Alf looked at me, smiled, and said, 'Well, at least it's consistent!' As a result we became occasional travelling acquaintances, since he was still England Soccer Manager and the Football Association's headquarters, like the College of Law, based at Lancaster Gate.

He was such an amiable chap, but I attempted purposely to avoid the subject of football and he addressed domestic matters at home e.g. faulty heaters. He often also enquired of my progress at college. It eventually, however, proved impossible, given that England were playing at Wembley one evening, and while sitting with him the following morning on the Central Line most of the occupants were reading newspapers adorned with photographs of the match and headlines that naturally included his name.

I became the subject of much banter e.g. that I'd been seen on Ipswich station wearing a tracksuit and carrying a football!

I consider myself extremely privileged to have known a true gentleman, and a legend in his own right.

Chapter Forty Two

During one of my return trips to Ipswich, a lawyer from another office in Ipswich spotted me and soon caused me concern when he enthused about a rumour circulating the various solicitors' offices in Ipswich that my boss (Eric) was the subject of a police investigation regarding forgery and/or attempts to defraud. I completely dismissed his assertions and his very clear intention to cause me distress, not least, as he was an opposition lawyer and the type of person one would attempt, if possible, to avoid. That said his comments *did* worry me.

I returned to work in August 1971 having completed law studies and exams. I was not optimistic. (Subsequently, after the third attempt, I actually passed Land Law).

Everything appeared normal save that on a few occasions, if in the main office, I noticed two guys in the waiting room fitting the archetypal, and unmistakable, description of police detectives.

I discreetly enquired and was informed by a colleague that our boss was indeed under investigation for alleged forgery and intent to defraud. Eric was adamant that he'd done nothing illegal and we all hoped that investigations would prove fruitless. Sadly, this was not to be, and a police prosecution followed, culminating in Eric standing trial in Ipswich, reasonably confident that at most he would receive a reprimand or possibly a period of suspension; not that either appeared appropriate or necessary, since clearly he was not a criminal, and if the court deemed that an offence had been committed then it would be the first for a man of impeccable background etc. Despite much reassurance from a then eminent London lawyer, who urged Eric to plead guilty, Eric was sentenced to nine months imprisonment. I was present in court and it was very clear that Eric was to receive no rationalisation or compassion from the Judge who was completely devoid of either virtue and simply deemed that Eric had abused a position of trust.

Eric, though pole-axed, took the verdict on the chin and handled the scenario with much courage, fortitude and dignity.

It's fair to say, at this juncture, that my understanding was that, allegedly, certain members of the Ipswich Police Force were not fond of Eric due to his ability to occasionally succeed in defending an accused and to also achieve an order for costs against the police.

Whatever the case, Eric was struck off. However, while within the confines of Ford Open Prison, he corresponded with Lord Denning, then Master of the Rolls (responsible, amongst other things, for registering solicitors) explaining, I *assume*, in some detail, the circumstances pertaining to the basis upon which the criminal proceedings were brought against him, and the subsequent miscarriage of justice due to the simple fact he had no criminal intent. Lord Denning eventually concurred and restored Eric to the rolls.

During much of his imprisonment, a locum attempted to run the practice, but with Eric absent, the drive and impetus had gone with him, and so too had the confidence that my job was secure. With a wife and child to consider – and another on the way – I felt obliged to secure a position with other solicitors.

This objective proved far simpler than anticipated as a

solicitor in Ipswich offered me the position of divorce lawyer with a long established firm. I was offered a very reasonable income, plus a car.

Having achieved this, my wife, son and I, headed for Cornwall for a short break, during which I contacted a mate whom I'd met while at Lancaster Gate, and he kindly invited us to stay a few nights with him and his family.

Having related the course of events that had taken place our host explained that coincidentally, his father, a senior partner with a firm in St Austell, had told his son that the firm would be requiring someone to take over their divorce department upon the retirement of their elderly clerk, culminating in a hastily arranged interview with his father and being offered the job.

This turn of events obviously required much deliberation, and much discussion with my wife. Given that our son was pre-school age we decided that a move to Cornwall would perhaps be beneficial.

Having been offered, and accepted, the post of divorce lawyer in Ipswich, I was faced with the unenviable task of informing – what would have been my potential new employer – of our decision. He was, not surprisingly, upset, a little annoyed, but accepted the decision.

While subsequently visiting and staying with my parents in Colchester for a short break with Glenys and (by then) our boys, I received, much to my surprise, a telephone call from Eric who despite being aware of our move to Cornwall was keen to establish whether I would consider returning to Ipswich with a view to joining him in resurrecting his practice. Sadly I did not consider it feasible, given all the circumstances. That said I appreciated very much his attempt to explore the possibility since he clearly thought I was worthy of reinstatement as a lawyer in his practice.

Whether it be my ability to play drums, or my chosen career,

I have always taken the view that whatever I did, and whatever level of success was achieved, one could always improve.. At the time of departure from Suffolk I did not, despite much effort, consider myself to be particularly good at my job until, that is, my final appearance before the then Senior Registrar (District Judge) of the Ipswich County Court.

Having concluded an application, I felt duty-bound to mention that I would shortly be leaving Ipswich for Cornwall. The Registrar, for whom I had much respect, responded with some sincerity, 'Well, Mr Ledbetter, it is Suffolk's loss, and Cornwall's gain!' Gobsmacked!

Continuing under 'Academic 'Talents' heading, I should perhaps dissect the two and focus on 'Talents', since I'm told I have a 'good eye' for photography – taking photos, that is. Gareth, in particular, has for many years provided praise and encouragement for my photography, latterly creating a website https://www.flickr.com/photos/187122735@No4/ devoted in part to my hobby, something I've enjoyed but never considered it to be of interest to anyone else. That said, I've had four published in 'Cornwall Today' and actually won a meal for two when my photo was voted best of the month.

Oh, have I mentioned that I played drums?

Chapter Forty Three

SHORT REFERENCE

Earlier I touched upon my role as a father. Gareth (pre Cornwall) was at this juncture (June 1970) two years of age. It is fair to say that the preceding two years had been thought-provoking and very much an education for his novice parents; we simply did not know what had hit us, in that as a beautiful baby (later as a young boy, much to his displeasure, he was sometimes mistaken for a girl) he demanded constant attention, but above all, uninterrupted stimulation. He was clearly very alert and intelligent and well ahead of any of his contemporaries. Our elderly neighbours, one of whom was a retired teacher, informed us that they had never encountered such a child. He was an early crawler and walker and we, as his parents, were mostly in a state of astonishment and indeed concern. During his first nine months Glenys would often be heard to say, 'If only he could speak, at least I'd know what he wanted.' We were left in no doubt that this dark wavy haired blue-eyed boy was to prove a challenge, in every sense of the word.

Obviously there's more to follow in due course.

Chapter Forty Four

UFO AND THINGS THAT...

I make no secret of the fact that I'm a non-believer, and that also applies to ghosts and the supernatural. However, I have to confess to possibly/probably having seen a UFO in Suffolk, and experienced a couple of unexplained events; one also in Suffolk, the other in Cornwall.

The UFO sighting took place, during daytime, in the back garden of our first matrimonial home (previously alluded to) in Somersham. I was in conversation with a neighbour, as an aircraft – probably from RAF Wattisham, a few miles from Somersham – was flying fairly low, and I commented that it had done several previous cicuits. I cannot recall what type of aircraft, save that it was a twin-engine jet with provision for passengers or equipment. As the plane passed over, a bright circular light appeared beneath the fuselage and proceeded slowly towards the nose of the plane. It then returned to the rear and travelled up to the tail of the aircraft where it remained for a few seconds before departing to the sky in a flash.

Neighbour and I stood transfixed, 'What the hell was that?' I enquired. What it clearly was not, given its position, was reflection from the sun.

The first 'unexplained event' took place about 30 years ago

when Glenys and I were visiting a former secretary of mine in Ipswich. She and her husband had recently purchased a property on a new development. No alcohol was consumed, but much tea required my seeking directions to the bathroom. As I ascended the stairs I experienced a very strange feeling that persisted and became slightly overwhelming when reaching the landing, culminating (post wee) in my relating this to Sue and Mick, (the owners) who eagerly related that part the new development had been built on a graveyard!

The second, and indeed, third, 'unexplained event' took place at our friends, (Bill and Libby's) house in St Austell. Their home: Old, quite large and imposing. Their son often referred to the property as his 'Amityville Horror Home'.

One afternoon, it was suggested that I use stairs at the rear of 'Amityville' to gain access to the back garden. The stairs were apparently seldom used (not the principal stair-case), and had received little attention since the house was built in the late thirties, and its primary use was then for kitchen staff and servants. About half way down the stairs I immediately experienced an errie and somewhat bewildering sensation. Best perhaps described as bizarre for the non-believer!

Neither Glenys not I were present when the third event took place at 'Amityville, but was described to us by our friends a day or so following a quite extraordinary incident while in the garden at the rear of 'Amityville'.

Libby and son, Mark (Bill was at work) heard tyres skidding and a collision. Both ran to the road (A390) situated beyond the front of their house, and were perplexed – there was no accident. Later that afternoon, when arriving home from a trip to Truro, they witnessed an accident that had taken place at the very same location, involving a motor-cyclist!

Chapter Forty Five

WHAT SOME PEOPLE...

Some years ago I was approached by Tom French - who at that time was the proprietor of a men's outfitters shop in St Austell – to do a spot of male modelling for a charitable cause. I, needless to say, forcefully but politely refused. However, a mate of mine had already agreed to help-out and persuaded me saying it would be a laugh, not to mention the incredibly lovely young ladies that would be part of the four gigs. Furthermore, once worn, the expensive suits etc would be offered at much reduced rates.

The first show was very well attended at the sixth form college in St Austell. However, I'd made it clear to Tom that I could not ponce about on stage in serious model mode, and would have to attempt to include humour. I decided to hang a rubber chicken from my belt so that its claws could be seen below the very expensive suit jacket, This was well received save that one guy found it hilarious and was laughing so much that one feared cardiac intervention. Later his wife explained that her husband had refused to attend but she'd persuaded him to do so. That, plus my subsequent appearance wearing sunglasses and walking into props, resulted in her husband saying it was one of the funniest things he'd seen for some time.

The final show was at the Cornwall Coliseum in St Austell. Our son James was about eleven and he accompanied his mother. Driving down the access road he thought there had to be some mistake given that this was the venue for very big bands of that era. However, I managed once again to prat about a bit, which appeared to be appreciated.

The next day, while in the office, I received a phone call from a lady who introduced herself as the proprietor of a local ladies' lingerie shop, and asked if I would be prepared to escort (scantily clad) young ladies at her next fashion show, as she considered me to be of James Bond calibre. In total disbelief I nevertheless said I would let her know my decision.

While obviously, and momentarily, taken aback with this compliment, I had to run this past my wife. Quite surprisingly she simply placed the ball back in my court saying that it was for me to decide. I telephoned that afternoon and declined the proprietor's offer. She thanked me and appreciated my courage in having the guts to let her know my decision. Subsequently the Cornish Guardian included photos of the fashion show. Had I made the right decision? Probably not, save that those young ladies may well have resulted in, at the very least, palpitations – my palpitations!

Chapter Forty Six

HUMOUR

Emotional White Male: I was, by 1970, eight years into my career, and while I have to accept that my working environment was safe and that I was never placed under any more pressure than would reasonably be expected of a young family lawyer, I was becoming increasingly aware that my genetically inherited emotional stability was sometimes restrictive in my aim and preference to remain rational and objective, particularly regarding the issue of children. Often I narrowly avoided embarrassment in Court when a client was reduced to tears due to the resurrection of the traumas previously or then confronting them, or alternatively when a client cried tears of relief at hearing that the child or children of the failed union, should remain in their custody.

It has been a lifelong wish of mine that my inability to control my emotions – that would invariably and so easily reduce me to tears – be at least moderated. However, when rarely confiding this desire to others, (who are mostly well aware of my emotional charge) I am often confidently informed that even a minor adjustment would result in an entirely different individual and persona. This may be an accurate observation, but I am bound to say that it can be awfully embarrassing when something that may appear to others to be effectively insignificant and wholly unmoving, results in tears!

Tears of happiness are, I'm sure, an acceptable response. Speaking personally, there are few things in life that can surpass the type of response to humour which results in crying with laughter, particularly if that laughter is exacerbated by prevailing circumstances that render it 'inappropriate'. Those, born with the gift of laughter, will of course first experience this type of scenario during their school days.

The Bawdens: Very soon (following our move to Cornwall) Glenys commenced conversations with a mother of a child who was attending Gareth's school and a friendship developed that lasted for many years. Margaret and Ken, both Cornish, lived in their cottage in Charlestown with their two boys. Glenys and I spent many enjoyable hours in their company, in particular visits following Margaret's regular invites for 'Yeasties' (Cornish yeast buns) absolutely delicious.

Ken didn't drive so one summer's day in the late seventies, Margaret and he took a bus ride to Fowey. When standing at the bus stop for the return trip, with many holiday makers, a Cornish ECLP work colleague (and real character) of Ken joined the back of the queue, whereupon Ken was ordered, and reminded several times by Margaret, that he should not look at or speak to the fellow.

Ken and Margaret chose to sit upstairs and were fortunate to find vacant seats to the rear. However, Ken's workmate also chose upstairs but appeared to pass them unnoticed and sat at the front. Every seat taken, Ken's workmate spotted the Bawdens, 'Ken, I'd 'ave thought by now you and yer missus would 'ave a tandem!' 'Do not speak to him,' reminded Margaret. 'I said I'd 'ave thought by now you and yer missus would 'ave a tandem! Receiving no response, and with a packed audience, he observed, 'Tis obvious they don't want a fucking tandem!'

Bowmans: It is perhaps essential that I relate an event that incisively falls within that age-old, tried and tested, category of humour involving one's mother-in-law.

Some years prior to the 'Happy Days' episode, I offered, one November 5th to oversee the lighting of fireworks for Glenys's brother Paul, who was then about eleven years old. All was going well, Glenys was preparing a meal in her parents' kitchen and could see the display through the kitchen window, and Alona, her mother, positioned herself at the upstairs open landing window.

Joe had arrived from work and was assisting me. It was decided to retain the rockets for the finale. Unfortunately (or perhaps fortuitously, depending on how one is inclined to view their mother-in-law) I trod on one of the rockets and broke its wooden tail. I was apprehensive about lighting it but Joe was confident that it would be ok. I placed it in a milk bottle and lit the blue touch paper. It burst into life, lifted about twelve feet in the air and abruptly projected itself toward the landing window. Alona ducked as the rocket narrowly missed her head, which together with the rest of her torso was brilliantly silhouetted against the flashes and resulting glare on the landing as the rocket erupted.

"You bloody fool – you did that on purpose!" drowned our uncontrolled laughter. "Don't be bleedin' stupid 'lona, he couldn't 'elp it", responded Joe.

Alona, was adamant that I tried to kill her. Naturally, I refuted this!

It is worthy of mention that as a child, Glenys would occasionally go *cockling* with her mother off the sea wall and would rest by sitting on a piece of metal protruding from the mud-flats. Some years later the metal was discovered to be one of the fins attached to a submerged unexploded German V2 rocket!

Sally: One afternoon (back in the sixties) the office receptionist, Sally, telephoned and whispered down the phone, 'Mr Ledbetter, Mrs P's husband is in the waiting room, and he has a shot gun with him.'

'Have you said that I'm in the office?'

'Yes, I'm afraid I have.'

Yet another occasion when I was not wearing brown trousers. To be honest 'brown' is not my colour!

I was acting for this guy's wife who alleged her husband's violence. With much apprehension and trepidation I confronted him, which was scary given that the butt of the gun was not concealed within the gun cover and while we conversed he persistently fingered it. However, he attempted to assure me that he was taking the gun to a local gunsmith as spent cartridges were not being properly ejected. I explained, very politely, that I could not discuss the matter with him as I was representing his wife, whereupon he became argumentative and somewhat threatening. Fortunately I was bigger than him, but he did have a gun! I wrestled him to the floor, grabbing the 12 bore as I did so. There was an explosion as the gun hit the floor, the mass of pellets embedding themselves in..... Sorry, for a moment, I became a fiction writer. In fact after my perseverance he left muttering obscenities.

Sally (office receptionist), was a very pleasant young lady who loved horses and spoke with precise diction. Without doubt a suitable substitute for Margot Leadbetter (Penelope Keith) of 'The Good Life.' However, despite being of similar age to me, she insisted on referring to me as 'Mr Ledbetter,' and even when attending a function at the Felixstowe Sailing Club, where I was performing with the band, she excitedly approached me during the interval.

'Oh, Mr Ledbetter you were absolutely brilliant, I had no idea...' Whereupon the guy with her says, 'Come off it, you're not in the office now - call him John.'

'Oh I couldn't possibly do that, could I Mr Ledbetter?'

Most mornings Michael and I walked from our office to the main office in Princes Street for coffee and an exchange of anecdotes and jokes. Sally ('Margot') invariably ended up crying with laughter and occasionally Eric (boss) would have to ask us to keep the noise down. However, she always attempted to maintain a prim and proper stance where smutty jokes were concerned. An already ruddy complexion would deepen, 'Oh really, do we have to?' was often followed by concealed laughter, but the most memorable was her response to a lavatory joke, 'Oh really Mr Ledbetter, once we're on toilets we can't get off them!'

One of Sally's anecdotal contributions related to her second driving lesson. The driving instructor, a guy in his early thirties, had asked her to pull into a lay-by where he attempted to seduce her. 'I wasn't sure what to do', she said, 'he really was quite nice, anyway, we were kissing and he asked whether I would like to go any further, so I said, 'Yes please, thinking that he was referring to the driving lesson!'

Mine's A Half. About two years into practicing divorce law I was taught a salutary lesson – one I would not forget.

It was a delightful summer's day, so I decided to have a half pint of beer with my lunch. I returned to the office to commence a consultation with a new young lady client, and chose to conduct the interview in a room that opened onto a small walled garden. The sun shone through the opened windows, the birds were singing, and with the exception of this poor unfortunate lady unburdening her troubles, in that stolen moment, everything in the garden was rosy. Her words, at first faint, then increasing in pitch and building to a clear and audible, 'Now, I realise you've heard all this before, but I wonder if you could stay awake!'

With the exception of one or two moments of weakness, lunch times have since been alcohol free.

I fondly recall the years with Eric Blakey & Co in Ipswich during the 1960's, not least the regular opportunities to drive at speed with highly tuned saloon and sports cars.

Fridays at Framlingham: Most Fridays Michael and I travelled to Framlingham in Suffolk where his father rented a room from an elderly lady to use as a branch office. The small room was adorned with various antiques, including a very nice glass lamp that we took great care to avoid hitting with our heads. One Friday morning I was recalling 'Top Of The Pops' that I'd seen the previous evening. I then emulated Pete Townsend's (lead Guitarist with The Who) 'windmill' action while playing, 'My Generation'. The 'windmill' involves winding one's elevated arm in a circle. As I did so my hand hit the glass lamp, smashing it to tiny fragments. Michael and I stood opened mouthed in shocked silence until he shouted, 'You're bleeding all over the rug.' The dear old lady owner dismissed her loss: 'accidents will happen.'

A Day at the Royal Cornwall Show: While much of the following describes an extraordinary event that is amusing, it also includes a father's (MINE) somewhat misguided intentions in regard to health and safety issues!

In June 1973, having successfully persuaded my wife, we duly attended the R C Show. Gareth was five and James seven months. It was a sunny day but a keen wind was blowing from the north coast. I was carrying James so he could see (at seven months, John - are you serious?) the Royal Horse Artillery display, galloping round the arena towing gun carriages. Upon completion they wheeled their field-guns into a line just behind the arena barrier, effectively pointing them at us, the spectators! 'They surely won't fire them there.' I confidently relayed to my wife, who was already in retreat with Gareth. *BANG!* James screamed with fright along with various children, and indeed, adults. The pieces of, what I presumed to be wadding, from the blank shells hit us, together with the smell of cordite.

Glenys suggested that it was time to go but I persuaded her to wait, at least, until the next event – a freefall parachute display.

The carrying aircraft circled above us and after three circuits the parachutists left the aircraft.

NOW, I emphasise that I'm no expert when it comes to prevailing weather conditions, but that said, I considered, given their drop-point, that these guys had been instructed to jump without thought for the wind direction. Furthermore this was before the introduction of directionally guidable parachutes, and I accurately surmised that there was not a cat in hell's chance of these chaps landing in the arena and that the wind direction would surely result in them landing just about where we were standing. I decided to stand my ground with James in my arms. The first to land demanded that I be agile, and swift of foot. I literally saw the studs of his boots just above me before dodging his fall. The second to fall, landed on the top of a refuse lorry parked behind us, and then fell from the back of the lorry while his chute caught overhead cables and promptly burst into flames, culminating in a complete power cut to the entire show ground. For my wife, and possibly others, a not entirely disappointing outcome.

Chapter Forty Seven

COMICAL

As a child I often took a bus to Colchester Town (you could in those days without fear) with a few shillings pocket money and would head for a Joke shop in Trinity Street to purchase – well, anything e.g. whoopee cushion, exploding pen (worked well on Dad!) to name but a few. The reason I mention this is because Gareth and James were soon introduced to the Trick Shop and were always keen to purchase an item of little, but effective, interest to the occupants of 1 Landseer Road i.e. Henry and Rose, their grandparents:

a) A trick glass that granddad attempted unsuccessfully several times to drink from while the contents ran slowly down his neck.

b) Vomit – James pretended to feel sick and wretched the fake vomit on the bonnet of Granddad's car. Henry quickly grabbed a newspaper and attempted to wipe the sticky lump of vomit eventually depositing it on one of Grandma's favourite rose bushes – Henry laughed.

c) Flies – three quite large plastic bluebottles to be precise, that G&J placed at teatime in salad on Nan's plate. She kept asking what we were laughing at while she, on three occasions, actually cut into the fake flies. It should also be mentioned that during teatime Grandma lent across and cut a huge piece of cheddar cheese thus substantially reducing the remainder – 'I've no appetite', she announced, with some sincerity!

d) My mother was a heavy smoker, so off to the trick shop for some small explosive capsules that, unbeknown to her, G&J carefully inserted in one of her Embassy Tipped, ensuring that it protruded slightly from the pack. The cigarette was lit and smoked for several puffs, and just as we thought, 'this is no joke', the fag exploded leaving an inch or so in mother's mouth with tobacco hanging in small strands, and the remainder of the contents covering her spectacles. 'You buggers!' she remonstrated.

e) I was first introduced to whoopee-cushions when I was about nine. During a visit, while in London, my parents took me to see Aunt Bird and Uncle Joe. I was sitting on the floor enjoying a glass of lemonade, when my aunt entered with a tray of tea. As she sat, my Uncle, without my knowledge (or hers) slipped the cushion beneath her, which provided a loud rasp and my lemonade ejected via my nostrils.

In the earlier 'Childhood/Post War Britian' chapter I spoke lovingly of my Nan Tyson, and although her passing in the early nineteen seventies left a void, her funeral has to be included in this chapter.

At the time of her death my nan lived on the tenth floor of a high rise block of flats in Shepherd's Bush, and on the day of the funeral all her daughters had gathered at my Aunt Lizzy's flat plus various grandchildren including my cousin Tony. I'm not sure why but I was privileged to be asked if I would accompany my aunts' in one of the leading cortege cars. I like to think that of all the very many grandchildren and great grandchildren, I was one of nan's favourites. I loved her, so I'm sticking, and resting of my laurels! I was also asked to keep a look out for when the florist's van arrived, and was told that the guy had been provided with my surname and, so too, had the undertakers. I kept a watch from the tenth floor but it wasn't the florist's van, but the funeral procession cars that were arriving. I waited at the lift door and as it opened I was met with two very solemn gentleman undertakers. 'You must be Mr Ledbetter, Sir, our sincere condolences.' followed by a pause while both remained in the lift, 'our *very* sincere condolences on the passing of your grandmother.' Thank you, most kind - I'm afraid the flowers haven't arrived yet.' Both looked at each other, still in the lift, and from the taller of the two, 'I'll fuckin' kill 'im!'

I can still see the piles of crispy bread rolls in my aunt's flat that were being generously buttered by my aunts. Well, to be precise, I could see the rolls through a haze of cigarette smoke – in all, about ten people smoking.

I sat in silence next to Aunt Alice with my mother and her sisters in the rear seats of the cortege car. On reaching the Church I waited for Glenys to arrive in the lift provided by Tony's father. Eventually she arrived and was clearly bursting to relate the drive to the church and was still laughing. She said that she felt bad because she knew I loved my Nan but she'd been entertained by Tony's constant quipping about his father's driving, other drivers and predictably getting lost enroute!

Later I joined Tony for drink at a pub on the estate where the Forman family, mostly males, were congregating. Something was said to Tony (former boxer) prompting an angry response, words were exchanged and I suggested that we return to Lizzy's flat for **smoked** cheese and ham rolls! Tony continued to threaten reprisals since he apparently never liked the Forman boys and wanted to knock a few blocks (heads) off. My intervention meant that the often customary punch-up for Londoners and their families at a funeral had been impeded thus, as I learned later, spoiling a good funeral!

I reminded Tony that our late grandfather, Tommy Tyson was also not one to shy away from a fight, my nan having told me that it was not unusual during their courtship to be out walking with Tommy and realise she was talking to herself, he having taken exception to the way another man had looked at her and a fight ensued.

Chapter Forty Eight

AMUSING YET...

I had formed a good working relationship with two fellow divorce lawyers. Perhaps surprisingly, they were in the employ of the principal opposition in St Austell, Stephens & Scown. One was a partner, Tony, and Glenys and I had formed a friendship with him, an extremely pleasant chap who'd suffered the tragic loss of his wife, leaving him with two young sons.

Tony left a message inviting us to meet for drinks at a local pub with a Radio 4 Journalist mate of his, and to go later to Tony's home for, what I thought, he said, was food, so I decided not to have an evening meal, culminating in me drinking on an empty stomach.

Having drunk three pints of beer, I was already feeling woozy and in need of sustenance.

We returned to Tony's and he commenced playing various Jazz classics from his extensive library, and it soon became clear that there was no food, just more booze.

I recall asking the well-rounded Journalist what weight he was just prior to blacking out and rather abruptly coming too when Glenys sensibly decided it was time to go. She drove me home and I commenced being sick, first in the downstairs toilet, where she witnessed her husband's pants round his ankles and simultaneously throwing up in the sink, which prompted Glenys, with a wry smile, to say, 'isn't it a shame the young lady couldn't stay.'

Earlier that afternoon, I was working on my car when a pair of shapely young legs appeared to the left of the open car bonnet, and something soft and French murmured, whereupon I actually lifted my head and smacked it on the bonnet. It was summer and the young lady was wearing tight shorts and was asking if I provided accommodation. Sadly (but fortuitously) I/we could not provide B&B.

Having left the downstairs loo, I made it to the upstairs bathroom where I proceeded to violently retch, due to lack of food.

Some months later I related to our friends (immediate neighbours), the evening's events, and they told us that they'd heard the most awful sounds coming from the woodland to the rear of our properties, thought someone was being assaulted, and were considering phoning the police!

One male client, who chose, come winter or shine, to wear a ('Flash Mac') raincoat and Wellington boots, sought to contest his wife's divorce petition but eventually accepted my advice given that some of his wife's allegations were acknowledged as true i.e. removing electrical heating elements from an oven hob and tying string across the banister at the top of stairs intending his wife to trip. On receipt of the Decree Absolute I'd not received Mr H's present address and knew that he was anxious to be told when it had arrived. I heard nothing, but about a month later I received a phone call. 'Mr Ledbetter, I'm calling from a phone box and have no change – any news?' 'I have your Decree Absolute, what is your......' was interrupted by a loud, 'So, I'm free – whoohay!' Followed by silence, as he hung up. I visualised Mr H in mac and wellies, on a promise, but checking that he was free to fondle.

While I continued to have concerns in regard to my employ with the Cornish firm, I was relieved and reassured due to two male colleagues, one a clerk, the other a Probate clerk (Malcolm, later qualifying as a Legal Executive). Ken was from Liverpool, having moved some years earlier to Cornwall. He was an experienced Conveyancer, and an essential fee earner for the firm. Likewise Malcolm was good at his job, and he, Ken and Les (another Conveyancer), were clearly instrumental in the firm's success *in spite of the partners.*

Ken was an extremely humorous upbeat guy, who had many business friends that clearly helped fuel the firm's profits. His office phone was faulty, often culminating in crossed lines. As an illustration of this guy's personality I merely relate just two of his incoming misdirected calls. Early morning he received a phone call from a local Cornish Pasty supplier believing that he was speaking to the Landlord of a local pub. 'Hello, how's it going? Will your usual 30 pasties be sufficient?' 'No, it's going to be busy, best double it.'

On another occasion I entered his room and he immediately signalled me to be quiet while he listened to what I realised was another misdirected call. He handed the phone to me and I gleaned that a couple were planning their next illicit meeting. Their conversation, however, was immediately interrupted when Malcolm passed the open door and called, 'Goodnight Ken'. Silence was followed by a female's voice, 'Did you hear that? Someone said, 'Goodnight Ken''.

Malcolm, from London, also provided many laughs and became a good mate. His sense of humour, however, sometimes misfired, or untimely, not least one morning while I was interviewing a new young female client.

My room provided two fairly large sash windows, one of which overlooked a toilet that was situated in the same building, and some mornings Malcolm liked to signify a successful bowel movement, which I purposely ignored. On the day in question, my lady client had commenced relating her matrimonial problems, was distressed, and in floods of tears – so much so that she was using tissues to mop the table, but was interrupted by the toilet window being opened with a bang and Malcolm first groaning with pleasure and then, 'success, success, success!' while waving a large mop out of the window. I immediately signified a cessation, but he appeared to be unaware of this lady's plight. I closed the window and attempted to redress the situation while this poor woman sat in shock and promptly burst into tears – again.

On another occasion I was awaiting the arrival of a lady seeking a divorce. She was a friend and known to both Malcolm and I. I then received a call from reception that my client had arrived, which coincided with Malc entering my room for a chat. I explained that I had to be quick as Vera was in reception. 'Come on,' he said, 'let's put our heads around the corner, and pull funny faces at her'. And that's exactly what we did – it wasn't Vera!

At least twice a week, during lunchtime, I played squash – not a particularly sensible pursuit given the cooling-off period. On one such occasion a fiercely contested game with Malcolm was in progress. We were both experienced players, but for an inexplicable moment, disaster struck in that he served and I returned a backhand that propelled the ball at speed, straight into Malc's left eye. He screamed and went down as if KO'd. I helped him to his feet and drove, in his car, to a small local 'Cottage' hospital. Despite Malcolm's distress and pain his plight was to intensify. 'I bet it'll be that fucking Doctor'. Yes, it was that, 'fucking Doctor,' which Malcolm had two days earlier lambasted in the street when the local GP had sounded his horn when it was abundantly clear that traffic was at a standstill!

Fortunately the 'lambasted' GP provided professional help and Malcolm was advised to travel to Falmouth to attend a small hospital that provided specialist eye care. During this time, not surprisingly, Malcolm was blind in one eye.

I drove as fast as his car, an ageing 1970's Rover, would permit given that the play (that part where there is no steering) in the steering exceeded an inch!

Having arrived and entered the hospital we were directed to the entrance of a ward where I explained Malc's plight to a male technician who, having made a few notes, indicated that a doctor would soon be with us. What was to follow was both extraordinary, but equally fortuitous, in that the doctor was young, blonde, female, and stunningly beautiful. As she approached I whispered, 'Malcolm, if possible, take a look – if you can – at your doctor.' Not only was she an apparition, she displayed compassion – she was simply very nice. Fortunately a test revealed that the retina, though somewhat precariously attached to the back of the eyeball, was still attached, thus improving the prospects of a full sight recovery.

Having spent some time with the doctor and Malcolm, it was time for me to depart and deal with what I feared would be traumatic – a nightmare scenario!

Mandy, Malcolm's wife, a former model, and a fantastic person, had fought cancer for four years, but tragically died at the age of thirty-nine leaving three young children in the care of Malcolm and other members of his family. Her extremely premature, and untimely, death occurred precisely one month prior to this incident, and it was for me to break the news to the children. On arrival at their home I was immediately greeted by Malc's sister, he having apparently telephoned her. The children were so forgiving culminating in an emotionally charged moment for me when leaving.

It's fair to say that Malcolm often helped me through some

very stressful work-related periods during which any reference to the problems confronting me were seldom mentioned as Malc was only too aware of my plight, and would assist with good humour, and regular internal phone calls, ' Right, it's coffee time at The Thin End,' a local café, just down the road, and where we sometimes entertained customers when leaving through a small confined area with two doors, by pretending to push a button and lowering ourselves in unison, thus emulating the use of a non-existent lift.

During a particularly stressful stage, Malcolm persuaded me, one summer's morning, to sail on the River Fal, he having acquired the keys to his brother's four-berth yacht. We moored for lunch and consumed a few pints. Having rowed back and managed to board, I was given instruction to push the accelerator control lever on his command i.e. when he'd weighed anchor. He called as I thrust the lever forward and immediately experienced the effects of the liquid lunch i.e. round and around and dizzy, until a shout from Malcolm who indicated that the boat was still anchored! Underway, Malc raised the main sail as the boom swung round taking my RayBans from my nose. I watched them, gently sinking while floating from side to side – never to be seen again. Now what is it my father would have said...?

Two weeks after starting this section of my tale I received the shocking news that Malcolm had died from cancer. I was not aware that he was unwell, and death must have come quickly, which is perhaps a small, or perhaps significant, relief. His funeral took place at St Paul's Church in Charlestown, St Austell, where **hundreds** of mourners attended, including yours truly.

[Given that I relate herein to Malcolm as a good friend, one may ask why I was not aware of his cancer and impending death. The simple truth is that following his wife's death, Malcolm, for a period of time, pursued a lifestyle that dictated that I distance myself from him. Subsequently he settled having married again. RIP Malc']

Chapter Forty Nine

CHUCKLESOME

Having mentioned squash reminds me that immediately following a lunchtime game, having showered, I walked swiftly to a clinic to give blood for the first time. 'Wow, that came out quickly', from the nurse, followed by, 'Oh I feel rather unsteady', as I attempted to stand. A lie down and a cup of tea rectified this. We learn from our mistakes, but mine was a bleedin' obvious one to make!

During a lecture (procedural and divorce law update) in Bristol I sat next to a (quite stunning) female solicitor from Truro. I was aware that she had a good sense of humour but was unaware that, like me, a moment of amusement could dissolve into tears of laughter. The young female lecturer was, I assume, fresh out of training, and struggling to keep our attention, thus resulting in one large gentleman falling asleep. At a whisper my colleague enquired, 'is Wayne dead?' Whereupon we both reverted to school days, and despite our completely uncontrollable laughter (Wayne wasn't dead) the lecturer attempted to continue for ten minutes until lunch break. Those ten minutes seemed to take hours during which time my colleague and I attempted, but failed miserably, to control our laughter while continuously mopping our tears.

During the afternoon I did manage to amuse the lecturer when she was relating the circumstances of a divorce that involved the husband's petition in which he alleged his wife's adultery with her GP. I simply observed, 'clearly she'd been under the doctor.'

Flying: Gareth agreed to accompany us to Florida for a holiday, but was concerned about flying. His initiation, having only flown once when a child, was not enhanced since his seat was situated behind to the rear of Glenys and I and occupied one of three middle seats. Next to him were, he was to discover, two well travelled young children, their mother, having sensibly booked seats away from her kids!

As the Jumbo taxied for take-off the children were chatting with Gareth while he attempted to communicate holding arm rests thus signifying a 'white knuckle ride' and thus creating much amusement for the young brother and sister, who were reminded by a Steward that they should fasten their seat belts. 'We don't normally bother.' exclaimed the girl.

On take-off Gareth showed courage and a colourless face.

Time for more 'white knuckles' during descent, which again was not enhanced when his accompanying young regular fliers decided, when hitting the runway, to have an unbelted scrap with each other.

Glenys and I had previously flown to Miami and explained to Gareth that the internal flight from there to Sarasota would probably be a fast passenger jet carrying fifty or so passengers, as previously experienced by us.

Nervous apprehension was then to be significantly increased when we were invited to leave the waiting area to join two very young 'red neck' pilots eating ice creams. 'Come with us guys.' (Us three and three other passengers!). Gareth was silent as we climbed into a twin engine propelled twelve-seater.

'Now, if you guys would kindly spread yourselves for best weight purposes – the John's (toilet) at the rear.'

The twin engines screamed on take-off, and the quite deafening sound did not diminish during the flight.

A small curtain divided the cockpit and passenger area but this (the curtain) was pulled back thus enabling us to watch the pilots as they joked and laughed with each other.

Gareth attempted to concentrate on a football alamanac. 'Look' said I 'at those wonderful spiralling clouds,' as we flew over the Everglades. His reply, through gritted teeth, 'I'm looking at nothing but this!'

On approaching Sarasota, the width of the runway appeared huge and dwarfed our little plane which was fortuitous since the aircraft on landing veered quite violently to the left, the pilot having successfully regained control i.e. the central position of the runway, the plane veered violently to the right. Eventually it slowed, and we were informed, 'that, was my buddy's landing, folks.'

Sitting to the rear of the plane was quite a large middle-aged guy who commented on one or two aspects of the flight and then enquired of me. 'Aren't you a film star?' (Not a 'film actor', a 'film Star!') I/we laughed but he insisted that I was, and that I lived in Sarasota. Sadly, I had to disappoint him.

Chapter Fifty

ANECDOTALLY

Attired appropriately: Being a lawyer naturally dictated that one should dress accordingly and this meant, particularly when walking in a small market town, that the public's response was a mixture of contempt and pleasure. Often when entering a shop I would be mistaken for the manager. However, on one occasion while in M&S in Truro (duly attired) an elderly lady asked if I would help her choose a shirt for her son. I immediately explained that I did not work there, but she ignored me, so I chose a shirt. She was thrilled and asked me to choose a tie, which I did, still reminding her that I wasn't the manager. She thanked me and I jokingly suggested to the sales assistant that commission was perhaps appropriate. However, I subsequently wrote a humorous letter to M&S relating the scenario. A few days later I received (by post) application forms for managerial position with M&S (another true story).

Perhaps, foolishly, I did not pursue their offer.

'A Sleeping Lyne': Prior to the large, and somewhat impressive new Court building in Truro that houses the Crown Court and civil actions, matters ancillary to divorce were often dealt with by a senior Court Registrar, sympathetically known to most lawyers as, *Granny Lyne*. He was an affable fellow who preferred a compromise i.e. a lawyer's suggestion that we meet half way or split the difference, would invariably result in settlement. However, the limited facilities within Strangeways Terrace, particularly the very small room where he heard cases, plus his seniority, often required a file to be dropped to the floor to wake him up!

During the latter part of the 1970's, and part of the 1980's, I submitted various articles that were published in the Law Society's Gazette, some of a serious nature, and some humorous. The following extract (and cutting) appeared in the Gazette on 22nd October 1980:

'The writer recently derived much pleasure from your article appearing in the Gazette (17 September 1980, p.869) which refers to the Be Well Advised book of legal cartoons.

In addition to the enjoyment to be obtained from the visual concern of clients when their legal adviser refers to a comic strip for guidance, it is perhaps worthwhile considering the benefit which could perhaps be derived from these comic strips when and if the recommendation of the Benson Commission is implemented in so far as it relates to advertising in the legal profession.

The writer considers the enclosed may give some indication of the available scope for advertising in legal services.'

The six cartoon pictures depict the doctrine of res ipsa loquitur (the facts speak for themselves) the first of its kind to be decided in the case of Byrne & Boadle 1863, effectively a breach of the defendant's duty of care. The cartoons reveal the falling bricks that hit a passer-by. The ballooned conversation: '...and I suffered severe injuries, and now the crane owners say they weren't negligent! What can I do? And the solicitor responds, 'That's nonsense!' I then take over by editing the next two sequences thus: *'This sounds like a job for Super Man – wait though, I have an idea.' 'Bloggs Junior, he's our man – res ipsa loquitur won't worry him, he's been vaccinated! Phone him immediately.'*

The LS Gazette also regularly included an item – 'Postbox – Humour in the Office' so given my increasingly stressful working environment and genetic ability to laugh in adversity, I submitted the following; an extract from the published article:

I am always delighted when something makes me laugh while in the confines of the office.

The days of long defended divorces are almost obsolete, so pleadings are now generally short. Recently, however, a colleague received an Answer and cross petition, the Answer ran to 43 paragraphs. According to the respondent wife the husband was a religious man, hence the customary array of obscenities never apparently left his lips.

The paragraph that reduced to tears read as follows:

On the 23rd day of November, the Respondent assisted the Petitioner to hang a very heavy metal gate in the yard. The gate was so heavy that the Respondent had great difficulty in hanging it, but was constantly upbraided by the Petitioner who said, 'Lift the gate, woman. Lift it higher; get another grip on it,' then 'A snail would move faster. Laziness and self-pity will not get the gate hung. Move the gate the other way, move it I say. No this is not right, put the gate down. Now next time do as I tell you.' Eventually the gate was hung, only to discover that he'd hung the gate upside down!

A Clouseau Moment, makes it imperative that I refer to an incident involving my former colleague's husband that took place during the popular 'Pink Panther' movies.

I was acting for a Frenchman (a particularly pleasant and personable chap) and as part of the proceedings, it was necessary for him to swear an affidavit in support of his divorce petition, so I took my client to Phil, a Commissioner for Oaths.

'Please take the testament, and repeat after me – I swear by almighty God.'

'I swear by er'mighty Gerrrd.' Phil began to laugh, but managed to proceed, 'That this is my name and handwriting.'

'Zat zees is my nam' an' 'and writing'. Followed by Phil, crying with laughter, and attempting, 'And the contents of this, my affidavit, are true...'

'An' ze contents of ziss my affidaveet are true.'

Phil was unable to conclude.

As I left with my client, he smiled and calmly responded, 'eet is best not to take zees zings too serious?'

I phoned Phil later and he said that he'd had to cancel any phone calls for at least an hour.

Oversight: One afternoon I received a message from reception that a lady needed urgent advice, she had a train to catch, and there was a baby to consider.

I agreed to see her and noticed she had a carrycot with her. While conducting the interview I pointed over the table, from a sitting position, and enquired, 'So, that child is not your husband's? She looked confused, finished the interview, hastily reversed through the door carrying a *suitcase*. I was dumbstruck – potential client never to be seen again.

My mate and work colleague, Malcolm (mentioned earlier) drew a cartoon with suitable caption showing the difference between a suitcase and carrycot!

It was around this time that I was consulted by a husband, he, in his late fifties, she, in her early thirties. The marriage had lasted only a few months. I advised that divorce proceedings could not be commenced until a year had passed. The remaining option was to seek an annulment, so I asked if his marriage had been consummated, to which he replied, with a broad Cornish accent, 'No me 'ansome, we was married in a Methodist.'

In an earlier chapter (Guns, War, Aviation) our friend and neighbour, Ernest Guest, is mentioned. One morning (many years since), as Glenys was entering our driveway, she was met by Ernest who was clearly eager to speak with her. At first he attempted a show of dignity when alluding to the sudden death of another neighbour, but then excitedly, and with muffled laughter, he explained how he was asked by the deceased's widow to attend and confirm her husband's passing. Ernest was divorced but despite his age, remained fit and active, and liked to have some Girlie mags since, as he put it, 'It wasn't on tap, so as to speak'. On inspection the deceased was apparently lying on his back and across his chest, the Playboy centrefold that Ernest had given him two days earlier!

Guinea Pig In Care: Relates to Kathryn, in her teens, and daughter of very good friends, and who asked if Glenys and I would look after her eight guinea pigs, while the family went on holiday.

A large wooden hutch with exterior cage would require moving daily to greener pastures.

On approaching the guinea pigs – including one very precious Albino – they quickly ran to their hutch thus enabling me to lift same, which was very heavy, so dropping it was a good option. Eventually the pigs ventured slowly out.

Where's the Albino?' enquired Glenys. Followed by, 'oh no John, you haven't, have you?' 'Of course, I haven't. There he is – oh bugger.' Flat as the proverbial pancake! Glenys fluctuated between manic laughter and total disbelief. I suggested, while not a perfect match, that I wear Al as a toupee.

Having buried Al, we walked home, Glenys oscillating between giggling and emotional turmoil. 'What are we going to tell Kath? You'll have to replace it.

Where the hell are we going to find an Albino, aren't they quite rare?'

Now, what happened next could be described as surreal.

Tony and his wife lived (still do) at the top of our close, and have perhaps been to our home once, the last time, twenty years ago. Within two minutes of entering our home, there was a knock on the door. It was Tony.

'John, we have a huge favour, we're going away for a week and wondered if you could look after our cat?' 'OK, I should just mention....'

We could not find a replacement for Al, but Kath was not too aggrieved at the loss of her pet, indeed we discovered subsequently that she'd dug him up and examined him. Perhaps given the fact that her dad was a GP, she performed an autopsy as well!

Chapter Fifty One

Still under the Humour umbrella

Observing: I make no secret of the fact that I am, and have been for as long as I can recall, a 'people watcher.' I have also a very good memory for faces which can be advantageous but often is combined with a bad memory for names which is very much an obstacle when a situation demands a person's introduction - a situation that repeated itself mostly when in conversation with lawyers. Indeed when experiencing some of those extremely embarrassing situations I considered emulating a Basil Fawlty faint (sic).

People watching, can be quite satisfying and does often stimulate the otherwise dormant part of one's brain. There are many instances, but I do particularly like to see young (or not so young these days) dads either at weekends or during holidays when the child-minder is not there to mind.

The highlights: a) Erecting a child's buggy. b) Failing miserably to silence a screaming child because he or she prefers the way Maureen (the minder) deals with mealtime. c) Not sure who dad is!

Joe Bowman, (featured in the Happy Days saga) my late father in law, provided an entertaining example of dad's in charge. One Sunday afternoon Glenys and I took him and Alona to Flatford (Constable Country) in Suffolk. Following a cup of tea in the café, situated next to the river, we strolled to a nearby bridge where we watched a father and three children in a rowing boat – one of several available to hire for an hour. The father was attempting to dock the vessel amid screams of concern from his children. 'Careful daddy we're going to sink!' And so on, and so forth. However, this father's plight was to accelerate beyond reasonable bounds when Joe decided to offer advice from the bridge, so with his clear unmistakable accent, and Londoners' charm, he commenced and continued thus: 'No mate, no, no, you'll never bleedin' do it like that – left hand down a bit, no, no, caw blimey, land ahoy – no bleedin' chance – left oar now – no, left, left, oh you'll be here......look try right oar, no right I say, right....' Alona suggested that her husband stop, 'that chap's going to punch you on the nose in a minute, Joe.' He'll 'ave to get out of the boat first!' Joe continued his directions culminating in the eldest child (about ten) on board, in sheer desperation, grabbing one of the oars in an attempt to help but hitting his father on the back of his head, whereupon Joe sensibly decided to curtail further instruction and retreat.

We'd noticed that a lady, also standing on the bridge a few yards from us, was laughing. She then approached Joe and said that it was one of the funniest things she'd ever seen!

Having been born in Colchester I was aware from an early age of the Essex accent but chose not to emulate it, probably due to my parents' slight London tones. The Essex (Colchester) accent has been described as 'sing-song' but whatever may, or may not, be the correct definition it can sometimes sound a little lazy, a bit tired, slow, but precise.

Glenys's older cousin, a particularly nice Essex chap, was asking about our holiday in Florida. I significantly précised our stay on Anna Marie Island and he responded very slowly with his wonderful brogue and very sad face, 'No we've never done anything like that,' concluding with the knock out blow, 'we lack motivation.'

On another occasion while visiting the Eden Project with Victor (our grandson who, when much younger, liked to travel to the biomes in carriages drawn by a tractor) three passengers seated in front of us were chatting and it was immediately apparent that these folk were from east Essex. Two, possibly husband and wife, were enjoying their first sight of the huge biomes. The lady brought a third person, sitting beside her, into the conversation and enthusiastically, 'isn't it wonderful, and to think they had the incredible idea to transform a clay pit into all this.' The chap rather wearily looked towards the biomes and with an expressionless face, replied in that slow Essex brogue, 'Why didn't they just fill it in?'

Annuals: Not a 'Round Robin' indeed quite the opposite. For several years I have sent my annual Christmas Message, mostly to friends residing in Suffolk, and which I haven't seen for a very long time, but have remained in contact annually. One year I failed to present my annual message and received complaints – well one, to be precise! Here's my 2019 message:

It's still looking a bit like Brexit, despite democracy having been redefined.

'First, MERRY CHRISTMAS, and secondly, will you, if 75, be buying a TV licence? I know I will since it's imperative that the likes of Lineker, Gregg Wallace, Winkleman, and many others, are properly remunerated by the BBC. I would willingly re-mortgage the house to ensure the continuation of fantastic programmes. Well, obviously keeping a bit in reserve for my lobotomy!

I make no secret of the fact that my patience and tolerance for *some* old people is often severely tested. I say this with obvious caution since I am one – an old person.

As part of our respective 75th birthday celebrations we decided to return to the Royal Weymouth Hotel for a 3 night stay. We'd stayed the previous year and indeed in 2017, and while we were fully aware that those also visiting would be old people, mostly coached in, we were fortunate to be seated at the same table in the large dining room for just two people in a quiet secluded position each year which meant that the scrum was behind us and even the exploding toaster with flames almost reaching the ceiling did not matter. Suffice it to say that the elderly lady remained close and in front of the inferno – she wanted her toast!

We arrived last Friday (20/09/2019) afternoon (by train – interesting) and were immediately met/confronted by an awfully fat chirpy cheery cockney chap, who'd just arrived. Having escaped we found our room in the western corridor which was not without obstacles but nevertheless encouraging - unsafe for old people. An easterly gale meant immediate stuffing of kitchen paper in the gaping Victorian Window frames.

Time for dinner: We chose the latest sitting, 4pm! Actually 7.15pm where we were ushered, not to our favourite table but with the old people, two of whom sat uncomfortably close i.e. 4 inches from our table! I was not a happy bunny – my face later described by Glenys as a 'smacked arse'. The stern and unfriendly face of the old lady (not Glenys) caused me, and wife, to consume and depart for alcohol.

For breakfast sitting, the same scenario, but for dinner my 'smacked arse' face resulted in our immediate neighbour's having changed (we presume) their meal time! What a relief. 'We'll have the Whitebait followed by the...' arrival of a very large old lady with greasy hair, and taking her seat at the table very close to ours. A polite but swift acknowledgement was followed by, at first, an unrecognisable sound, then shuffling and puffing as her partner - my immediate and very, very close dining partner – weighing in at approximately 30 stone! White Bait and main course were hastily consumed while thirty stone 'Ox-Man' coughed and spluttered his way through mealtime.

Time to speak with the table-planner who kindly arranged for Glenys and me to occupy a table for two in the adjoining, and somewhat more elegant, dining room area the following day for dinner, but not for breakfast. A dilemma – which breakfast sitting, early or late? There's only one - perhaps later, say 5 minutes to nine – all clear, and breathe... just like 'Ox-Man', who'd just joined us for breakfast!

Well at least we had a dinner table reserved for two in the 'somewhat more elegant' part of the dining room, so we entered and true to the table-planner's word our reserved table was there – and so was 'Ox-Man' with missus seated at our very table!

Retreating immediately in fits of concealed laughter, we returned to our original seats in the not 'somewhat more elegant' part of the dining area – job done – no one wanted to sit with us!

Retribution, John? Probably! However, one much younger female friend actually confessed to having wet her knickers when reading the above – result!

Meantime, the Santa's on motorbikes mentioned last year have just passed the top of the Close en-route to the children's Hospice a mile or so from us. However, the numbers of riders have trebled to about 150 – fantastic!

Have a good one. John x

P.S. Frankly, the poor guy and his missus were quite probably the recipients of bad travel advice in that the hotel and facilities were wholly unsuitable for their needs.'

Chapter Fifty Two

CATS

I have to confess my love for the feline species, and have done so since childhood. These creatures are simply vastly superior. They are intelligent, manipulative and incredibly shrewd. All these qualities, I absolutely adore.

Of the many cats sharing our lives, and those of our sons, one in particular merits inclusion.

In about 1978 a large male cat commenced visiting us, and within a short time we allowed him into our home, perseverance effectively achieving his/our adoption.

We discovered that his territorial sector was vast, once being approached by him on our departure from a pub a mile or so from home.

He was un-neutered, resulting in *much* fighting and fucking.

Given his size and bulging cheeks (the result, we were advised, of fighting and scar tissue) we named him Bag Puss.

One evening we received a phone call from a resident about half a mile from our home. She knew that BP was our adopted cat because she and her husband had recently moved from our Close. 'Please, can you come and collect Bag Puss, he's attacked me and I have to have a tetanus jab. I feel like a prisoner in my own home.'

It transpired that BP regularly entered her property through a cat-flap, terrorising her two cats, eating their food, and settling down for a nap in their bed.

In May 1980 we received a note from our friends, Jo & Sally living on the Porthpean Beach Road, about 600 yards from our home. The note read, *'Could you defend a paternity suit on this evidence?* In addition, three photos of BP copulating with their cat, Rosie. Now, some might enquire why steps were not taken to prevent this happening, perhaps a bucket of water. No, my good friend, and local GP, decided that photography was far more interesting.

The matter required a legal response:

Dr J Leigh, 6th May 1980
(Address provided)

Dear Sir

We have been consulted by Mr B.A.G. Puss with regard to the intended affiliation proceedings of one (cup of) Rosie Leigh.

Mr Puss (otherwise known as Gingernuts) denies paternity or inference thereof in the event of conception.

We have seen the photographic evidence that will doubtless be relied upon by the Complainant in support of her application, but are bound to say that this pornographic material has CATastrophic implications. Furthermore our client states CATegorically that it is not he who is portrayed in res dictus and any similarity between himself and the accused is purely coincidental.

Our client wishes to emphasise, in any event, that although he is a CATholic he always wears a CAT-mac..............'

I'll save you from the remainder of this very foolish/infantile attempt to be funny, not least the use of adjectives, such as, 'tight pussy', and 'only a whisker in it'.

Before departing from our friends I must relate amusing events involving Bookers (retail suppliers to shops and businesses). Glenys had commenced G&C Catering, and was provided with a Bookers pass thus enabling her to purchase items to further her business. However, it came to the company's notice that certain items did not fall within the category of Catering – her pass was withdrawn. On relating this to Jo and Sally both found this scenario hilarious, culminating in Jo repeating, *'you've been chucked out of better places than bloody Bookers'*, while crying with laughter. A fortnight later it was our turn for hilarity since Jo's pass, providing strictly for provisions for his surgery, was also cancelled.

Now, I should point out that my mate Jo – like me – were/are massive Fawlty Towers followers, so it was time for frivolity - it was time to write a further letter to Dr Leigh. I photocopied Booker's business address from an invoice and wrote a letter of apology from the management explaining that there'd been an oversight. One paragraph referred to sausages, and utilising part of the 'Corpse' script, I wrote, 'Dr Leigh complained, *'I'm a doctor, and I want my sausages'*. On receipt of the letter, Jo, as senior partner to the practice, having merely read the opening paragraph, immediately approached one of his partners, and voiced his glee at the foolishness of Booker's mistake, but was calmly interrupted by his partner. 'Jo, have you read this letter? It says here.........' Jo allegedly left muttering, 'fucking Ledbetter'.

[Please see closing reference to my mate Jo]

Chapter Fifty Three

LOOKS LIKE

Have I fired five or six shots? Well in all this excitement, I kinda got confused myself... well, do you feel lucky – punk?' (Courtesy of Dirty Harry – Clint Eastwood) This somewhat extraneous reference is because I've been told that I bear a likeness to Clint, resulting in the most extraordinary episode taking place some years ago while shopping in Tesco during a Whitsun Saturday. While searching for a shorter queue I noticed a very tall guy (total stranger) towards the front of a queue looking at me, and then leaving the queue and asked, 'What the hell's Clint Eastwood doing in Tesco?' He then asked if anyone else had ever thought this. Yep, our son Jim, when about ten years old. A croaky voice from the rear of our car, 'Dad, as you walked across the car park, you looked like Clint Eastwood.' Feeling quite pleased about this, was followed by his quite brilliant observation, 'Yeah, you've got all those lines on your face.'

Glenys cannot endorse my 'lookalike' status, and frankly, neither can I, but it's cool, and while at Vic's junior school some of the young mothers called me 'Clint'.

In an earlier chapter I alluded to my lady client and her sister (in the 1960's) laughing at my apparent likeness to

Tom Jones.

My office was situated across the road from reception, so a client, having entered and climbed some stairs to the landing, would always be met by me, and then shown to my room.

I was aware that a new female client, of British nationality, was seeking my advice regarding her child who continued residing in France following the death of her French husband.

As she climbed the stairs I introduced myself, and she froze. Eventually, and very slowly, she entered my office in the company of her father. I completed the interview, but sensed that something was wrong, particularly as her father did most of the talking. The following day I received a phone call from her father apologising for his daughter's inability to converse with me. 'She was in shock, Mr Ledbetter, you are the spitting image of her late husband.'

It's truly amazing how others see us: Glenys's niece, Jodie, has for years compared me with Chevy Chase, and four years ago while in a tapas bar in Seville with Glenys and friends, enjoying flamenco dancers, three smiling Senioritas asked where I was from and then imparted that I looked like Charlton Heston. 'Isn't he dead.' I asked, 'Yes, she replied, 'but when he was...' was immediately interrupted by my mate Paul, 'do they mean Bobby Charlton?'

A new male client sat for a few minutes staring at me and not listening to what I was saying. 'I'm sorry, he blurted, 'are you sure you weren't previously a builder?'

Chapter Fifty Four

LA-RUINE FOR CHRISTMAS

This followed the kind invitation of Barry and Judy Greegrass, Gareth's parents in law, to stay in their home in Frangy (France) close to the Swiss border in 1999.

Departure was planned for Christmas Eve, 1999, so Glenys and I prepared ourselves for a train journey to London from St Austell one day prior thereto. Now, it's fair to say that we'd travelled numerous times by train to visit our sons in London from St Austell and *rarely* achieved a successful journey, often receiving a refund from GWR. This was to be a repeat performance. However, before we arrived at the station Glenys dropped a bag containing a jar of pickled onions that she'd pickled herself, and that she hoped to eventually give to Barry, and that I'd advised strenuously against carrying, culminating in the large jar breaking and filling the sports bag with onions and a pint or so of vinegar. Having disposed of the bag, and its very smelly contents we mounted the platform – 'We regret to inform you that the Penzance train for Paddington has been cancelled, please leave the station and await bus transportation to Bodmin for onward journey'.

Eventually we arrived in Paddington, but not before I'd developed a cough, a ticklish cough, with an apparent desire to prevail, indeed I coughed all night at Gareth and Sophie's, coughed through the flight and coughed a greeting to Barry and Judy on arrival, by which time I was ailing and awaiting influenza. However, I'd had flu as a teenager, and also during two previous Christmas's, so while my symptoms were similar i.e. aching limbs, high temperature, sweating one moment, and chilled the next, I was, unlike previous bouts, able to stand. That said, I eagerly awaited their invitation to place our luggage in the guest's bedroom, and collapse upon the inviting bed for a snooze, but had forgotten Barry and Judy's kind reservation to stay at a Gite down the road.

Sophie had been recommended, by her sister, the room to secure, leaving the next available for Glenys and I. Suffice it to say that the horsehair mattress smelt of poo, possibly human.

We returned to La Ruine for an evening meal and were joined by Emma and Simon, Sophie's sister and brother in law, plus friends of Barry and Judy's. We assembled at a large dining table, and while my appetite was far from normal, I did manage to drink some very nice red wine. Simon, a solicitor was in good form, but sadly the sound of laughter was to end abruptly by Emma who was concerned that their child would awaken.

Situated in the centre of the dining table was a 'Lazy Susan' which was ladened with goodies, including bottles of wine. I began to rotate Lazy Susan to reach a bottle of red wine, but Simon, larking about, held Lazy Susan thus preventing me from reaching the bottle. Not to be beaten, I persevered and Simon let go resulting in Lazy Susan heading rapidly in my direction and the bottle of red rapidly heading in the opposite direction as it was propelled, thus spraying Barry's very expensive white shirt. Fortunately, he's a gentleman (a Diplomat in fact) and dealt with this scenario with dignity and good humour.

Following the meal we adjourned to the *grand salle (hall)* a large annex adjoining the rear of La Ruine. When I say 'large', I mean 'large', since the hall was big enough to accommodate our detached three-bedroom property in its entirety, with room to spare.

Off to bed with, the smelly mattress, a gale outside, preventing the opening of windows, feeling awfully unwell, oh, and the need of some warmth.

Sophie reminded us that her parents would be up early and ready for breakfast.

I rose early and attempted to shower, but could not stop shivering. At one point my back came into contact with the (freezing) glass surround; 'FUCK!'

On *early* arrival at La Ruine, we were met by Barry & Judy, attired in their dressing gowns and carrying out some domestic chores - mopping!

The various dishes that followed for breakfast were there to impress, and were doubtless well received by their guests, with the exception of yours (ailing) truly who was unable to find the Shredded Wheat.

A very large turkey was apparently in the oven, having been purchased from the local butcher. We'd been invited to view it hanging in the shop window – we missed it.

The fire, with a large and quite stunning brick surround in the sitting room was lit and I sat nearby oscillating between cold and colder, while obviously running a temperature.

I then, with reluctance, rose to join family and guests for drinks, and in accordance with apparent Greengrass tradition, Christmas presents were laboriously given singularly to each recipient for unwrapping while the dozen or so family members and guests could watch their (the recipient's) reaction.

Back to the fireplace while Barry and Judy returned upstairs to their kitchen. Sophie then joined us having checked that her parents were coping with the Christmas dinner preparations, not least the roasting turkey.

A sigh of relief from Sophie was immediately followed by a deep sounding thud from upstairs. Sophie left and returned to announce, sadly, that her father, while attempting to baste the turkey, had dropped the roasting pan and said turkey thus covering his expensive trousers in fat – hopefully Santa had included (expensive) trousers and *shirt* in his sack.

During the afternoon, Barry invited me to take a telephone call from our good friend Jo Leigh. 'Hello Jo, Merry Christmas'. 'Who the hell is it? Is that you John?' He'd simply phoned because it was unusual for us not to celebrate with Sally and he during the Christmas break. However, my ailing health had rendered my voice unrecognisable.

Adjourning once more to the Grand Salle where we were provided with an incredible display (an exhibition no less) of various bottles of spirits, possibly acquired by Barry, and possibly categorised as forming part of the 'Diplomat's Bag'. Either way, the various, and many, bottles placed strategically throughout the hall appeared to be unavailable since they remained untouched. Irony dictated that Glenys would await the arrival of her offered G&T, well, that is, having waited half an hour, I went and made one.

Off to bed with a borrowed hot water bottle. This, sadly, but obviously, increased the smell of shit from the offending mattress.

Boxing Day and La Ruine, were to experience gales and rain resulting in a power failure, and poor Barry and Judy struggling with the dire weather and the workings of an exterior Calor gas cylinder.

Having achieved this, it was time to light the living room fire. Regrettably the force and direction of gales had since changed, resulting in smoke billowing into the sitting room. Barry was left with no alternative; he shovelled the fire from the grate, depositing it outside the French windows, but not before much coughing, and one's attire smelling strongly of (obviously) smoke!

Lunch finished, and the rain having subsided, Judy sensibly suggested that we all take a walk into Frangy, and perhaps a cup of tea at a café.

The rural track leading down to Frangy was situated much lower than the sloping fields to our left which provided a somewhat hair-raising episode when two large horses, having spotted us, decided to run down the extremely muddy, and precarious, slope towards us while skidding, and eventually leaping to the track just to our rear. The very large steeds followed us and one commenced nuzzling the back of Gareth's neck, while he complained/observed, 'I don't like large animals'.

Passing over a small wooden bridge – the horses having deserted us – Judy decided to abandon our visit to Frangy, and suggested that we return through dense woodland. A quick assessment confirmed the density, but also revealed an extreme gradient. Having earlier consumed some red wine and insufficient water with our lunch, we were invited to climb a very difficult, indeed dangerous, terrain – 'should I be doing this?' I thought. Not least as our location was already several thousands of feet above sea level, and mountaineering is sometimes best avoided.

Closing in on the summit I glanced back at Glenys - who was being assisted by Gareth - as she promptly slumped back against a tree trunk and passed out. Sophie (a nurse) ordered, 'put your head between your legs!' which is a little difficult when you're unconscious, and not, given the circumstances, what all medics would advise.

We survived – that said, an earlier medical/health episode would question the suitability of such pursuits. (All will be revealed in the fullness of time!)

I **stress** that I have much respect for Barry and Judy

Greengrass and have simply related the above scenario since it deserves anecdotal inclusion, and I'm confident they would find it amusing and wholly inoffensive.

Chapter Fifty Five

VIC'S BITS AND MAISIE'S MOMENTS

In February 2008 one Victor Bainey Ledbetter was born to Jim and Cathy in Truro, which meant that Glenys and I would spend much time with him during his infancy and beyond. We soon gathered that this good looking chap would often remind us that genetics can sometimes bite again i.e. a reincarnation of another family member - our son Gareth, who would argue that black was white.

Like Gareth, Victor has a good brain, but is a little lazy. However, the subjects he enjoyed, he excelled in. His parents were to discover that sex education had clearly been absorbing stuff when ten years old.

While watching a programme about Oliver Cromwell (Vic loves History) he enquired, 'What's a Whore?' 'She's a lady that sells herself for sex.' responded his Community Matron mother. 'Wow, she must be full of sperm.'

When eight, Victor persuaded his parents that he was capable of making a cup of tea. All proceeded well for two weeks but one evening having bathed he entered the kitchen naked and promptly spilt boiling water over his lower regions. Fortunately Cathy, his mum, was able to deal with this without a visit to A&E.

Glenys and I visited him at home and Vic was eager to show me his injury that included a very red penis and trimmings. 'Oh dear', I observed, 'so no sex for you tonight'. 'Unfortunately not, and I don't have a wife'.

I'm mindful that my next related Victor episode (given his age) may create the impression that he's a bit ahead of himself, but apparently his knowledge of sex is on par with other children of his age as the result of sex education.

I had a lesion removed from my face in 2015 (not my substantial nose) by a very nice young lady surgeon, and every six months she invited me to have my scar (very cool) checked. Having received my appointment, which she explained was not absolutely necessary, I mentioned to Jim that I was off the next day to see Mrs D in Truro, and stressed that while it was not essential, she was very attractive and a very nice person. However, failing to note that big ears, Vic, was listening, I continued, 'I simply thought, well I...' was immediately interrupted by Vic who finished it thus, 'Want to have sex with her?'

There are many, but I'll close with a simple scenario. When nine, Victor entered our bedroom and noticed a box containing ladies' Panty Liners. 'You didn't tell me you had a sensitive bladder, Grandma!'

Maisie Alberta: Relates just two of many observations of our beautiful granddaughter when only a few years old.

During pre-school days, Maisie often received Nursery care and was asked where she was born. 'The Dick hospital', she replied. When collecting her, the childminder asked Maisie's mum, Sophie, where Maisie was born? 'At the Whittington in north London'.

When about five years of age, Maisie very much enjoyed the film Annie. While walking in town she sped ahead and was reprimanded by her concerned parents. On catching-up with her, sat in the doorway of one of the numerous estate agents, she was asked what she was doing. Maisie looked to the sky, and sighing, exclaimed, 'I was just asking God to make me an Orphan.'

Chapter Fifty Six

ADVERSITY

Inside No. 33: From 'Humour' to another facet of one's life, ***adversity*** – the adversity, in this instance, endured by my wife during her childhood and adolescence.

Very sadly, all that is good that I have to say in regard to my wife, cannot be said of her parents who ensured that her childhood would predominantly be a miserable one.

However, an incident, involving her mother's son, prompted a response, and in 2005 I scripted (just under 10,000 words) that traumatic scenario, ***'Secrets – The Final Straw'***, simply because (like many of us) I hate injustices. Suffice it to say that Glenys, and to a lesser extent, her sister, Dilys, were to experience a loathing and rejection by both parents – ***particularly their mother.***

It's reasonable comment when I say that Gleny's father was not the father she'd have chosen but during a conversation several years ago, he confided in me – and apparently no one else in the family, including Glenys – that when about 7 years of age he was taken by his mother from his home in Acton, London, to a house where he was told to go to the end of the garden and watch passing trains. Later the occupants of the house (total strangers) provided his tea and showed him to his bedroom, his mother having abandoned him – he would not see her again for four years!

Joe thought that his parents were simply unable to accommodate or financially support him and his brothers.

Irreparable damage, and a possible contributory factor to his conduct, but given what I know, it was wholly inexcusable.

Given that my wife would prefer not to recount this entire and upsetting period of her life – I obviously respect her wishes, and suffice it to say that due to another child born to her mother, following an affair, that child would be insanely idolised culminating eventually in both Glenys and her sister, Dilys, being disinherited i.e. their parents' home conveyed without notice to the male child – a spoilt child that persisted into adulthood when his mother and Glenys's father appeared to fear him.

Excluding the (undisclosed here) conduct of the parties (Glenys's parents) it reminds me that French law does not permit the disinheritance of children unless they specifically document their consent to disinherit. It's difficult to raise issues of injustices in this regard particularly as French law provides a very fair solution in regard to dividing a deceased's estate.

As an example of my mother in law's staunch socialist (communist actually) views she persisted in attempting to persuade me to obtain a copy of a will under the terms of which her grandson and granddaughter were to inherit. Eventually I acquiesced and upon reading the will she complained vehemently that her grandson – who'd worked on the farm since a child – was receiving more than her granddaughter!

'Pot and kettle', I respectfully submit, and to close: *'I've treated my kids all the same!'* A statement of Alona Bowman regularly delivered to those present, either outside, or *inside No. 33*.

It is an extraordinary achievement that my wife survived, what was, for her, a traumatic childhood and adolescence. She showed inner strength and indisputable fortitude.

Adversity is of course, also an aspect that most people experience during their lifetime at one time or another. However, I'm now focusing, if I may, on the misfortune of children who sadly experience adversity, in this instance, my/our children, Gareth and James.

In an earlier chapter I dealt with Brian's (guitarist) paedophilia. Prior to this episode I had little knowledge of paedophilia, indeed, neither my wife nor I were really aware of such a crime. However, our awareness would manifest itself on our doorstep, thus indelibly imprinting it upon us for the rest of our lives.

Gareth commenced Charlestown County Primary school in 1973 and James started at the same school in 1976. The Headmaster was one David Holman, a personable type of fellow, and well liked by the parents.

I recall my Aunt Phyllis, who was holidaying in Cornwall, and Glenys was singing the praises of the school and saying what a good Headmaster the school had, whereupon Gareth – who was, despite his age, known for his bolshy responses – interrupted with, 'Oh, he's a Bender.' Having reprimanded him, and reaffirming Glenys's praises for Holman, my Aunt simply asked, 'Are you sure?'

I was late one afternoon when collecting James and he was clearly concerned and said that he'd kept moving within the school building in an attempt to avoid Holman.

Starting to have concerns but, busy, busy, lawyer with much to do and no understanding or knowledge of what *some* adults are capable of doing to children, Glenys and I merely acknowledging the fact that Gareth and James simply did not like their Headmaster.

However, close friends, one a local GP, unbeknown to us, at the time, apparently questioned Holman in his office making it clear that their daughter did not like his (Holman's) cuddles. He naturally denied any wrongdoing.

Gareth and James *very sensibly* attempted to keep clear of Holman.

A good mate of mine, Ronnie Rubin, an electrician, was asked by Holman to install a light above his office door and to provide an internal switch thus enabling Holman to let other Teachers know that he or she should not enter while the light was on. Fair to say that Ronnie would rue the day when he innocently accepted the job, not least as his own children attended the school.

Eventually further complaints from parents resulted in Holman's arrest and imprisonment, following and during which he died of AIDS.

My failure to fully comprehend this man's paedophilia prior to arrest and imprisonment will remain very much a *failure* since I feel we let our boys down.

My mitigation has already been alluded to, added to which was the fact that most parents, some very intelligent and professional people, all failed to recognise this man's criminal activities. However, my/our then ignorance of paedophilia will sadly remain as 'inexcusable'.

Given the fact that the school was a new building of modern open-plan design, I still consider it a mystery, indeed incomprehensible, that none of the teachers were wise to, or questioned, Holman's conduct.

Society now realises that paedophiles are often sufficiently intelligent to enable them, as predators, to capitalise on their position of trust.

Suffice it to say that my perception of those who commit offences against children is disgust, and devoid of any compassion whatsoever.

***

While remaining with education, I'm bound to make mention of a recent incident, not on the same scale as particularised above, but nevertheless involving a teacher at our grandson's junior school. I stress, however, that this is a significantly abridged account of a serious breach of conduct.

Suffice it to say that a Headmistress having severely traumatised a child dictated that a formal complaint be made following which we (parents and grandparents) attended a Stage 3 meeting, Predictably it was not upheld so I further pursued our complaint initially through Ofsted and subsequently the TRA (Teaching Regulation Agency) our principal objective being a formal caution against the Headmistress thus hopefully safeguarding other children's welfare during their education.

My final letter: 'We appear to be chasing our tales in that we have attempted, post Stage 3, to pursue a complaint, but each time have been referred to another department.

I fully appreciate that you are bound by the provisions of the Education Act which deals with the issue of misconduct but, we are advised, is limited to prohibition orders. There appears to be nothing that can be utilised as a deterrent to those teacher's who act unprofessionally but who may not be categorised as being subject to a prohibition order. At the very least there should be provision for disciplinary action......'

Immediately following the Stage 3 meeting the teacher was inducted as Head of another private school!

It was obviously quite normal for me, as a lawyer, to encounter events that were distressing, but one case in particular epitomised the depths of despair.

I was acting for an extremely pleasant middle-aged lady who sought a divorce from her hoarder husband.

She was at her wits end due principally to her husband's refusal to stop hoarding newspapers and other items, mostly rubbish, thus cluttering much of their home and making it almost impossible to access the house through the front door. He was also of a violent and threatening disposition.

She was receptive to my advice to divorce and to possibly pursue injunctive measures.

Shortly after I commenced proceedings, my client committed suicide.

Out of respect for her, and any surviving family member, I choose not to detail her chosen route of self-destruction. Suffice it to say that her desperation was of unimaginable magnitude.

Chapter Fifty Seven

MOVING ON

I commenced my new job in September 1972, staying initially with the senior partner's son and family and returning home at weekends. Later we moved to Cornwall but were forced to rent accommodation as the property that we'd purchased was subject to possession taking place in November.

Our furniture and belongings were in storage and it proved necessary to move three times while in rented accommodation, which was hardly conducive to commencement of life in a completely new environment. To make matters worse, we had prior to vacating our property in Suffolk, sold it subject to contract to a young couple, keen to take possession in October, but the sale was not proceeding.

Various phone calls to the Estate Agents achieved nothing resulting in my phoning the prospective purchaser, who was less than helpful, leaving me in no doubt that there was a serious problem afoot. I eventually established that the couple were experiencing matrimonial problems due to the husband's affair with a female work colleague. This, needless to say, was devastating news, not least as we were expecting our second child in December, I was earning less than was offered in Ipswich, band earnings had ceased, and in addition to paying rent, I was attempting, at one stage, to meet repayments on two mortgages and a bridging loan!

We were to take possession of our new home on Friday the 16th November 1972 with a view to moving in the following day. However, during lunch (liver and onions) with the boss's son and his wife, Glenys's contractions commenced. She was admitted Penrice Maternity Hospital and later that evening, despite almost strangling himself with the umbilical chord, James Bainey was born, albeit prematurely. He was placed in an incubator and as they wheeled him passed me I thought, *'Blimey, he looks just like my dad.'* (Henry Bainey). This was to prove an accurate observation, in more ways than one.

The following day, with the kind help of a trainee solicitor, and van hire, our furniture and possessions were moved into our new home.

Prior to purchasing the property we were advised that although it had no central heating, we would not find the climate as chilling as that previously experienced in Suffolk. Quite how Gareth and I survived the freezing conditions (immediately after moving in) that November, I really don't know!

Just prior to Christmas the prospective purchasers apparently attempted a reconciliation leading to contracts for our sale being exchanged and the sale completed shortly thereafter, by which time we were in dire straits financially, and it would be some years before those straits were escaped. While I was fully aware that by vacating Suffolk I forfeited band earnings, I had not fully appreciated how much this would impact on our lives since the resurrection of any supplementary band earnings would not take place until the 1980's, indeed, recently I discovered diaries that contained details of all band bookings during much of the sixties. Suffice it to say that fitness and perseverance prevailed and proved extremely beneficial, particularly, financially!

Prior to my predecessor's retirement, my caseload had been light, but given **his** emphasis on pressure of work I anticipated an increase in work after his departure. However, on gaining access to his room and filing cabinet, I discovered few files, of which, only three were pending. It then became abundantly clear that it was down to me to build a more productive and, despite various pitfalls, a more lucrative divorce practice.

The firm appeared to be successful primarily with conveyancing (the legal process required for land and property transactions) and probate, which was in part due to experienced and capable (clerks/legal executives) fee earners. Accordingly, with the exception of some criminal work, the firm pursued non-contentious work, which meant that regular court appearances and advocacy were not a fundamental part of its agenda, which also simplified caseload management, unlike the litigation lawyer who knows that while he or she is in court the files are piling-up in the office.

I recall attending a new client (a local businessman, with matrimonial problems) in the company of one of the senior conveyancing clerks who was a personal friend of this chap. It was soon apparent that my advice was well received. He smiled and said, 'It's interesting, Ken, how successful the firm is *in spite* of the partners.' This concerned me as I'd already started to form a similar impression. However, with a four-year-old son (having commenced school) a baby, plus severe financial pressures, I naturally persevered.

It is fair to say, however, that the senior partner of the firm was a personable and pleasant chap, and I'm sure that some, or most, of the firm's success was due to him and fee earners.

I took on more and more work, mostly as the result of clients recommending my services to others. Initially my hard work and conscientiousness appeared to be appreciated, at least by the then senior partner. I received no indication from the other partners that my efforts were either acknowledged, or appreciated. I felt alienated, and that feeling would not diminish with time.

Chapter Fifty Eight

One of the inherited cases related to an elderly lady whose husband had deserted her. However, he had been absent for about eleven years so I made application to the court for leave to present a petition for divorce based on presumption of death. Given the husband's age, and the fact that she'd heard nothing from him for many years, I considered that she had a case for seeking dissolution of her marriage as she had reasonable grounds for supposing that her husband was presumed dead.

I duly appeared, for the first time, before His Honour Judge Chope in the Truro Divorce Court and he dismissed the application, muttering, 'they've merely lost touch with each other.'

His decision, I surmised, was based either on his reluctance to presume the death of the respondent, his antipathy towards the basis of any application of that nature, rare as they were, or perhaps his intention to show this young whippersnapper, from up country, that he should not expect a smooth ride through his court.

I therefore advised my client to instruct me to file a petition based on five years separation. However, this would not be a simple solution since we had to dispense with service on an AWOL husband. Eventually, following notices in the London Gazette and other newspapers, by way of substituted service, I was able to proceed and my client obtained her decree nisi. She was a lady of very modest means living in poor rented accommodation, and yet, to show her gratitude, she gave me a very nice cased biro.

Save for appearances with counsel at Truro, I did not then – with the exception of the above application – personally have to perform advocacy skills before His Honour Judge Chope. That is, until the case of P v P.

I acted for the petitioner husband who was granted a decree nisi but had commenced a relationship with a young woman who was expecting his child, and both were anxious to remarry before it was born. It was therefore down to me to make a rarely used application for an order expediting the granting of the decree absolute. It would take three attempts (two in Truro and one in Plymouth) before Judge Chope to achieve the order. In fairness, he apologised for his somewhat inflexible approach to my application. It is also true that, over time, he would gain my never diminishing respect.

Many years later (having regularly conducted cases before him) I received a request from solicitors, based outside Cornwall, for me (as agent) to represent their lady client whose former husband was seeking an order that he be given custody and care and control of their twelve year old daughter who had, since birth, been living with her mother.

The request was made at the behest of the lady whom I'd previously represented while living in Cornwall, but I'd forgotten who she was.

I prepared my case, which included a detailed Welfare Officer's Report, that supported the mother's case i.e. that her daughter remain living with her, so I was reasonably confident that the father would not succeed.

On entering the court building I was immediately welcomed by John Neligan, a senior, and very experienced Barrister, who informed me that he was acting for the applicant father. He then handed me a further report that had been prepared by a Welfare Officer based in Cornwall and had been delivered that morning.

I was extremely concerned to note that this report supported the father's application. In addition I had been led to believe that a solicitor for the father would be presenting the case, and not Counsel. My concerns, however, significantly increased upon meeting my client, having immediately recalled what happened about two years earlier when attending court for her divorce i.e. while waiting with my client (a very pleasant lady) prior to entering Court, she sighed, 'Oh no, he's turned up.' He certainly had, as he ran the length of the large waiting area and then threw himself to the floor, while screaming dementedly. Given the noise, the adopted foetal position, and obvious concern to the waiting public, which included a few children, I decided to approach him. Now, I'm not one to pick a fight, but when a prone man attempts to kick me twice, I tend to get a bit rattled.

Given that the father's questionable mental state had not been flagged by her present solicitors, and the late arrival of the further Welfare Report, I sought an adjournment..

Neligan and I appeared before His Honour Judge Chope who listened to my concerns that excluded, given the lack of any evidence, my principal observation that the father was probably mentally unstable.

John Neligan responded with gusto, 'I appreciate Mr Ledbetter's concerns, but he, as we *all* know, has a vast amount of experience in these cases......'

'Yes, yes, Mr Neligan' The Judge Interrupting, 'we all know about Mr Ledbetter,'

Judge Chope kindly suggested that I proceed and that if I still had concerns, he would consider them, possibly in his Chambers.

Neligan opened the case and the applicant father gave his evidence and I then cross-examined him, suggesting his inability, given his circumstances, to provide the essentials that a female child approaching adolescence would require. I was making good progress when Judge Chope, with a rye smile, asked if I was content to carry on.

Following the luncheon adjournment, John Neligan congratulated me and reminded me that I had to provide a closing speech.

Neligan's speech lasted about 40 minutes, mine about five, during which I emphasised the status quo, the limited access sought by the father, and the importance of the child's education and stable home environment; continuing where she'd been living with her mother prior to, and since, the divorce.

Judge Chope found in favour of my client.

Chapter fifty Nine

'CARRICKOWL'

Subsequently to be renamed 'Blue Waters', for reasons, as you'll gather. Carrickowl was/is an impressive property overlooking the sea on cliffs at Porthpean, Cornwall.

I discovered that the large antique table/desk I'd inherited from my predecessor had previously been the property of Charles Giffard, a solicitor who, during the 1940's and 50's, provided legal advice while sitting (like me) at the desk.

Mr Giffard was no longer alive, having been murdered, along with his wife, Elizabeth, by their son Miles, in November 1952.

Charles and Elizabeth Giffard were then living in Carrickowl. Both were held in high regard - pillars of society, he a local solicitor and clerk to the St Austell Justices, and she, of Irish descent, attractive, and an active member of the local Conservative Party.

Miles Giffard, was a troubled young man who had experienced problems throughout his childhood and was, during his teens, considered by a doctor to be a schizophrenic with psychopathic tendencies. Whether this culminated in the murder of his parents was a crucial part of his unsuccessful defence.

Between 7.30 pm and 8.30 pm on Friday 7th November 1952 Miles attacked his parents, first his father, in his garage, striking him on the head with an iron pipe, and then his mother, from behind with the same instrument, in the kitchen.

On returning to the garage he discovered his father regaining consciousness, so he struck him again – the final blow. He then re-entered the kitchen and similarly dealt with his mother, who was also coming round, resulting in a massive splattering of blood.

Miles then disposed of the bodies, one at a time, by wheelbarrow, tipping them over the cliffs, his mother first and then returning and trundling his father, this time a slightly easier route, to the cliff edge above Duporth Beach where he cast his father and wheel barrow to the rocks below.

Miles confessed to the murders, was tried at Bodmin Assizes the following February when Mr Justice Oliver sentenced him to death. Miles was subsequently hanged in Bristol.

It is truly coincidental that situated for many years in the garden of Blue Waters, formerly Carrickowl, which was open to view when gaining access to Porthpean Beach, was a very old wooden wheel barrow that I attempted to convince (scare) my young sons that it had been used to dispatch the victims over the cliffs.

(During 2016-17 Gareth prepared an excellent and detailed script for screen, radio or stage-play, dealing with the murders. Given the location and the era it would be equally tragic if this true story was not dramatised. Thus far his script has received very good reviews and achieved quarter final status).

Chapter Sixty

FRIENDS AND NEIGHBOURS

During the early years in Cornwall it was still necessary for divorces to be heard and granted in the divorce court, and as my caseload continued to increase I often briefed Counsel in London to appear on behalf of petitioner clients. One barrister, namely Nicholas Wilson, was always my first choice. He was of exceptional competence. He exuded charisma, and Judge Chope liked him! I do not recall a slight hesitation, a pause, or the smallest deviation when he addressed the court.

I was always hesitant when asked to act for friends and this cautiousness was highlighted when I agreed to act for a friend and neighbour. I arrived at court, having briefed Nicholas Wilson to represent my neighbour and as he arrived, he called, "Hello John, we have six of your cases today, one of which will fail."

I instinctively knew that *Sod's Law* would ensure that my friend and neighbour's case would fail – it did.

Despite the fact that the parties had lived apart for many years my client (the neighbour) was unable to satisfy the court that he'd at all times considered the marriage to have broken down irretrievably, in other words, had his wife returned he would have done his best to save the marriage.

Subsequently I was able to petition the court for divorce on an alternative basis.

While under the remit of neighbours I am firmly of the belief that if one is fortunate enough to live with decent immediate neighbours – don't move!

Our first home in Somersham (semi bungalow) included a carpenter who occasionally pursued DIY late evening. Our peaceable enjoyment of our second home, a detached/linked home in Capel St Mary, was often disturbed by the immediate neighbour's huge, and somewhat neglected, Pyrenees Mountain dog that they kept outside in an alleyway – its booming bark often reverberating around our home.

Our third (and final) home in Cornwall enjoyed good immediate neighbours, mostly including new and current neighbours. However, in the interim we experienced the 'nightmare neighbour' scenario when a local solicitor acquired number 9, and we at number 10. The various episodes (far too many to mention) included fights with his wife and others, police intervention, and wholly irrational and indeed, threatening behaviour, that we assumed would eventually result in their moving on, which is precisely what they did. However, his conduct actually resulted in doing us a favour since we would have never contemplated having an extension to our home, but his presence, not least his need to discuss or dictate private matters very close to our boundary, resulted a in very nice large utility room being built close to the offending area.

Though professionally qualified, one had to assume that this guy had some serious psychological problems – perhaps a connection with his surname and origin. Answers on a postcard, please – no prizes.

Chapter Sixty One

GOOD SECRETARIES

They are, needless to say, absolutely essential, particularly when providing for the very demanding needs of a divorce lawyer that includes the secretary's trust and absolute integrity. Without reservation, I confidently say that I was only as good as the support provided by my secretaries. During twenty-seven years practicing in Cornwall I was fortunate – with one exception – to work with hard working loyal and diligent secretaries – six in all!

Chapter Sixty Two

STRESS/ILLNESS

On the 6th February 1974, following a court attendance the previous day, I awoke to find myself covered from head to foot in spots. I was advised by my GP not to return immediately to work but I chose, due to my caseload, to return the following day, which resulted in much of my office table being adorned, by my secretary, with hundreds of small red adhesive seals where it was assumed I would touch e.g. dictaphone, telephone, chair etc!

On the 21st February 1974 I attended a specialist who diagnosed psoriasis, a condition that was to eventually clear and not return. However, he advised that my working environment, plus the type of work I was undertaking, were possible, or probable, contributory factors.

Following this, I decided that the stress and pressure of the work, and the sustained feeling of insecurity, due mainly to the partners' (with the exception of the then senior partner who was soon to retire) inability to exercise, in particular, any degree of appreciation or communication, it would be necessary for me to adopt a disciplined approach to diet and regular exercise. I simply felt that such course of action was imperative if I were to survive the adverse affects of stress in the workplace. Given that

I was in good shape physically meant that these measures were not burdensome and Glenys ensured that a well balanced diet was provided.

Most days commenced with at least thirty minutes of aerobic exercise, plus some jogging, but mostly walking evenings and weekends with Glenys.

Despite my working environment, and the resulting problems experienced by me, I mostly drew on my hidden strength i.e. a sense of humour that I'd thankfully inherited, and which enabled me to often defuse the level of stress.

However, that 'hidden strength,' was sometimes severely tested, not least in 1982 when finances had improved, albeit slightly, enabling us to take Jim (Gareth declined the invitation – another story) to the Costa Del Sol on a package holiday.

Glenys and I were invited to a wedding reception a week prior to our flight. The following Monday I was approached by a junior partner (and mate?) who alleged that during the wedding reception Glenys had complained to a guest, who subsequently informed his wife, that I was not being paid enough. I was incensed, not least, as I was confident that Glenys would never make such an audible observation. Suffice to say – he'd been set up!

It's pertinent to mention that the aforesaid wedding was a remarriage ceremony the parties having divorced many years earlier. In fact I'd acted for the wife during which my conciliatory approach had obviously succeeded, hence the remarriage/wedding invitation.

I'd adopted – on the advice of a senior, and very experienced, divorce lawyer with Stephens & Scown – a simple routine that provided a degree of stability and a boost to one's morale: A letter/card thanking me for my advice and assistance would be copied and retained for future reference. How I worshipped that letter! Fortunately, I jest, and as an illustration, disclose just one of several clients who took the trouble to express their thanks. However, this letter was sent the then senior partner, who passed it to me. It was handwritten by my client, a gentleman living in Redruth, and is dated 17th September 1985.

Dear Mr Follett

Mr J.C. Ledbetter

During 1984 I met and discussed with Mr Ledbetter in your offices at St Austell the procedure necessary for me to obtain a divorce. An immediate rapport was established and since that time Mr Ledbetter has acted promptly, efficiently and with genuine interest on my behalf, culminating in the successful conclusion of the divorce action at the beginning of last month. I cannot speak too highly of the impression I formed and I am extremely pleased I had the good fortune to have him acting on my behalf.

It is because of my pleasure and gratitude that I decided to write this letter to you as I think it fitting that my appreciation of his diligence and efficiency should be a matter of record in your files. Needless to say, Mr Ledbetter has no knowledge of my intention to pen this letter to you.

Yours sincerely
T. H. C.......

Now, I know what you're thinking, how much did this cost, and did he write it himself? Well, no money or gifts were exchanged, and my letter writing skills are no match for this gentleman's.

Frankly, I think this well intended letter fell on deaf ears.

A previous reference to Counsel, Nicolas Wilson, reminded

me that the then senior partner told me that Nicholas had sung my praises and stressed the importance of my being properly remunerated!

During this time of unsettling concerns, I had considered moving, as I was twice offered work in Essex by a solicitor friend who was keen to employ me. In addition I had asked the firm to consider employing a lawyer to assist me with my ever increasing caseload.

Further, in December 1986, while conducting a complex case for an extremely irate and difficult chap, I was approached by the senior family law partner with Foote & Bowden in Plymouth who was acting for my client's wife. He was impressed with the conciliatory way I dealt with the matter and invited me to be interviewed, following which he phoned and offered me the position of senior matrimonial lawyer. Sadly I felt unable to accept because a move would have proved detrimental to our two sons, in particular our eldest, who was attending sixth form college in readiness for A and S levels. He's an intelligent chap who profited from his mother's genes!

I have always taken, indeed practiced as a lawyer, the view that children should come first.

In later years I would discover that my decision would prove wholly detrimental on more than one count. However, I do NOT regret putting my children first.

Chapter Sixty Three

PERSEVERE

Perseverance eventually (years later) paid off when I was given a freehand in advertising for, and interviewing, applicants.

A partner, (an acquaintance of mine) with another firm of solicitors informed me that his wife, a qualified solicitor working in Truro, was keen to secure a job in St Austell. It was immediately clear during the interview that she was the ideal candidate, and we subsequently forged an excellent working relationship that commenced in September 1987.

As anticipated it would take time for her presence to impact on my caseload, but she was helpful and considerate. Moreover, she had a good sense of humour and personality, which did not impress one of the younger partners, who was (for whatever reason) unhappy with her joining the firm, culminating in my being asked, within a relatively short time of her joining the firm, to attend a partner one Saturday at his home where I was informed that she would have to go. I spent about four hours advocating on her behalf and attempting to dissuade the partner from dismissing her, stressing that it was a colleague's problem, not hers. I left in a distressed and anxious state given that he (the partner) was not prepared to budge. First thing Monday morning *that* partner informed me that he'd changed his mind and she would be staying! To this day I do not know if she was aware of her planned premature departure.

While it was a huge relief to know that I now had a competent and intelligent colleague, with a good sense of humour, to assist me, I was by this time beginning to feel out of sorts, but continued disciplined exercise despite experiencing fatigue and anxiety.

In June 1988 I began to feel very unwell – I was forty-three – and circumstances dictated that I continue to work hard with no sick leave for fear of caseload problems or letting clients and their children down, but also for fear of the adverse reaction from the partners, particularly their total lack of appreciation, causing an ever-increasing vulnerability that deemed it essential that I persevere. My colleague did her best to help, but there were obvious limitations.

Regrettably, I had no alternative, and made a few visits to my GP revealing nothing untoward following two ECG's (heart monitor) but I continued to feel ill and attempted to convince myself that it was the affects of a virus, so I continued to work and exercise.

One morning I experienced difficulty in climbing the stairs to my office and was in some discomfort. While leaning against the filing cabinet my colleague entered, took one look, and suggested that I go home. Foolishly, I indicated that I'd be ok, and continued working.

My problems were exacerbated when my mother's mental health deteriorated culminating in her being sectioned and I attempting to achieve some sort of favourable solution that involved much travelling, including driving to various locations in Colchester, consulting her GP and psychiatric hospital, while feeling very unwell and overwhelmingly anxious. Needless to say, I had the unfailing support of my wife.

Further exacerbation would confront me as the result of two

separate threatening and abusive home telephone calls from males, resulting in our number being removed from the next telephone directory. While I had no proof, I was nevertheless reasonably certain of their identity given the circumstances pertaining to the cases in which I was representing their wives. However, having acted for many, many wives, I have to consider myself fortunate that very few cases resulted in deranged and threatening husbands. Oh, when acting for females, I was very occasionally informed that their husbands were alleging my impropriety with their wives! Not so, my conscience is clear!

In early August 1988, Glenys, Jim and I spent a short break with my cousin in London (Wimpole Street!) and during one night I became ill and had difficulty breathing. The train journey home was a nightmare but despite this I returned to work the following day.

Three days later I attended a case in Plymouth and had to ask Glenys to drive and to help me climb stairs to the court.

In retrospect I realise how ridiculous I'd been, but given my circumstances e.g. dependent children, a mortgage, and the overriding feeling of insecurity, I was left with no other realistic option.

I began to feel better and continued daily exercise to combat stress. However, in March 1989, while travelling to Cardiff for Gareth's 21st birthday (he was at University) I felt ill again and on my return consulted my GP. A further ECG revealed something untoward and I was immediately referred to Dr Mourant, Consultant Cardiologist, in Truro, who carried out a thorough examination, including a further ECG, concluding that I'd suffered, and *worked through*, a heart attack in 1988. He advised I should speak with the partners with a view to easing my caseload; an exercise that would simply increase my vulnerability, so chose not to do so.

Following a treadmill test, Dr Mourant suggested

Angiogram/plasty procedure in London, but I declined, particularly as this procedure was in its infancy, my GP didn't favour it, and I was feeling better, so I continued my routine of regular exercise and sensible diet.

I am a non-smoker. My parents died in their eighties, so nothing congenital. It is mystifying, and alarming, that at no time, during the above tests, were my blood pressure or cholesterol levels too high. However, in my working environment, I'm confident my blood pressure, at times, exceeded safety margins.

Save for one emotional outburst by me to a junior partner in October 1989 when I raised certain issues, including the total lack of communication between partners and fee earners, and an earlier reference to my having worked through illness in 1988, I chose not to confide in my employers regarding my health issues.

Needless to say, the diagnosis caused my wife, sons and family much concern. It persisted in haunting me – however, 'Perseverance' is my middle name!

Following my 'emotional outburst' the firm, did at least, suggest I take a paid sabbatical which enabled Glenys and I to celebrate our twenty fifth wedding anniversary in Florida.

Chapter Sixty Four

STRESSED TO KILL

Aptly describes what was to follow in that during the early period - and for much of the nineties - the country was in recession. Notwithstanding this, the firm was actively in the process of expansion while lucrative conveyancing was curtailed and significantly replaced with repossession. A four-day week was introduced, together with a reduction in salary – I worked five!

One Friday in September 1992 I was summoned, late in the day, to attend the senior partner. Suffice it to say that the need for much more productivity and the dire consequences in the absence thereof – the loss to the firm of my two colleagues and myself – formed the basis of his discourse. I immediately prepared an attendance note and disclosed same to my colleague the following morning. She then spoke with the senior partner and he denied the content of his conversation with me!

At least, however, it was *communication* from a partner. Predictably though, any communication was extremely rare, and invariably, negative.

If I appear to be labouring this scenario, I do so in the hope that others, who may experience similar scenarios, can take steps to eradicate and/or minimise

the minefield of workplace stress that is endemic in many jobs these days. That said, I fully appreciate that achieving this may well be easier said than done and I would struggle to provide constructive advice, not least for my grandchildren!

During 1997/98 I continued to undertake more new cases during which caseload problems were exacerbated because my colleague was now working part-time and a young female solicitor who'd been engaged to assist, also working part-time. This naturally didn't help to alleviate the unremitting pressure and stress, and by the end of 1998 I was at breaking point – thirty-seven years' experience, and I was not coping.

In addition to numerous pending cases, I had a number of complex child-care cases and the usual array of urgent injunctions that required my attendance/ advocacy at Court six times in the ten days leading up to Christmas, plus the emergency preparatory work. At commencement of one of these attendances before a senior District Judge I opened my application with a weary, 'I'm getting too old for all this!' resulting in his response thus, 'You don't look any different to what you looked like ten years ago when I commenced this post,' followed, a few days later, with a congratulatory observation by another District Judge, that I was providing an extremely lucrative practice for the firm, thus effectively providing a precursor for the *death knell!*

I was experiencing anxiety attacks and a feeling of helplessness, and I feared the consequences of mental exhaustion i.e. a breakdown.

One afternoon I was feeling unwell and went home having checked that my diary was free of appointments, and having left instructions with my secretary to hold all outgoing letters until the following day. The next morning I learned that a fee earner had complained to a partner that no one was available the previous afternoon to see a lady seeking advice in regard to her matrimonial problems. I was incensed and made my feelings very clear to the fee earner – a conveyancer! I recall, during my time in Suffolk, the often repeated observation of Ted Glasgow, a senior litigation lawyer practicing in Ipswich, 'Fucking conveyancers – they don't know they're born!'

My problems were further exacerbated by administrative work and, in particular, one voluminous case that occupied an entire drawer of my filing cabinet! The client, a personal friend of the senior partner, considered anything short of undivided attention, wholly unacceptable. The scenario that followed, I still find oppressive.

I enjoyed the Christmas break but dreaded returning to the 'sinking ship' as I knew that in addition to many urgent cases, priority had to be given to this case in readiness for a conference with Counsel early in January.

Stress levels were maximised when a fee earner (had letters after his name –T.W.A.T) communicated a message from a branch office partner who required me to attend Court the following day. I attempted to suppress my displeasure and explained why I was unable to assist. The fee earner left but returned. 'Mr G sends his compliments, but says that some bugger's got to do it!' I was incensed and felt I would explode.

I sat for a while to calm myself but this episode caused me much distress. I experienced unparalleled anger due to circumstances that had fuelled it. I returned home that evening feeling distressed and anxious. As was customary I went to bed exhausted at 9.30 pm, but slept for only two to three hours.

The following day I again knew that I was not coping. I felt soul-destroyed and desperate. My inner strength that had previously provided a safety net was deserting me, together with my sense of humour. I felt that I would be unable to continue, but what followed left no room for manoeuvre or doubt.

At about 3AM that night I awoke to discover an arm that did not appear to belong to me, also a leg. I could not explain to my wife what was wrong as I was unable to speak coherently but she realised that something serious was afoot – an arm and a leg, to be precise! Fortunately our GP friend, Jo Leigh, promptly attended and confirmed that I'd suffered a probable stroke and resulting paralysis. By the time he left, feeling had returned to my right side and I was able to speak more coherently. When leaving he paused, and calmly said, 'they call it being conscientious, John.'

While Glenys made a cup of tea, I muttered to myself, 'I'm not fucking surprised!' Whereupon Glenys retorted, 'that's it, there's no way you're returning to that bloody office!' Meantime our cat Sunny jumped on our bed and promptly attacked my moving feet beneath the duvet!

Chapter Sixty Five

OP TIME

Various tests and consultations followed, culminating in an angiogram, an exploratory operation to establish narrowing, or blockage, of the arteries, which was performed by a consultant cardiologist at Derriford Hospital in Plymouth in early June 1999.

Attired in obligatory gown with ties at the back for opening, I was wheeled to a lift to descend for x-rays i.e. the lift for public use, for all to see. Then to a waiting area in a wheel chair that, it and I, began to tremble due to my apprehension and insufficient attire. An elderly lady, waiting with me, kindly explained that, like her, I should be wearing slippers and bed-jacket!

Eventually a fit, but somewhat manic (four days beard growth and tattooed) looking guy, viewed the line of wheel chaired patients, looked at me, grabbed the back of my chair, and grunted, 'you'll do'. He reversed me at speed into the x-ray department. I couldn't stop shaking and he remarked that his work area was mostly freezing.

Later, it was time for the procedure to take place and as I kissed and waved goodbye to Glenys a swell of emotion hit me and I began to cry. Given all that had preceded me since 1988/9 – particularly the stroke – I felt I was going to die, and I would not see Glenys or our sons again.

A couple of theatre nurses were far too nice, thus exacerbating the problem. They kindly asked if a 'G&T' would help, reducing me, again, to tears and observing, 'it's fortunate females have the children – if it were the males, there wouldn't be any.' The nurses apologised telling me that the consultant said that I didn't need a 'G&T'.

The Cardiologist then showed me on screen the arteries that were blocked, but I have to confess that I could neither comprehend what I saw nor hear what he was saying, save for, 'Get your backside on the operating table A.S.A.P!'

An angiogram can involve an incision in the area of the groin to gain access to a major artery thus necessitating immediate pressure to be applied to stem bleeding, following the procedure. The young lady nurse, while doing this, asked what I did for a living and when I told her, she promptly confided in me her own matrimonial problems. I attempted, despite the circumstances, to adopt compassion and professionalism, whereupon she blurted, 'I can't believe I'm doing this, it's so unprofessional. Your problem is; you're too nice!' Fear can make you *nice*!

In their favour, my employers, very fortunately, had implemented, as part of the wage structure, group membership of BUPA, so having gathered my senses and having obtained some helpful advice and guidance from Jim's future wife Cathy, who was then an intensive care nurse at the Wellington Hospital in London, I was admitted there, and on 19th June 1999 I underwent a quadruple heart by-pass operation. Five and a half hours later the surgeon telephoned Glenys and told her that I could have dropped dead at any time prior to, or during, the operation, but that fortunately, a further stroke during the op did not manifest itself.

Cathy had kindly attended me with a nurse colleague prior

to the operation when I was given a pre-med, following which I apparently gabbled on about my younger days with Nan Tyson, regularly buying her plastic table cloths from Shepherds Bush market, and also toilet rolls as I was concerned that I used far too much of her toilet paper!

No 'out of body' experience during the operation, no dreams, just black. In the distance I recalled Glenys calling to reassure me and, subsequently, opening my eyes when an attractive nurse said, 'Oh, what lovely eyes, you have!' ('All the better to see you with, my dear.')

On regaining consciousness I was in intensive care for a couple of days, but was soon able, momentarily, to stand prior to being wheeled to another room, where I was joined by Glenys, Gareth, Sophie, Jim and Cathy. Both Gareth and Jim checked their emotions but Jim nearly had a 'John' moment! Soon I was joined by Mr Edmundson, my surgeon, who enquired, of two somewhat perplexed nurses, 'Why is Mr Ledbetter yellow – jaundiced?' He left, but soon returned. 'Mr Ledbetter, I've done over nine thousand of these operations and have never had a jaundiced patient, however, it's a fairly rare condition called the *Gilbert's Syndrome*, which coincidentally I also have. The good news is that it's often a sign of intelligence.' Whereupon, Gareth retorted, 'Well, it looks as though it worked in **your** case, Mr Edmundson!'

Which enables me to succinctly conclude the final part of our 'La Ruine' at Christmas 1999 i.e. that just under five months earlier I'd undergone quadruple heart by-pass surgery following a stroke.'

It occurred to me later why the nurse had complimented me on my apparently *lovely eyes*. Yep, they were blue and yellow!

During the early stages of recovery morphine was evident in that the clock at the end of my bed persisted in climbing up and down the wall, while open curtains revolved. One afternoon

I drew Glenys's attention to the strange aircraft in the sky that would proceed forth and then back again. Perhaps a, 'Lucy In The Sky With Diamonds' (Sergeant Pepper's Lonely Hearts Club Band) moment.

I was well cared for save that one very pleasant, but careless, nurse culminated in a course of anti-biotics being prescribed prior to my discharge.

Having injected various liquids (drugs) into a canular affixed to my wrist, she proceeded to check my blood pressure thus attaching an arm wrap and inflating it. She then left to attend to something and I recall wondering what would happen if the inflated pressure wrap became locked. 'Nurse, the wrap has locked!!!'

I was advised that when leaving my room I should wear footwear to provide some protection since the hospital was obviously open to visitors. One early morning I decided to take a stroll to reception. I wore only boxers so I put on my dressing gown, and as I had no slippers I donned my (type of) baseball boots, size thirteen. As I passed a small room I could hear various nurses chatting. For a moment there was silence followed by much laughter. The Staff nurse – or whatever she was – very pleasantly observed, 'Sorry Mr Ledbetter, we're very naughty; your legs will return once you've recovered.' 'No', I said, 'what you see is what you get.'

Very simply my legs from my shins are tiny, but I've been blessed (previously mentioned during a foot inspection) with large feet that appear even larger, perhaps clown like, when in boots and without trousers.

I mentioned my dressing gown. I was advised by my daughter-in-law that the Wellington Hospital was often extremely warm and that a lightweight gown would be sensible. I utilised my (late) Uncle Albert's silk paisley dressing gown and for at least five days I wore it while walking the corridors as (rehab) instructed. On the penultimate evening before discharge I was allowed to wear clothing i.e. black T-shirt and black jeans. Coming towards me was a young Australian nurse – wonderful girl, got to know her very well, always upbeat and brash – as she passed she glanced and clearly did not recognise me. 'It's me.' I called. 'Blimey,' she responded, 'I preferred you in yer dress!'

It would be remiss of me not to recount our train journey to and from London.

Glenys was insistent – given our return train journey experiences from St Austell to Paddington many times during the preceding years – that we travel first class.

The late arrival (so no change there) at St Austell from Penzance met us with an engine and rolling stock, circa 1960's. The interior of the first class carriage, needless to say, had seen better days, but at least it provided somewhat premature passenger communication shortly after commencement. Indeed, it's fair to say that those participating in conversation with Glenys and I lessened the severity of the purpose of my trip.

All were requesting reimbursement claim forms, quickly followed by a Steward with a refreshments trolley that would not fit in the aisle, resulting in him, the Steward, removing all the contents and slamming them, with some force, on the first available table, occupied by a very well presented/dressed lady who, until she moved, could not be seen behind boxes of refreshments. Needless to say, she was not impressed, the Steward chose not to apologise, and she chose to seek our support.

One lady begged me not to speak to her elderly husband as he had previously owned a train company in India and considered the service provided here was far worse!

Our return journey, following my op' eight days later, showed little improvement, save that the engine and carriages were post Brunell. Gareth accompanied us to Paddington to carry our luggage as I was not permitted to lift anything.

Prior to this Glenys had telephoned Paddington Station to ensure that first class accommodation was available. A particularly unhelpful and incoherent chap of Asian dialect caused wholly unnecessary distress and concern for both of us, but thought we had achieved the confirmation sought. However, on boarding the train we were ushered to the rear first class carriage.

I decided to take advantage of a free tea or coffee offer, and newspaper, for first class passengers and felt sufficiently confident to approach the buffet carriage, despite my fragility and the rather unsightly dressing attached to the underneath of my left arm where a cut of six inches long had been performed to remove an artery.

'Yes mate, how can I help?'

'Two teas please - I'll take advantage of the offer of free teas.'

'Sorry mate, only at weekends.'

'Newspaper?'

'Sorry mate, weekends only.'

A lady standing behind me was laughing so much that she had to vacate in haste, I presume, to the nearest loo.

On approaching St Austell station we were advised that we should immediately move forward three carriages as the station at St Austell was too short to accommodate the rear section of the train!

Insurmountable embarrassment as I had to witness Glenys struggling with the luggage.

My father's saying when describing poor or badly run businesses, sprung to mind. 'They couldn't run a coconut shy!'

Chapter Sixty Six

POST OP

I worked for forty years, thirty-seven, as a lawyer, twenty-seven of those in Cornwall, which proved, indisputably, to be injurious to one's health and wellbeing.

Following my sudden, and premature, cessation of work, I have at all times attempted to maintain a good level of physical fitness. However, the psychological damage attributable to my working environment and the absence of a duty of care remains – it is *not* a distant memory.

If there's anything to be learnt from my scenario then, as confirmed by my surgeon and consultant cardiologist, if you are a *conscientious* male (females apparently have their pre-menopausal hormones to afford some protection) then keep fit, watch your diet, and do not smoke or drink excessively since these measures probably saved my life. Furthermore, a good level of physical fitness would appear to be beneficial in the recovery period following major heart surgery – oh, and a sense of humour!

I corresponded with a professor at University College London with regard to possible, or probable, link with work related stress and heart disease, and he and his co-researcher's objective was then hopefully to establish the existence of such a link. The principal stumbling block is proving causation but I'm confident that research will result in a successful litigated claim based on an unsafe working environment due to an employer's failure to exercise his/her duty of care.

We are, after all, dealing with the balance of probability as the burden of proof. Although perhaps an over-simplification, the following criteria, applicable to me, is of some relevance:

1. Smoker – NO
2. Dangerously high cholesterol levels – NO
3. High blood pressure (out of work!) – NO
4. Overweight – NO
5. High sat-fat diet – NO
6. Lack of regular exercise – NO
7. Heavy drinker – NO
8. Something congenital – NO
9. Matrimonial (married 56 years!) or family problems – NO
10. Miserable git – NO!

It is, however, acknowledged that stress can increase the risk of heart disease, (and other contributory factors) and this is supported in various research findings e.g. In January 2001, *'When people are stressed, their blood pressure increases and their blood vessels constrict, which can cause plaque in the artery walls to break loose and block blood flow to the heart or brain. Stress also increases the possibility of blood clots forming – which causes an increase in platelet activity....'*

I have no doubt whatsoever that my near demise was directly attributable to **unrelieved** stress in my workplace, and steps should, have been implemented to afford relief. However, I also have no doubt that the lack of care which I experienced, was far from unique.

Following my op', and return to Cornwall, I was advised to

attend a weekly session with a cardiac rehabilitation nurse. As a result I attended eight sessions of light exercise and reassuring discussions with the very able nurse, and it was during one of those sessions that she suggested I watch a short Disney animated film that highlights the issue of stress, in particular workplace stress. I sat completely absorbed while mostly shaking my head in total disbelief, and when it finished I turned to the nurse and said, 'that was me – been there done that!'

I acknowledge that conscientiousness is an inherit part of my persona thus preventing me from shirking my responsibilities. However, my persona also denies me obsequiousness, a trait, I'm sure, would have proved beneficial in certain quarters!

I decided that I should seek advice of an employment lawyer and chose to consult a solicitor with Foote & Bowden (the firm that offered me a job as mentioned earlier) and he considered that I'd been treated disgracefully but sadly any financial provision was unlikely unless my employers chose to make such provision (in your dreams!) since they were not obliged to do so.

He then enquired of my closing income and also asked why I'd chosen their firm to provide advice. I explained that I'd been offered employment with F&B but had chosen not to accept their offer. 'Oh, what a pity, our trainee solicitors are earning more than you!'

In November 1999 the firm offered me a leaving get-together at St Austell Rugby Club. I was, needless to say, hesitant in accepting but eventually agreed as some colleagues, staff and other lawyers, were people I respected. In addition, others with whom I'd shared my lengthy career were also invited. A very short speech of the senior Partner excluded two words, *'thank you'*.

In January 2004 the Legal Executive Journal published my

two page article (approximately 1,700 words) detailing my downfall and the related issues of stress in the workplace. As a result the following month Hilary A Tilby of LawCare responded under the heading: *'Stress Can Be A Killer.'*

A small extract reads thus: ***'I do not think that it is any exaggeration to say that Mr Ledbetter was lucky to survive this catalogue of horrors. Others reading that article, and this, and recognising similar symptoms in their own lives, may not be so lucky unless they radically change their approach to their work.'***

While my working environment was indisputably linked to my downfall and premature retirement it's essential that I mention again the firm's senior partner ('pleasant and personable') who interviewed and offered me the position of divorce lawyer in 1972. He, I discovered, had very astutely secured a policy of insurance for fee-earners resulting in my receiving approximately four thousand pounds that enabled Glenys and I to utilise towards the redemption of our mortgage. Much appreciated Jimmy – R.I.P.

Prior to my published article I'd been going through various personal papers collected from my office desk and discovered my final Appraisal and Development form dated the 27th November 1998. The Professional Competence category included an, 'Excellent'.

Under Appraiser's Comments, she had written, 'Another year of hard work'. Under Appraisee's Comments, I'd written, ***'Hard work never killed anyone – fingers crossed!'***

Fair to say, that circumstances dictated a prevailing bitterness. That said, however, the love and unwavering support of my wife and sons, has been instrumental in providing stability, and a mellowing with age.

Since my op in 1999 it has been necessary for me to seek regular advice and assistance of Consultant Cardiologists, including various procedures, not least in regard to ectopics, heart rhythm irregularities and angina, necessitating, in 2013, the implanting of a pacemaker just below my left shoulder, the procedure having been performed by Dr Slade, Consultant Cardiologist in Truro.

I was offered a sedative but declined in an effort to accelerate the procedure, a procedure that would clearly assist the surgeon if the patient were sedated! However, with the exception of my reacting to one or two discomforts, he completed the job. My daughter-in-law (experienced nurse) considered my rejection of a sedative as a typical moment of macho stupidity – she's probably right, particularly as the chap in the bed opposite, having the same procedure by another consultant, slept for hours following the procedure.

Mentioning 'angina' resurrects for me the time we were enjoying another trip to France, staying again with Barry and Judy Greengrass (Gareth's in-laws) in Frangy, during the summer of 1998. It was suggested that we take a walk in the French Alps. As we climbed, to spectacular views, I experienced an alarming discomfort, in particular with my right wrist, but this gradually cleared at rest. I'd previously experienced this type of episode on a few occasions, not least the time, alluded to, when experiencing difficulty climbing the stairs to the office and the trip to Court in Plymouth. It naturally caused me much concern, but, as usual, I persevered, and hoped it would pass. It was of course – 'YOU STUPID BOY' – angina!

Chapter Sixty Seven

I WAS OK UNTIL...

Medication (quite a lot!) became an integral part of my life, including an anticoagulant that required me to regularly attend a nurse for blood tests. For ten years I encountered no problems whatsoever, and during that time I was mostly level at 5mg of warfarin. However, in 2012 the procedure for test results was changed following the introduction of a computerised system. Prior thereto I would hand the nurse my anticoagulant record book in which the result was inserted and initialled by a GP, and the card returned me by post, mostly within a day or so of the blood test. I was unaware of the change in procedure but knew that results had become erratic/unstable and somewhat incomprehensible, so much so that I mentioned my obser-vations and concerns to a nurse who too was confused given that I'd been stable and level at 5mg of warfarin for many years. Prior to Christmas 2012 I attended a new nurse (Polkyth Surgery St Austell) for my blood test, but did not subsequently receive a result. On the 4th January 2013 I went for my annual medical that included blood tests for cholesterol etc. I mentioned to the (very senior and extremely experienced) nurse that I'd not received my earlier blood test results and asked if she'd kindly include an anticoagulant blood test. She had known me for many years and was responsible for my annual check-ups since 1999. Her response to my not having received the previous blood test was emphatic: 'This is one of the reasons why I shall be glad to leave this place.'

Later that day, at about 5 pm, I received a phone call from reception at Polkyth and was instructed to omit my dose of warfarin as my INR was 3.1. I explained that I'd already taken my usual dose of 5mg at my usual time of 4.30 pm. I was then instructed to omit Saturday's dose and reduce dosage as instructed. I was confused, not least, as a reading of 3.1 did not seem excessive. However, on Monday 7th January 2013 I received printed Dosage Instructions and ensured that I followed them. At about 8.30AM on Wednesday 9th January I began to feel very unwell, and Glenys rang for an ambulance. I was rushed to A&E in Truro where on arrival I could not recall my name, date of birth or my wife's name, and promptly burst into tears! A doctor attended me following blood tests and enquired, 'what the hell's been going on here?' My INR had dropped to 1.3. A scan and other procedures followed, including warfarin injection.

I'd suffered a stroke, and remained overnight in Treliske Hospital where the only available bed was in the company of three paraplegics, one close to death. Above the bed of the guy opposite me was a notice that I was unable to read. At about 4AM I remembered my date of birth, and later that day was able to read the notice. Comprehension tests followed, that I failed, but I'd made it clear that, 'I was getting the hell out of here!' My son Jim drove me home with Glenys, and I experienced a panic attack when close to home.

The paramedics and A&E staff that provided rapid response clearly saved my life or probable paralysis. Initially I was undecided, but obviously realised how the Surgery's error could have been catastrophic. In addition, I assumed that other patients were at risk. Accordingly I sought legal advice and eventually, supported by expert evidence, a claim against the doctor and Polkyth Surgery for medical negligence was commenced.

Six years later and a compromise settlement of a nominal sum was paid me following the rapid departure of my experts who felt unable to significantly oppose the Defence's causation argument. It had taken the Defence six years to submit their causation response, an aspect that could, and should, have been raised at least within two years of commencement of my claim.

Their defence was based on my stroke having been the result of an earlier TIA in 1999, **fourteen years earlier**, and not caused as the result of bad warfarin management. Needless to say, having been on the receiving end of their alleged incompetence, I know what caused the 2013 stroke – wrong levels of anticoagulant advice following the introduction of computerisation – *not* a coincidence! Fortunately, save for my quite regular inability to readily comprehend a conversation, reoccurring night time hallucinations, and a somewhat debilitating and very annoying right hand tremor, I survived what could have otherwise been catastrophic consequences.

I think it fair to say that in the absence of a cocktail of daily medicines, mostly suggested by my Consultant Cardiologist, Dr Slade, plus the implanted pacemaker, I would not be here.

Chapter Sixty Eight

WIND IT UP

I conclude my memoirs at the age of 76.

I attempt to maintain a good level of fitness walking most days with Glenys. Jim provides drum lessons for pupils in our home, and occasionally gigs, so I am still very much a part of drums and drummers, though I seldom play.

We attempt to continue to maintain our home and garden despite the aches and pains.

Glenys mostly agrees with my rantings but occasionally tires thereof.

Despite the fact that I'm on the way out, I still have concerns and merely summarise certain issues thus:

- This Government, and previous Governments have, due to fundamental failings, written-off this wonderful **small** island (known to some hopefuls as 'Treasure Island') that used to be **Great Britain**, and which, in parts, is now over-populated.
- Very simply, **common sense has not prevailed.**
- The NHS is likely to implode.
- The Government's answer to a population crisis is to build more homes despite the indisputable absence of workable

infrastructure and jobs.

- Prisons – no obvious comment necessary.
- Parts of cities resemble a Ghetto theme.
- Integration is fundamentally essential but is often difficult to achieve.
- Cultural differences: **_Understandable_** but sometimes also difficult to achieve e.g. recently my wife was diagnosed with Macular Degeneration (deterioration of one's sight) and having twice attended the RCH Truro for tests, it was time for the Consultant Ophthalmologist to see her. The Doctor, a brisk, small, and extremely agile Indian, having checked Glenys's eye through apparatus, instructed, 'You have to have an injection in your right eye.' Glenys calmly, but with obvious concern, enquired, 'what will this entail?' _'What do you want to know that for?'_ he asserted. Stunned, we sat speechless. What we should have said is, 'my wife is 78% British and we British always like to seek clarification before someone sticks a needle in their eye!' However, that said, we Brits and the NHS, would be in a <u>right old pickle without ethnic nursing and overseas expertise.</u>
- Brexit (when eventually fully implemented) is probably too late.
- The UK, we are informed, is the second highest contributor to Europe. On leaving could we possibly see what we've paid in and what Europe has paid out (us) during our membership?
- As an example, about six years ago the A390 at Tresillian in Cornwall would, we were advised, involve traffic delays due to major work. The 'major work?' A cycle-path courtesy of the EU. Two to three years on and we've seen one cyclist, a portly gentleman struggling up hill, and recently two guys on racing cycles choosing the road as opposed to the cycle-path!

- Revert to Universities and admission grades thereto as provided prior to the amalgamation of Polytechnics. As a local (late) GP (not Jo Leigh) once observed (prior to amalgamation) when advising a lad who was under pressure from his parents to achieve University status, 'you've either gorrit, or you haven't gorrit, and if you haven't gorrit, forgerrit.'
- Apprenticeships, are for some, absolutely essential, and can be extremely beneficial.

I'm OLD, so best ignored. A recent email contained various amusing observations, one of which I particularly like: **'Ageing sure has slowed you down, but it hasn't shut you up!'**

Chapter Sixty Nine

A FOLLOWER?

I make no secret of the fact that I am an atheist and have been since a child.

The Bible is an extraordinary story, and an exceedingly clever piece of work that provides inter alia an array of exemption clauses.

Common sense dictates that religion has a track record that leaves **much** to be desired. Some religions even provide forgiveness for sins and we are advised/assured that Islam is a 'Religion of Peace,' but sadly not for all Muslims given the availability of the Quran and Shari Law.

Please be assured that I do **not** have a problem with people who need to follow a religion, particularly if they find it provides mental stability and support during their lives.

In the absence of a God I have attempted throughout my adult life to ensure, to the best of my ability, that I've provided love and security for my wife and two children. I've worked extremely hard, and have always put my family first – they are paramount. I would also like to think that many of those who sought my help during their matrimonial or family problems, found me compassionate and constructive. Very simply, I could not have achieved this without morals and principles, effectively living a life in tune with **_Christian values_**.

Chapter Seventy

I conclude when this country, and much of the World, is attempting to combat a virus, the Corona Covid 19 Virus, to be precise. We are in lock-down and are advised to stay home unless you have an essential trip for shopping or medication, and further, to work from home if possible. Exercise is limited to an hour each day during which strict distancing rules apply i.e. at least a metre apart, and no physical contact with any family member or person not residing within your household.

The present Government, led by Boris Johnson (who suffered but survived the virus) has, in my opinion, done mostly all that has been possible given the nature of this global pandemic. I compare the crisis with Pearl Harbour when America was attacked without warning. However, the crucial difference is that they were immediately in a position to retaliate – the British Government had no obvious means of retaliation – they were confronted with an unknown enemy, and no vaccination. Despite this, journalists, continue to criticise the Government, in particular those in the employ of the BBC. They are mostly individuals who appear to be unaware of how inane and ridiculous some of their questions are – some meriting a 'bleedin' obvious' response! Further, one could be excused from thinking that any *good* news during Covid 19 should, courtesy of the BBC, be well and truly suppressed.

My/our son, Gareth, having achieved a law degree at Cardiff University, pursued a Post Graduate course in journalism, following which he secured a journalistic post with a local newspaper in Wales. His career was short-lived since he foolishly thought, inter alia, that providing a truthful and accurate account was what sold newspapers!

Covid 19 is, to say the least, surreal and, frankly, a wake-up call for an over-populated, and extremely vulnerable and fragile, planet.

Chapter Seventy One

WIFE AND SONS

I find it extremely difficult to script this chapter, simply because words are inadequate. I also know that Glenys is unlikely to ever venture into the realms of a biography – her biography, so I sincerely hope that Gareth and Jim will eventually prepare biographies of their respective lives.

My wife of 55 years, is virtuous and of unique qualities. I love her immeasurably. To attempt to provide my sincere feelings for her would require a separate script. However, it would be remiss of me not to recount the findings of our good and longstanding friend, Bill Price, who, while sheltering from the heat of Atlanta, enjoys exploring one's ancestry/genealogy, which has resulted in some quite extraordinary findings in relation to Glenys's family tree i.e. that she is an ancestor of Capt William Pierce 'Mariner' (1591-1641) who captained the second voyage of the Mayflower. His biography describes his second voyage as Captain of the famed Mayflower, plus many other voyages, and may have been instrumental in bringing about the first **real** Thanksgiving observance some ten years later in 1631.

Bill (semi-retired physicist) is confident of the connection which, needless to say, has nothing to do with the Ledbetters, but stems from her (Glenys) mother's family tree bearing the surname FRY, which also reveals an ancestral connection with Norfolk, the Duke of Norfolk, the ancestral home of Arundel Castle, plus the burial of Henry Collett, in Tewkesbury Abbey. Glenys, needless to say, stresses that she needs hard evidence – while Bill observes, 'so you have 'Blue Blood!'

Our sons – suffice it to say that our sons are similarly virtuous and of unique qualities.

Gareth has achieved so much, is of outstanding intellect – inherited from his mother! But always retaining his basic qualities i.e. humour, kindness, respect, honesty, and much more.

In September 1999, Gareth married Sophie in London. It was a lovely day and we celebrated in Prue Leith's restaurant in the grounds of Regent's Park adjacent to the Zoo. Jim did a brilliant Best Man speech that was very well received. Glenys and I provided a three tier cake, the top eventually falling to the floor but sadly not filmed for 'You've Been Framed!' On leaving, Gareth gave me a hug, momentarily forgetting that heart procedures include splitting the sternum. Ouch!

Gareth is a prolific writer, and in 1990 prepared, 'We Are Still Married.' To celebrate our 25th Wedding Anniversary. An extract reads thus:

'.......In the spring of 1968, while Hendrix wooed the flower children, she gave birth to a baby boy. Conceived in the bowels of hell the child grew to utter his first words, "No, No, No!" A definite problem, they soldiered on. In the Autumn of 1972 she gave birth to another bundle of fun. He grew to utter his first words none of which can be translated. The family was now complete, and poverty stricken. They soon discovered the joy of parenthood and the acidity of inconsequential bank managers. They poured hours of effort into their children.

It is 1990, it has been twenty-five years of intense

matrimony. He continues to struggle with a yokel law firm, she has gone into catering. They are my parents and my brother Jim's. We are forever in their debt. In our strange ways, we love and respect them.

Despite 25 years together, despite financial hassles, despite strange relatives and lunatic children – they are still married.'

Jim, as previously mentioned, is a brilliant drummer, and is now self employed as a drum tutor.

Following departure from London in 2005 with wife Cathy, Jim commenced work at a local garden centre. Sadly his duties were beyond the call, culminating in a back injury at work during the afternoon of the 23rd December 2016. Glenys and I spent Christmas Eve with Cathy and Victor – it was not a Merry Christmas – Jim was in a very bad way but hoped during the break, rest and pain killers would help in recovery. Suffice it to say that Jim's problem did not go away so appropriate intervention was implemented.

Gareth John Ledbetter LLB can now add MBE (Member of the Order of the British Empire) to his letters (not that he ever will, unless essential!) he having been included in the Queen's Birthday Honours List on the 8th June 2018. The short published (as opposed to the detailed unpublished) citation reads, 'Gareth John LEDBETTER, Lately Head of Screening and Research Team, Home Office. For services to Border Security.' This, I would merely add, is obviously a vastly over simplified account of what he, and his loyal team, achieved for the security of this Country. He led a team that achieved significant advances in the punishment and extradition of war criminals. As an example I include a short extract from Victor's, 'War Hero's Prep V1 Assembly' recital that he performed on the 9th November 2018: 'My Uncle Gareth set up a War Crimes Unit in the Home office, to bring today's war criminals to justice....'As a result of this case (as detailed therein) –

and hundreds of others – my Uncle has been awarded an MBE from the Queen.....

The following is my account of Gareth's official recognition, plus the quite extraordinary coincidence that followed:

'It's Saturday 9th June 2018, the Queen's Official Birthday, and Gareth Ledbetter is attempting, unsuccessfully, to contact his parents to let them know that he was to receive an MBE for his services to the Home Office. Having eventually made contact, his mother was so disbelieving that she needed confirmation from someone sensible in the house. Fortunately her granddaughter was around and she responded, 'yes Grandma it's true he is getting and MBE.' It had been a shock to him, and obviously a shock to his parents, but they were aware of his years of service to the Home Office which often required his team's leadership 'twenty four seven'.

On 7th December 2018 saw Gareth's investiture at Buckingham Palace, receiving his medal from Prince William.

When earlier entering the huge ballroom the Countess of Wessex's String Orchestra was performing in the elevated Minstrel Gallery. The investiture programme named the conductor as Major David Hammond and while it was considered extremely unlikely that Major Hammond and David Hammond, former school mate of Gareth, was one and the same, a seed had been sown.

When leaving the ballroom Gareth's father glanced up at the Conductor and realised that he, while still conducting, was looking down and smiling at him. Subsequently, Gareth made contact with Major Hammond who expressed his pleasure that the Ledbetter family had successfully perceived the quite extraordinary coincidence.

Gareth lost touch with David when he commenced studying for his law degree at Cardiff University and David commenced his studies at the London College of Music and York and

Cambridge Universities. Subsequently he joined the British Army, culminating in David leading the mounted bands on the Queen's Birthday Parade in 2014. He was promoted to the rank of Major and holds the position of Director of Music.

Having achieved his law degree Gareth completed his law finals, and sought employment with the Home Office. He has had a fascinating career with much of his work focusing on issues such as international law, criminality and national security.

Gareth and David both grew up in Cornwall and attended Penrice School when a Comprehensive. They shared a passion for music and both recall attending their first gig in 1980 at the Cornwall Coliseum – The Specials, a literally riotous event. Indisputably – not bad for a couple of comprehensive kids.'

Back row: Gareth, Jim, Cathy, Me. Front: Maisie, Sophie, Stanley, Glenys & Victor (2017)

Since concluding my memoirs, my best mate, Jo Leigh, has died of a head and neck (ENT) related cancer. He was – until an apparently aggressive cancer intervened – an extremely fit and active man, and for me it will remain a mystery as to why he did not, at the very least, seek *early* second opinions of consultants at specialist hospitals.

I was invited, indeed honoured, to accompany family members, as pall bearers at his recent funeral. Jo and I had been close mates for 43 years, and his passing has left a massive void. I could write much in regard to Dr Jonathan Rupert Leigh but emotions dictate a simple epitaph: He was a loyal and genuine friend – he will forever remain, for the Ledbetter quartet, a *LEGEND*.

Given my age, my medical history, I wish, if I may, to utilise a Spike Milligan adage, 'I'm not frightened of dying, I just don't want to be there when it happens.'

Printed in Great Britain
by Amazon

53075980R00176